Addiction & Reco[...] For Dummies®

Recognizing Addiction in Yourself

Get honest with yourself and take a real look, a hard look, at your behavior. Don't waste your time and energy on self-deception. Are any of the following true?

- Your substance-seeking behavior is increasing (you are going to places where you can score), or your compulsion to do the problematic behavior (such as gambling) is increasing.
- Your main reason for living is *using*.
- You lose touch with important aspects of your life, such as friends, work, school, and family responsibilities, because of substance use or addictive behavior.

Recognizing Addiction in a Loved One

The following list presents signs that your loved one has a substance addiction or is engaging in a self-destructive addictive behavior. Answer yes or no to the following questions. Does your loved one . . .

- Turn up late for functions or dates?
- No longer follow through on his/her commitments?
- Have more trouble with illness than usual?
- Have more problems at work than usual?
- Appear to be withdrawing from intimate contacts?
- Have unexplained absences from or inconsistencies in his/her usual schedule?
- Appear to have a new set of friends who he/she is highly involved with but who you don't get to meet?
- Have major financial fluctuations (like carrying more or considerably less money than usual)?
- Have lapses of concentration or memory?
- Stay up later at night and sleep in more during the day?
- Have more trouble than usual getting it together in the morning?
- Appear surprisingly secretive about specific aspects of his/her life?

While this checklist cannot diagnose an addiction in a loved one, the more "yes" answers you produce, the greater the chances are that your loved one is suffering from an addiction.

For Dummies: Bestselling Book Series for Beginners

Addiction & Recovery For Dummies®

Deciding on Help

All addiction programs draw from one or more of these seven views of addiction:

- **Moral:** People can sacrifice anything to feed addictions.
- **Disease:** Addiction is like other diseases that cause unhealthy brain function.
- **Pharmacological:** Addiction stems from chemical imbalances which non-addictive drugs can overcome (for example, antidepressants and anti-anxiety medications).
- **Cognitive-behavioral:** "Stinking thinking" or cognitive distortions drive addictions and can be replaced with "healthy thinking" and non-addicting satisfactions.
- **Learning:** Different levels of learning cause addiction. Conditioning is important as it can be largely automatic and dominant, involving little or no thinking.
- **Psychodynamic:** Difficulties in emotional regulation cause psychic numbing, emotional flooding, and other extremes. Addictive substances are then used to numb, calm, sedate, excite, and sexualize.
- **Biopsychosocial:** Physical, psychological, and social aspects of addiction are addressed in combined treatments.

These views are structured into programs taking place in residential treatment centers (for example, 28-day program) or outpatient centers, guided by professionals or self-help trainers who apply twelve-step and other treatment approaches.

For Dummies: Bestselling Book Series for Beginners

Addiction & Recovery FOR DUMMIES®

by Brian F. Shaw, PhD, Paul Ritvo, PhD, and Jane Irvine, DPhil

Foreword by M. David Lewis, MD, FASAM

ASAP Family Programs, Malibu, California

WILEY

Wiley Publishing, Inc.

Addiction & Recovery For Dummies®

Published by
Wiley Publishing, Inc.
111 River St.
Hoboken, NJ 07030-5774
www.wiley.com

WILEY

About the Authors

Dr. Brian F. Shaw is one of the originators of applied cognitive-behavioral psychology for clinical practice, the performance of elite athletes, health promotion, and coping with significant illness.

As one of the developers of Cognitive-Behavior Therapy (CBT), a psychological treatment for the depression, anxiety, and substance abuse, Dr. Shaw adapted this technology to help people learn to recover and refocus their lives.

In sports, Dr. Shaw is well known for his work with the NHL/NHLPA Substance Abuse and Behavioral Health Program, Major League Soccer in the U.S., and Major League Baseball's Toronto Blue Jays.

Dr. Shaw is an expert on how the mind works, how it gets derailed, and how to get it back on track. More importantly, he understands how people refresh their thinking to gain new perspectives on their life, their world, and their future.

Dr. Shaw is a Professor in the Departments of Public Health Sciences and Psychiatry at the University of Toronto, Toronto, Canada.

Dr. Paul Ritvo is an innovator in the application of cognitive-behavioral psychology, particularly in telephone-based counseling with corporate executives, elite athletes, and individuals confronting life-threatening illness.

A researcher who studies cancer and AIDS prevention, Dr. Ritvo is a Career Scientist at Cancer Care Ontario and Associate Professor in the School of Kinesiology and Health Sciences, York University, and in the Department of Public Health Sciences at the University of Toronto.

Dr. Ritvo is active in innovative projects in North America and Africa, where his research addresses AIDS prevention and vaccine testing. He is an active developer and disseminator of health-promotion software and compact discs through Interactive-Health.Com, Inc.

Dr. Jane Irvine has devoted her research program and clinical practice to helping individuals with complex medical conditions live productive and satisfying lives. She has pioneered the development of cognitive-behavioral interventions for smoking cessation, health behavior change, medication adherence, and personal adjustment to chronic illnesses. Dr. Irvine has authored more than fifty publications on health behavior change, cardiovascular health, and cancer prevention.

Dr. Irvine is a clinical psychologist with Interactive-Health.Com, Inc., and an Associate Professor in the Department of Psychology, York University, and the Departments of Psychiatry and Public Health Sciences at the University of Toronto, Toronto, Canada.

Drs. Shaw, Ritvo, and Irvine are available for speaking engagements and workshops. They also offer individual counseling as well as a Web-based cognitive-behavioral therapy program for relapse prevention and recovery from addictions. You can visit their Web site at www.interactive-health.com. *You can also call their toll-free number: 1-877-577-2778.*

Dedication

This book is dedicated to our families and friends, particularly those who have struggled or are currently struggling with addiction.

Authors' Acknowledgments

We would like to thank our families for supporting us during the intense and challenging work sessions when this book was first taking form. We especially want to thank Nicolai Geilich for his insightful edits to earlier drafts of the chapters and Marnie Shaw for her constructive reviews. Thanks also to Dan Cronin for his expert consultation regarding interventions and treatment facilities and to Sabine Johnson for her research.

We also want to thank all of the editors at Wiley, especially Natasha Graf for her very helpful guidance during the early days of writing this book and Tim Gallan and Jennifer Bingham for their outstanding editorial assistance.

Finally, our special thanks and appreciation go to those of our friends, family members, and clients who have taught us at firsthand about the various forms of addiction and shown us the real possibility of overcoming addiction and maintaining recovery.

Publisher's Acknowledgments

We're proud of this book; please send us your comments through our Dummies online registration form located at www.dummies.com/register/.

Some of the people who helped bring this book to market include the following:

Acquisitions, Editorial, and Media Development

Senior Project Editor: Tim Gallan

Acquisitions Editor: Mikal Belicove

Copy Editor: Jennifer Bingham

Technical Editor: Lin Ames

Editorial Manager: Christine Meloy Beck

Editorial Assistants: Courtney Allen, Melissa S. Bennett, Nadine Bell

Cover Photos: Attracted to the Light © Douglas Whyte/CORBIS

Cartoons: Rich Tennant, www.the5thwave.com

Composition

Project Coordinator: Maridee Ennis

Layout and Graphics: Andrea Dahl, Clint Lahnen, Barry Offringa, Heather Ryan

Proofreaders: Leeann Harney, Joe Niesen, TECHBOOKS Production Services

Indexer: TECHBOOKS Production Services

Publishing and Editorial for Consumer Dummies

    Diane Graves Steele, Vice President and Publisher, Consumer Dummies

    Joyce Pepple, Acquisitions Director, Consumer Dummies

    Kristin A. Cocks, Product Development Director, Consumer Dummies

    Michael Spring, Vice President and Publisher, Travel

    Brice Gosnell, Associate Publisher, Travel

    Kelly Regan, Editorial Director, Travel

Publishing for Technology Dummies

    Andy Cummings, Vice President and Publisher, Dummies Technology/General User

Composition Services

    Gerry Fahey, Vice President of Production Services

    Debbie Stailey, Director of Composition Services

Contents at a Glance

Table of Contents

Foreword

Addiction in Our Times

by M. David Lewis, MD, FASAM
ASAP Family Programs, Malibu, California

● ●

*A*ddiction is a chronic and dangerous disease. It strikes in many forms, feeding on our obsessions — everything from drugs, to gambling, to sex, to money. It is responsible for the devastation of families, the destruction of livelihoods, and countless deaths.

There is no cure for addiction. Nonetheless, there *is* hope for managing it.

The basis for this hope, as the authors of this book tell us, comes to us through *knowledge*. When we are knowledgeable about the traits and treatments for the disease, we can see it for what it is, take action, and control it. We can help those we love — and ourselves — to live freely rather than as slaves to addiction.

Becoming knowledgeable is not easy. Addiction is a disease of lies and disguises, difficult to understand because of the press it receives and the prejudices we have about it. It is both a glamorous byproduct of fame and an affliction of the destitute. It is a psychological disorder, a family dysfunction, a physiological need.

This book helps to strip the mask off addiction so we can stand face-to-face with it. In the following pages, Doctors Shaw, Ritvo, and Irvine address the important questions from a clear, straight-forward perspective. By reading this book, you will understand the origins of addictions, the risks of addiction, and the most effective treatments.

But books alone can't do the job of alerting our society to the range of addictions problem, which have no simple solutions. As parents, teachers, citizens, and health professionals, we must engage in a vigorous campaign of communicating openly and non-judgmentally about addiction within our homes, our schools and the halls of government.

We need to arm ourselves with important information about addiction expressed as clearly and simply as it is in this book. We need to be open to talking with youth about their addictive and non-addictive difficulties. We need to have more effective teen treatments.

I commend the authors for opening the door for more people to put their prejudices aside, understand addiction, and be able effectively and openly confront it wherever it lies in their lives. I believe this book and our own efforts to care for people with addiction can make a major difference.

Even though there is no cure, there is healing. And it all begins with knowledge.

Introduction

● ●

Some of our friends, family members, and clients have overcome addiction. These folks are in recovery and live interesting, useful, and compassionate lives.

Some of our friends, family members, and clients are still struggling with addiction. We care for them and worry about what will happen to them. We know we can't control their lives or decisions — we want to help, but know that sometimes we must watch and wait. We've learned that wishes and hopes don't necessarily resolve addictive problems.

Our experiences of successful recovery *and* continuing struggle have convinced us of the great need to *destigmatize addiction.* As technology progresses, newly developed substances powerfully target pleasure centers in the brain, mostly to ease the pain of severely ill people. As a result, addictive substances have become even more accessible, tempting, and common.

We believe that addictive behavior will increase during the 21st century. But so will knowledge of how addiction problems develop and how professionals can help people recover from them. We, as scientists and caregivers, will use our collective understandings to neutralize the powerful effects of society, technology, marketing, and the very human drive to consume.

You may often hear people say that they're battling an illness or an addiction. This analogy of a battle helps them focus energies on overcoming troubling and life-threatening addictions.

But there is another analogy to consider: A journey through life where loving people support you in finding your natural life-path — a path *free* of addictions. As you take this journey, you find obstacles to confront and overcome. However, you can rediscover non-addictive pleasures in the company of caring companions. These pleasures will dwarf past experiences of addiction.

Recovery is, in many ways, an inner journey, and people with addictions often feel alone. In their aloneness, they ache and yearn for another state of mind and body. People with addiction must find inner strengths again, and they need help in doing so. We wrote this book to communicate with your strengths and to offer what we know about recovery — to help you and your loved ones recover your lives and your freedom.

About This Book

This book is written for people seeking freedom from addiction. You may be deciding whether you need help. You may have already tried to overcome your addiction, but failed. You may have decided that now is the time to confront addictive behavior, but you don't know where to start or what options are available. This book addresses all of these issues. It helps you determine how big a problem your addictive behavior is. It helps you assess your readiness for treatment. It describes all the common professional and self-help treatment approaches, which include:

- ✔ Detoxification treatments
- ✔ Residential treatment models
- ✔ Pharmacotherapies
- ✔ Psychological treatment models
- ✔ Treatments programs based on the AA model
- ✔ Different types of self-help treatment approaches

The book has specific information for teens and adults, and it addresses substance (for instance, drugs and alcohol) and behavioral (for instance, gambling and sex) addictions. It helps you break free of addiction by helping you find the best solutions for your recovery at this time.

This book is also written for family and friends of addicts. In our experience, the family often first seeks help for a relative's addiction. This book guides family members in considering treatment options for their loved one. It provides information and direction on how to communicate with a family member who is addicted. It also provides support and guidance in helping family members ensure that their own needs aren't neglected despite the desperate needs of the addict.

The book is written so that you can read whatever chapters are of interest at the moment. You need not read the chapters in any particular order. Nor do you need to read the entire book. The book is meant as a reference guide on how to recover successfully from addictions. You need only refer to the chapters that are relevant to your needs. But of course, if you want to read the whole book cover-to-cover, we won't stop you!

Each chapter provides cross-references to related topics in other chapters.

Conventions Used in This Book

This book is written for you, the person struggling with an addiction or the family member or friend of an addict. Chapter titles and chapter subheadings let you know who this particular section is addressing. We have tried hard not to use professional and medical jargon. When jargon or medical terminology is used, we highlight and define these terms and mark them as *technical stuff.*

We incorporate many case studies of individuals to illustrate specific issues. The identities of these people are carefully disguised to protect confidentiality. In many instances, an individual in a story represents a composite of experiences with many clients. When these case examples are used to embellish a point and aren't central to the information or guidance being discussed in the section, the story is highlighted in a sidebar. Sometimes the case examples are part of a point we are trying to make. In those cases, you find them in the regular body text. You should consider the sidebars as extra material that you don't have to read if you don't want to.

Start with whatever chapter is of most interest to you. Most chapters assume that the primary audience is the person struggling with an addiction. However, some chapters are specifically written for the families of addicted persons.

Foolish Assumptions

Who is reading this book? We assume that the primary readers of this book are people with addictions or family and friends of an addict. We also assume that the readers are struggling to get free of addictions or are family members searching for help for their loved ones. If these descriptions fit your situation, then this book is for you.

How This Book Is Organized

We organize *Addiction and Recovery For Dummies* into 4 parts and 20 chapters. Each part is described below.

Part 1: The Hole in the Heart: Detecting Addiction

Chapter 1 defines key terms used in this book, including the distinctions among addiction, dependence, and abuse. It also provides a brief overview of all of the other chapters in this book. Chapter 2 focuses on addictive substances and describes the different classes of drugs (for instance, uppers, downers, and hallucinogens). Chapter 3 focuses on addictive behaviors and discusses what is addictive about certain behaviors like gambling, sex, eating, and yes, work. In Chapter 4, we talk about how experimenting with certain substances can easily escalate to an addiction, and we review the risk factors for experimentation. We also go over the risks from experimentation and the risks and costs of addictions. This section is a must-read for people who are experimenting with addictive substances or behaviors or who are questioning the addictive potential of certain substances and behaviors.

Part II: Taking Those First Steps

This part of the book focuses on helping you decide whether you need treatment. We begin in Chapter 5 by helping you assess your risk factors for developing addictions and then assessing the severity of your addictive behaviors. We also offer guidance to family members on how to detect addictions in a loved one. Chapter 6 focuses on helping you assess your readiness for treatment at this time and informing you of the general characteristics of different treatments. Chapter 7 focuses on helping you understand the different aspects to your addiction so that you can assess your treatment needs fully. It also gives you information to help you avoid falling for common myths about quitting an addiction.

Part III: Examining Treatment Approaches

This part of the book is a reference guide to a wide range of treatment options for addictions. In Chapter 8, we go over the specifics of different treatment approaches and models for addictions. You can identify treatment approaches that best fit with your personal beliefs and philosophies. Chapter 9 focuses on inpatient and outpatient treatment options. We include a firsthand account of what it's like to undergo residential treatment. We also provide information that helps you assess the pros and cons of inpatient and outpatient treatment. Chapter 10 addresses physical dependence and gives information on how long it takes to detox from specific substances. It helps you assess your risk of severe withdrawal symptoms and learn about medications that can help. Chapter 11 provides a very detailed description of the twelve-step program. Chapter 12 describes the array of self-help and peer support treatment approaches for addictions. In Chapter 13, we focus on alternative treatments for addictions including ibogaine and acupuncture. Chapter 14 is especially for teens. It focuses on treatment considerations for teens.

Part IV: Life in Recovery

Part IV focuses on longer-term recovery issues. In Chapter 15, we go over methods for overcoming barriers to successful recovery. Chapter 16 provides guidance in handling slips and relapses during recovery (slips are common, so you need to be prepared to handle them). Chapter 17 provides guidance in dealing with relationships during recovery, including repairing relationships and starting new relationships. It covers relations with family, friends, and colleagues. The chapter also delves into financial issues. Chapter 18 is specifically written for family members. It provides guidance to families in handling relationships with the addicted member as well as with each other. It also focuses on the all-important issue of ensuring one's own well-being.

Part V: The Part of Tens

This is the final part of the book. It provides quick tips to overcoming addictions and ensuring a successful recovery. Chapter 19 covers ten quit tips for families and friends. We conclude with Chapter 20, which provides an extensive list of self-help books and Internet sites with information on different addiction programs and information resources.

Icons Used in This Book

Throughout this book, we use icons in the margins to quickly identify different types of information. Here are the icons we use and a brief description of their meaning:

This icon highlights information that we don't want you to forget.

As the name implies, the tip icon alerts you to pieces of practical information or things you can do to handle your addiction problem.

This icon alerts you to things you should avoid. The warning icon is also used to highlight cautionary points about addictions.

This icon is used to indicate that the information in the paragraph is of a technical nature, and you need not read it unless you want to find out more about the professional and scientific aspects of addictions.

Where to Go from Here

You can go straight to whatever chapter is of most interest to you. If you're seriously considering treatment, we suggest that you review Part III to get informed about the wide array of treatment options available to you. We also want to draw your attention to Chapter 7, because it helps you get a full understanding of the factors that you must address to free yourself from your addiction.

Part I

The Hole in the Heart: Detecting Addiction

"The blues I can handle. Usually, I can express it with a simple 12-bar guitar lick. Depression, on the other hand, takes a 3-act opera."

In this part . . .

We help you detect the signs of addiction and determine whether you or someone else is addicted. We provide surprising facts about how common addiction is and about the many forms it takes. We especially focus on substance addictions (such as drugs and alcohol) and behavioral addictions (such as gambling, sex, and eating).

One of the challenges is knowing whether your use of a substance or reliance on a behavior is a problem. In this part, we explain the differences among use, abuse, and dependence. Finally, we discuss how costly addictions are — to you personally and to your family.

Chapter 1

Addiction: What Is It?

*A*ddiction robs you of freedom and control. You may think that you *choose* to use — but just try to stop. See if you can. See whether you have control over the addictive substance or behavior you're thinking about. If you find you do, great. Abstain for a while. Be sure that you've got the control you think you have. If you don't have control, if abstaining is unthinkable or impossible, read on.

In this chapter, we tell you about the different types of addictions, especially about substance addictions and behavioral addictions. We tell you about how the medical community views addiction and how your personal view, when it's all said and done, is what you'll most likely follow. We also briefly overview what the rest of this book can offer.

We've designed this book to help you gain an understanding of where you are right now in regard to your control over addictive substances and behaviors. This understanding can help you develop a strategy for seeking freedom, well-being, and control in your life.

Substance Use, Abuse, and Addiction

A number of addiction-related terms are used throughout this book. We want to be clear about what they mean before proceeding.

Addiction: The definitions

In 1964, the World Health Organization suggested the term *addiction* be replaced. The group wanted to replace it with the word *dependence,* because *dependence* describes the feeling that, physically and mentally, you *have* to use the substance. Your brain and body cry out. You gotta have it!

We however, don't agree with the World Health Organization entirely. So in this book, we use the term *addiction* to refer to a *combined* experience of mental and physical dependence. In *addiction,* as we see it, you're compelled to use a substance or behave in a certain way, even though you know you face considerable harm by going through with it.

You're addicted when you can no longer direct yourself out of harm's way. You're addicted when you continue to use a substance or engage in a behavior that *puts* you in harm's way.

Simply put, addiction causes a *change in your brain.* A change that we, and other scientists and clinicians, are trying hard to understand. Make no mistake; although this change is something of a mystery, it's still powerful. When the change occurs, you lose control over your urges to use a substance or engage in certain behaviors. The urges are irresistible. You can become so compelled by your addictive behavior that nothing else matters. It doesn't matter how smart you are, how accomplished you are, or how physically strong you are. It can happen to anyone.

Dependence is really one step along a slippery path that leads to addiction. At a certain point, a prolonged dependence results in another switch being thrown. The experience you have after that switch is thrown is what we call addiction.

It's important now to talk about both mental and physical dependence. *Mental dependence* refers to associations that develop in your mind between specific events (called triggers) and emotional and physical urges to use the substance or take part in the addictive behavior. These triggers are actually memory traces that are set off by various stimuli. When set off, they exert a powerful influence on your behavior. Moreover, they're not just in your mind — through a series of chain reactions, they induce biochemical changes in your brain as well.

What is the difference between mental and physical dependence when both cause changes in brain chemistry? The main difference is that the changes in chemistry brought on by the effects of mental dependence are due to mental associations. Put bluntly, just thinking about getting high changes your brain chemistry. Then the brain changes affect your whole body so that you feel physically excited.

Physical dependence, on the other hand, doesn't require any thinking at all. It's simply related to the physical effects of the addictive substance on specific brain chemicals called neurotransmitters. Certain neurotransmitters get altered by the substance. The brain adjusts — it tolerates the drug. And then you don't feel normal or good unless you take the substance. Physical dependence describes your brain's physical adaptation to the drug.

As you can read in Chapter 10, you can detoxify your brain (get rid of the foreign chemicals) from a physical dependence relatively quickly (a few days). However, your mental dependence can last a lifetime.

We describe more of the differences between mental and physical dependence in Chapter 5.

The difference between abuse and dependence

The difference between abuse and dependence is a matter of time and degree. The medical criteria for substance dependence and substance abuse are summarized below in the following sections. Essentially, the difference is that *dependence* is associated with tolerance (you need more and more of the substance to get the same effect) and withdrawal symptoms (you experience substance-specific withdrawal symptoms when you stop using), and *abuse* is associated with continued substance use despite adverse health, social, or financial consequences.

Abuse can occur without dependence but the reverse is rarely true; dependence almost always leads to abuse.

Medical criteria for substance dependence

From the medical perspective, dependence is defined as experiencing at least three of the following criteria occurring within a 12-month period:

> ✔ Experiencing tolerance, which is defined as either a need for markedly increased amounts of the substance to achieve the desired effect or a markedly diminished effect with continued use of the same amount.

✔ Experiencing withdrawal, as evidenced by either the characteristic withdrawal syndrome for the substance or when medication is taken to relieve withdrawal symptoms.

✔ The substance is taken in larger amounts or over a longer time period than initially intended.

✔ There is a persistent desire or unsuccessful efforts to cut down or control substance use.

✔ A great deal of time is spent in activities necessary to obtain the substance (being preoccupied with how and when you're going to get your next fix dominates your daily thoughts).

✔ Important social, occupational, or recreational activities are neglected or abandoned because of substance use.

✔ The substance use is continued despite knowledge of having a persistent or recurrent psychological or physical problem related to substance use.

Medical criteria for substance abuse

The medical definition of abuse is one or more of the following criteria within a 12-month period:

✔ Recurrent substance use resulting in a failure to fulfill major role obligations at work, home, or school.

✔ Recurrent substance use in situations where it is physically hazardous (for instance, while driving a car).

✔ Recurrent substance-related legal problems.

✔ Continued substance use despite having persistent or recurrent social or interpersonal problems caused or worsened by substance use (for instance, arguments with spouse about the consequences of use).

 If you have both the criteria for substance abuse and substance dependence, you would be diagnosed as having a substance dependence problem.

Nonsubstance or behavioral addictions

Nonsubstance or behavioral addictions are behaviors you engage in that meet many of the same criteria as substance addictions. They are behaviors that dominate your life: You feel compelled to do them. One example is pathological gambling, another is sex addiction.

When we apply the medical criteria in the preceding two sections to behavioral addictions, the definitions, however, become less clear. You can readily see how a behavioral addiction meets criteria for abuse (for instance, pathological gambling) but the dependence criteria don't apply as readily with addictions like workaholism, overeating, and excessive sex. Still, tolerance does build up with behavioral addictions. You need to do more and more of the activity or engage in riskier and riskier aspects of the behavior to get the same high. (For more on behavioral addictions, see Chapter 3.)

Your personal definition

Regardless of medical criteria, you know if you have a substance or behavioral addiction. You know because the actions involved in getting the substance or doing the behavior dominate your life.

The line between heavy use and abuse or dependence is fuzzy. The case examples of Joe and Mark in the following sections highlight just how fuzzy the line can be.

Case example: Is Joe abusing marijuana?

Joe smoked marijuana every day — his first joint was in the morning. Smoking was his way of approaching the day in a mellow frame of mind. Joe was in his third year of college; he'd started smoking marijuana at the end of his sophomore year. He enjoyed college and felt in no hurry to finish, partly because he was still uncertain about what he wanted to do after college. At least, this is how he rationalized taking half the course load he should have been taking in his third year. At this rate, it would take him twice the normal time to complete college.

Joe supplemented his income from a student loan by working as an assistant in the college library on Saturdays and Sundays. He tried getting other jobs, but found that the hours of work conflicted too much with his recreation time. Other than paying for a steady supply of marijuana, he figured he had few financial needs. The student loan paid for his tuition and rent. He even had some money left over to sustain a pretty simple diet of bread, peanut butter, jam, and an occasional hamburger. The money he made at his part-time job on the weekends financed his drug habit.

Joe was a bit of a loner. He only had a few friends to get together with on Saturday nights. They often went to a bar to play pool and drink beer, and, of course, smoke a joint or two. During the weekday evenings Joe kept to himself. He rented a room in a house near campus. The other rooms were also rented out to students, but Joe didn't socialize with his roommates. What he most liked to do in the evenings was smoke marijuana and listen to music. He rarely got to bed before 2 a.m.

Is Joe abusing marijuana?

Case example: Is Mark abusing marijuana?

Mark's situation was very similar to Joe's. Like Joe, Mark smoked marijuana daily, and Mark was also at college. However, unlike Joe, Mark was very outgoing and sociable. He started smoking marijuana at parties (he met his girlfriend at one of these parties). He and his friends usually socialized as a group, sometimes partying at the local dance club and sometimes getting together at fraternity houses. Mark lived at home, so he seldom had the opportunity to host these parties himself. He worked on the weekends, but because his living expenses were low, he could use most of his earnings to buy marijuana.

By his third year, smoking marijuana had become a daily habit. Mark's room was in the basements of his parent's house and so he could sometimes smoke at home without being detected. However, most of the time, he had a few joints in the evenings when he went out with his buddies.

His girlfriend sometimes joined in, but increasingly she complained that she was tired of these pot parties. They had been fighting a lot lately because she wanted them to branch out and do a variety of activities. Mark didn't want to fight with his girlfriend, but he also didn't want to cut back on seeing his buddies and smoking marijuana.

Mark started to experience problems at college in his third year. He rarely got home before 1 a.m., so getting up in the morning became a big problem. He couldn't keep up with a full course load and dropped two of his classes. He kept his afternoon courses, reasoning that they were scheduled at a more reasonable time of the day. It wasn't long before his parents noticed the major shift in his sleeping pattern. Arguments became increasingly more frequent between Mark and his parents, who complained that he wasn't taking his studies seriously. He complained that they were old fashioned.

Is Mark abusing marijuana?

The answer

Both Joe and Mark are abusing marijuana. Because Joe is a loner by nature while Mark has a sociable personality, and because Joe's lifestyle is so closely aligned with his drug habit, the problems he's having with marijuana use may seem less obvious. Nevertheless, both young men are abusing marijuana. In both cases, marijuana use has interfered with their school and occupational activities. The adverse consequences are more apparent in Mark's case because his drug use is causing problems with his girlfriend and family. Although his parents may not yet know the underlying cause of the shift in his schedule, they have certainly picked up on the problems he's having with meeting his school responsibilities. Thus, Mark's drug use may appear more obvious because it is affecting many areas of his life. However, in actuality, both young men's drug use meets criteria for substance abuse. In both cases, marijuana use is interfering with them fulfilling their school and occupational responsibilities.

You only need to have one of the medical criteria for substance abuse to be diagnosed as having a substance abuse problem.

The line between use and abuse can become blurred because of the gradual nature of addiction. It's very easy for you to rationalize substance abuse as normal. The first step toward freedom from addiction, however, consists of taking an honest look at how the substance you use is affecting your life.

The role of experimentation

Drug use typically begins with experimentation ("Hey, try this. It will make you feel so good!"). When you're young, saying no is hard. After all, you're young only once! The good news is that in the last ten years, drug use has been declining among youth. Unfortunately, alcohol use hasn't shown a similar decline. We've heard estimates that say 50 percent of adolescents ages 12 through 17 have tried alcohol.

All people with an addiction started by experimenting. No one sets out thinking that he's going to become an addict. Substance use affects the chemistry of the brain. You may not even realize that your brain is changing just as you may not realize that your liver is changing. Before long, experimentation becomes dependence. After a while, dependence becomes addiction.

Assessing Your Addiction Risk

The first step toward getting help is recognizing a problem. Part II of this book focuses on recognizing and assessing your addiction risk and what parents and friends can look out for. It also discusses many social influences that induce you to experiment with addictive substances and behaviors (see Chapter 4 for information on these social influences). Knowing what may have lead to your addiction problem can help you avoid relapse following treatment. If your use hasn't yet progressed to abuse and dependence, this information can help you avoid developing an addiction problem.

Warning signs of addiction

The defining sign of addiction is that you feel compelled to do it. In Chapter 5, we provide a tool that assists you in assessing the likelihood that you're addicted. We also discuss the risk factors for developing an addiction problem. Some of the factors that you need to be aware of are:

- **Your family history:** The attitudes, behaviors, and genetic vulnerabilities that you pick up from your family render you more or less susceptible to developing an addiction problem.

- **Your willingness to experiment with risky behaviors:** If you're a risk-taker by nature, you're more likely to experiment with drugs. Experimentation is always the first step toward addiction.

- **Your mental states:** If you have problems controlling negative mood states like anxiety, depression, and anger, you're more likely to turn to substances (for instance, alcohol) or addictive behaviors (for instance, overeating) as a way of regulating your moods.

- **Your choice of drugs:** Some drugs are more addictive than others (check out the addictive potential of different substances in Chapter 5).

A comment for families and friends of the addicted person

Families often notice that something is wrong without knowing the specifics of the problem. In Chapter 5, we provide an assessment tool that helps family members and friends determine whether their loved one is battling an addiction problem. Uncharacteristic and negative changes in your loved one's moods and social habits are the real clues. But ultimately, your only way of getting to the bottom of the problem is a sincere talk.

Be careful not to enable your loved one's addiction. Family members tend to want to protect the addicted person and reduce potential harm. This may take the form of bailing your loved one out of jail, offering housing, or ensuring proper nutrition. All of these actions, although they reduce the harm, can enable your loved one to continue to abuse substances. Helping your addicted relative prevents the person from hitting bottom. Harm reduction efforts are important, especially when addiction treatments have repeatedly failed. However, be mindful of the fact that your good intentions may be allowing your loved one to continue to abuse drugs. Get good advice from professionals about how to best handle addiction in a loved one. In Part II of this book, we talk about addiction treatment options. In Chapter 18, we provide specific information for family members and friends.

 Look after your own needs. A loved one's addiction problem can quickly dominate the lives of family members and friends. Moreover, family members and friends can quickly become discouraged by their loved one's repeated failures at stopping the addiction. Thus, you need to look after your own needs. In Chapter 18, we provide information on how to protect your own welfare when battling the consequences of a loved one's addiction.

Exploring Methods and Models of Treatment

Do I have an addiction problem? Am I ready for treatment? Do I need to be hospitalized to safely withdraw from a substance addiction? After I've kicked the physical dependence on the substance, can I kick the mental addiction on my own? What are my treatment options? Who typically undergoes this or that type of treatment? What treatment options are available on an outpatient basis and which ones involve residential stays? What are some of the myths about overcoming an addiction? When are self-help treatment approaches helpful?

These and other questions are addressed in Part III of this book. Fortunately, a very wide range of treatment methods and models are available for assisting you. A few of these are previewed in the following sections.

Treatment centers and professional help

Shame about the addiction is the major barrier to seeking professional help. Most likely, you've tried to quit on your own and sought advice from trusted advisers (friends, family doctor, minister, priest, or rabbi) before seeking professional help. Unfortunately, many advisers don't have the expert knowledge or resources to help you withdraw. Nor can they provide treatment for the mental aspects of addictions. However, they're often a good resource for learning about specific addiction treatment options in your community.

In some situations, you may not be seeking help on your own. Rather, it's your family or employer who is confronting you with treatment options. Thus, your initial exposure to treatment may not have been the treatment of your choice.

 You must want to change to successfully recover. No amount of external persuasion will help overcome an addiction if you don't want to change. After you do get to the point of seriously engaging with treatment, seek out the treatments most suited to your needs.

Things to consider when deciding on your treatment

Many treatment options are available to you. What you choose depends on a number of factors:

- ✔ Can you afford the time and money it takes to go into a residential treatment facility? Most require a minimum stay of 28 days. Can you afford not to?

- ✔ Residential treatment centers offer some advantages over outpatient programs. They get you away from many of the social and environmental triggers for your addiction. You're exposed to treatment information from the professional staff and from peers within the center. Your peers can share their firsthand experiences about what has and hasn't helped them, and they can be an unconditional source of support.

- ✔ Quitting an addiction is often easier than staying substance- or behavior-free over the long-term. Relapse rates are alarmingly high. The mental aspects of addictions are usually harder to treat than the physical dependence. Addictions affect every aspect of your life. Triggers are hidden deep within your family and social environments. Therefore, consider a variety of treatment options for help with all of the different aspects of an addiction problem.

- ✔ When it comes to treating addictions, take a variety of approaches. Most treatment options allow you the freedom to combine different approaches.

✔ Abstinence is usually the goal of treatment. In some cases controlled use is possible. Chapter 9 provides information on controlled drinking approaches.

If you are physically dependent on a substance like alcohol, controlled use is not an option for you. Your treatment goal needs to be abstinence.

The twelve-step program and other self-help approaches

Almost everyone has heard of Alcoholics Anonymous (AA), but you may not know everything about what a twelve-step program involves. The twelve-step program is perhaps the most common treatment model for overcoming addictions. Although it started as a peer-support treatment program for alcohol addiction, it has rapidly proliferated as a treatment for both substance and nonsubstance addictions. You can find an AA program in virtually every community. Many AA groups address multiple types of addictions, so you may not need to find a specific group for your addiction. We have devoted a whole chapter (Chapter 11) to describing the twelve-step program. We also include a self-assessment tool to help you determine whether the twelve-step treatment approach is likely to work for you.

Self-help approaches generally aren't sufficient to help you get clean. You may well need to start with a residential treatment approach early in your recovery program. You can also consider combining various treatment approaches. Because addictions affect every area of your life, you may also need psychotherapeutic approaches to help you unravel the emotional and social aspects of your addiction problem. Chapter 8 provides information on some of the psychotherapy approaches to treating addictions.

The Ins and Outs of Recovery

As you begin the journey of recovery (whether it is the first time or the umpteenth time), we hope that this book will help you find the means to free yourself from addictions.

The treatment of addictions involves both getting clean and restoring a normal way of living. Therefore, recovery means not just abstinence from the addiction but also repairing the damages that the addiction has brought to your life and addressing some of the vulnerabilities in your emotional makeup and social background that rendered you susceptible to addictions. Effective recovery, therefore, also means building awareness and strategies to resist your triggers. In Part IV of this book, we focus on these recovery topics.

Overcoming fears and obstacles to recovery

What will it mean to go into treatment? What will your friends and colleagues think about you? How will you cope with the loss of comfort you associate with your addiction? You need to be aware that your anxiety, shame, anticipated loss, and other issues will act as barriers to getting help for your addiction. Chapter 15 provides guidance to you in overcoming these barriers to change.

Remember that solutions you use to deal with your addiction will also need to address the specific issues in your social and psychological environment that present barriers to successful recovery.

What to do if you slip

You need to know that recovery is a work in progress. As you repair and rebuild your life after an addiction, you will come face-to-face with temptations and triggers to slip back. You may slip off the wagon once, twice, or even more, but treat slips as temporary lapses in your recovery process and look for what you can learn from the situation. For example, a longer passage of time of abstinence between the slips is also positive feedback. Thus, learning about your triggers (when you feel down, for example) can help you plan how to handle the same situation (trigger) more effectively next time. Chapter 16 provides specific guidance in handling slips and relapses.

How to relate to family, friends, and colleagues

By the time you find yourself in treatment for an addiction, a lot of hurtful things have probably been said and done by you to your family as well as by your family to you. If these relationships can be mended, your recovery may have an easier path. Therefore, we encourage you and your family and friends to consider actively participating in the forgiveness process. Chapter 17 deals with handling these relationships in recovery.

Recovery can also be a time for the start of new relationships. You've seen the damage that addictions can do to intimate relationships. You may feel anxious about when to trust yourself enough to start a new relationship. You may have questions about how much to disclose to new friends. These and related issues are addressed in Chapter 17.

Many successfully recovered addicts liken their process to a rebirth. It's normal and natural for you to seek new friends and relationships. Frequently, you may connect with other ex-addicts that you meet in peer group therapy settings.

What family and friends can do

Addiction isn't just the problem of the person battling addiction. The personal problems of the addicted individual cause collateral damage to family, friends, and colleagues. Thus, many sections of this book provide tips for friends and family. Chapter 18 focuses specifically on guidance for families and friends.

Chapter 2

Substance Use, Substance Abuse, and Addiction

Substance use is part of our heritage. We humans have experimented with mind-altering substances for some time. And substance use is even part of our prehistory because monkeys, gorillas, chimpanzees, and other primates ingested alcohol after discovering fermented fruit. Unfortunately, substance abuse also goes far back. The first record of abuse dates back to 6th century BC in regard to an alcohol-abusing Persian king.

In this chapter, we discuss current *substances of abuse* — those that people use to alter their minds. First, we go over the basics of what drug and alcohol substances are and what they do. Then, we present an in-depth list that covers most substances abused today.

The Basics of How Substances of Abuse Work

To understand substances, you have to think like a chemist (for a little while). A molecule is the smallest unit of a substance. At the molecular level, the substance is pure, but "on the street" it's rarely pure — all street drugs are contaminated. By *contaminated*, we mean mixed with other substances that dilute effects and increase the profits of distributors! Less frequently, an additional substance is used to enhance the drug's effects.

Drug and alcohol substances consist of *active ingredients* (the actual molecules that cross the blood/brain barrier), *buffers* (chemicals that neutralize or even reverse the effects of the active drug), and *fillers* (substances that come along for the ride). The active ingredients of most drugs and types of alcohol are well-known, usually leaving a detectable chemical fingerprint within our bodies.

The active ingredients in drugs and alcohol are *psychoactive,* meaning they influence mental functions such as thinking, remembering, and sensing. Substances may also affect breathing and the function of your heart and other organs. Some drugs, if taken excessively, are toxic or poisonous, and, yes, they can kill you!

Addiction occurs when you need more of a drug to get high and you suffer withdrawal when the drug level in your system drops. Add these biochemical changes to the loss of control that you'll likely experience (when you feel controlled by the drug instead of vice-versa), and you're on your way to understanding addiction.

The Drug Lineup

Taking nonmedical drugs and other substances requires an experimental attitude. We discuss the different characteristics of people who are likely to experiment in Chapter 4. If you ingest substances, they tend to have predictable effects on you: some rev you up, some calm you down, and others trip you out. However, for some people, a given drug may also be a dud with little or no effect.

As we proceed to discuss the menu of available substances, we want to make the point that all of them can be dangerous. But some are more dangerous than others. Exactly *how* dangerous depends on how much you take, for how long, and how you react to the dosage (meaning the concentration of the drug). Some people have reactions to even small amounts of a drug (due to genetics, allergies, and other sensitivities).

You may see references in the addictions field to *controlled substances.* This term refers to the legal status of certain substances. Typically, nicotine and caffeine aren't designated as controlled substances because they've been used for a long time and are more socially acceptable.

In this book, we discuss the commonly abused drugs. The major categories include: sedatives, stimulants, narcotics, psychedelics and hallucinogens, anti-anxiety and antidepressant drugs, volatile hydrocarbons, dissociative anesthetics, and steroids. We go over the major players in each category in the sections that follow.

Marijuana (THC)

Marijuana is a mixture of dried and shredded leaves, stems, and seeds of the hemp plant, *Cannabis sativa*. The mixture can be green, brown, or grey in color. Marijuana's key chemical (the one influencing brain function) is THC or tetrahydrocannabinol. But 400 other chemicals are present in marijuana. In any case, THC works by releasing the pleasure-causing chemical, dopamine, in the brain.

We know of more than 200 street names for marijuana. Some of the more common ones include: *pot, grass, weed, reefer, Mary Jane, skunk, boom, kif,* and *ganja.*

Marijuana is used in many ways. It may be smoked in a cigarette, known as a *joint* or *nail.* It may be smoked through a water pipe called a *bong,* or in a *blunt* (a hollowed out cigar filled with the plant). It may also be brewed in a tea or mixed with food (yes, brownies seem to work for some folks).

Marijuana has a relatively low addiction potential because the withdrawal effects aren't very severe and tolerance builds slowly. Psychological dependence, however, can be a significant issue. You may feel that you *must* use the drug in order to relax. Using marijuana depresses your brain function to the point where chronic use results in lethargy and a reduction in motivation that may affect functioning at work, school, or home.

Sedatives and tranquilizers

Tranquilizers are *depressant* drugs (they slow down and depress brain function). Sedatives are often used as sleep aids, relaxers, and anti-anxiety calmers.

Alcohol

Ethanol is a particular type of alcohol produced by the fermentation of foods and grains. The most common sources are barley, hops, grapes, and potatoes. Other commonly available alcohol types are highly poisonous even in smaller quantities. These include methanol (usually found in glass cleaners), isopropyl alcohol (rubbing alcohol), and ethylene glycol (automobile antifreeze solutions). In this book, when we refer to *alcohol,* we mean ethanol.

Alcohol depresses the actions of the brain, causing progressive impairment and basically reducing the flow of signals. In addition to disinhibition, the most common effects are memory loss (and sometimes blackout), confusion, disorientation, uncoordinated movements, lethargy, coma, and respiratory shutdown (often fatal).

Date rape drugs

Two other drugs in the pharmaceutical sedative class are known as date rape drugs because of their properties (colorless, odorless, only slightly salty to taste), their knockout potential, and their effects on memory.

✔ GHB (also called *Georgia Home Boy* or *grievous bodily harm*) is a sedative-hypnotic that causes sleepiness and dizziness. With an overdose, breathing slows, and you may experience a loss of consciousness. Combining this drug with alcohol is particularly risky because breathing slows dangerously. You will feel the primary effect between 10 minutes and 1 hour after ingestion, but it will last 2 to 3 hours with residual effects for up to 24 hours.

✔ Rohypnol (often called *Roofies*) is the brand name for a benzodiazepine, fluni-trazepam that is many times stronger than Valium (diazepam). Sedation occurs usually within 30 minutes after ingestion and lasts for several hours. Roofies, like GHB, are dangerous when taken with alcohol. If you ingest this drug, chances are that your memory will be impaired, and when the drug effect wears off you won't know where or when you took it.

Alcohol, although legal in most countries, has about the same addiction potential as cocaine. Surprised? Unfortunately, the legal status of a drug doesn't necessarily indicate how potentially addictive it is. Tobacco, another highly addictive substance (even more addictive for lab animals than cocaine), is also legal.

Pharmaceutical sedatives

Sedatives are usually prescribed for sleep problems and anxiety. These drugs should generally be used only over a short-term, usually five to seven days, because they carry significant risks for dependence and tolerance.

Over the longer-term, use of this class of drugs may bring about irritability, lethargy, decreased motivation, vivid and disturbing dreams, nausea, headache, skin rash, tremors, a change in appetite (loss or increase), and sexual impairment.

The commonly known pharmaceutical sedative drugs are Valium, Librium, BuSpar, Equanil, Miltown Serax, Clonapin, and Halcion. These drugs, known as benzodiazepines, are taken by mouth in pill form and give most people a sense of relaxation and well-being. They also lead to drowsiness, confusion, slurring of speech, and memory problems.

Methaqualone (Quaaludes, Sopor, Parest) was at one time a popu-lar party drug that has fallen into disfavor. It will probably be back some day because drugs, like fashions, often go through cycles of favor and disfavor.

Sedatives have a high addiction potential because they're short-acting and you quickly build up a tolerance to them (you eventually require more drug to get the same mind altering effect.)

Barbiturates

These drugs include Mephobarbital (Mebaral) and Pentobarbital sodium (Nembutol). They're used for sleep disorders and (at higher doses) for anesthesia. Acting on the GABA neurotransmitter system, they slow brain activity, thereby producing a calm feeling. Like all depressants, they have a potential for tolerance, physical dependence, withdrawal (watch out for seizures), and addiction.

Barbiturates are controlled substances because they have a fairly high addiction potential. They effectively numb your mind and, over time, they require higher and higher doses to achieve similar effects.

Stimulants

Stimulants are a class of drugs that increase alertness and physical activity. They include amphetamines (pharmaceuticals such as Dexedrine and Biphetamine also known as *speed*), methamphetamines *(meth, chalk, ice, crystal, glass)* and cocaine *(blow, bump, coke, Charlie, rock, snow, toot)*. If you start using these drugs, chances are high that you will develop intense cravings for more.

Stimulants may be taken in different forms: swallowed, snorted, smoked, or injected. Injecting stimulants is the riskiest method (due to HIV needle infection, and so on) and swallowing is the safest — from the immediately physical viewpoint, at any rate.

Stimulants increase heart and respiration rates, increase blood pressure, *dilate* (expand) the pupils, and decrease appetite. The last side effect was once a sought-after attribute of stimulants in their use as weight-loss drugs. Now we know better!

Amphetamines

Amphetamines are psychologically addictive because people become dependent on taking more to avoid feeling the down of withdrawal (got to keep that rush going or you'll crash and burn!). If you suddenly stop using the drug, you end up feeling tired, sleepy, irritable, and depressed. The severity and length of time that you experience these effects vary depending on the degree of abuse. (See Chapter 10 for more information on withdrawal effects from these substances.)

What do amphetamines, tobacco (nicotine), diet pills, laxatives, steroids, and diuretics all have in common? Answer: girls. Yes! They're all used by adolescent girls who are trying to stay thin.

Cocaine

Cocaine Hydrochloride is a white powder derived from the leaves of the coca plant. Cocaine used to be sold over the counter in many forms (yes, including Coca Cola!). Crack cocaine is made chemically by altering cocaine powder into crystals or *rocks* that can be smoked. Cocaine is short-acting (the effects are fairly immediate and peak after 15 to 30 minutes), so users are very motivated to keep getting another hit every 15 to 30 minutes to maintain the buzz.

Entactogens

This class of drugs was originally developed to help people who have experienced trauma. Ecstasy, for example, (MDMA, also called *Adam, Eve, STP, X*) is a mood-elevating drug that can also produce hallucinations. MDMA takes effect 20 to 40 minutes after ingestion, causing exhilaration (and often nausea). You may feel empathy for others and an enhanced feeling of warmth and self-acceptance. For this reason, MDMA is sometimes referred to as a love drug.

Using MDMA carries two main risks. The first is contamination with other drugs during manufacturing (everything from amphetamine to PCP to fillers). These fillers may create toxic effects. The second risk is the tendency of users to overheat from heavy exertion (for instance, dancing) and not enough water. In extreme cases, these effects, individually or in combination, can result in coma and death.

Yet another entactogen, called 2 C-B *(bromo, nexus, spectrum)*, is also a psychedelic drug. It was developed in the 1970s and has the effect of making you feel more "in touch" emotionally. You may readily experience certain erotic sensations and feel acutely responsive to music and color.

The drug 2 C-B is taken orally in pill form. Although it's generally well-tolerated (nausea and chills are the main side-effects), there is a greater tendency for a bad trip than there is with MDMA. What is particularly dangerous about 2 C-B is any combination with alcohol, or with other depressant drugs. Although difficult to predict, the effects include elevated body temperature and high blood pressure.

The entactogens, generally, are associated with mental confusion and anxiety-provoking experiences that can add up to a *bad trip* —

feeling scared and out of control. The combination of a psychological state of relaxation, sensitivity to music and color, and your body overheating to the point of collapse, is a significant risk.

Opiates and narcotics

Heroin and morphine are the most common drugs in this family. Heroin (*smack, horse, junk,* and *dope*) is made from the opium poppy and is a white or brownish powder (or a brown sticky substance known as *tar*). Heroin is typically cut or mixed with other white powder additives.

Heroin is snorted, smoked *(chased),* or injected (the most common route). After ingesting heroin, you may feel a sense of euphoria, contentment, well-being, and warmth. Heroin and morphine are painkillers. The side effects you may expect are nausea, vomiting, itching, and slowed breathing.

Two other powerful painkillers, oxycodone hydrochloride (OxyContin) and hydrocodone bitartrate (Vicodin) are increasingly popular substances to abuse. OxyContin is a controlled-release drug that provides approximately 12 hours of pain relief. The drug has a high potential for abuse, because the more you take, the better you feel. This effect is different from other pain relievers like aspirin or acetaminophen; these drugs have a threshold to their effectiveness.

People who abuse OxyContin avoid the controlled release by chewing, snorting, or injecting the drug to get an intense high.

 Painkillers such as OxyContin and Vicodin act on the same parts of the brain as does heroin. There has been a troubling increase in reported abuse of these drugs in high school students. Parents, grandparents, and other adults should keep a close eye on medicine cabinets if anyone in the house is taking these drugs.

The opiates, particularly the newer painkillers described above, have a very high addiction potential. These drugs seem to pull you back to chasing the high you experienced. And the tolerance effects ensure that you will need to use more and more of the drug to get to the same state.

Psychedelics and hallucinogens

Direct from the Age of Aquarius, with a history going back thousands of years, hallucinogens take people on far-ranging trips inside their own minds. Hallucinogens (also called psychedelics) cause your brain to generate experiences that are profound distortions of reality.

We have five senses: seeing, hearing, tasting, touching, and smelling. Hallucinogens distort these senses, and particularly change your impressions of time and space. Hallucinogens specifically disrupt the neurotransmitter serotonin and interfere with the way your neural cells interact. Serotonin can be found in many places in the central nervous system (your brain and spinal cord) and assists in the functions controlling mood, hunger, body temperature, sexual behavior, muscle control, and sensory perception.

The trips caused by hallucinogens can last for as long as 6 to 12 hours. Some trips are good, some are bad. A good trip is dependent on your mindset when you take the drug. Your reaction may differ from time to time, even though you take the same amount of a drug. A *good trip* often involves visual hallucinations (seeing things that aren't really there or that are distorted). These images may be seen as funny or inspiring, or just odd. Colors may be especially intense and intriguing patterns may emerge on surfaces, like tables or ceilings. Distortions of objects, faces, and other body parts may be experienced. A heightened sexual drive — an aphrodisiac effect — has also been reported.

A bad trip on the other hand, may be set off by similar doses of drug that in the past provided a good trip. A *bad trip* is a frightening experience with surging anxiety and fears of being out of control and vulnerable. Terrifying images and hallucinations have been reported. At different times, under controlled conditions, hallucinogens have been used in experimental forms of psychotherapy, because they seem to bring underlying conflicts to the surface. The bad trips may be linked to these conflicts surfacing, especially when they take symbolic forms and distort reality (these distorted thoughts and images are like a very bad nightmare).

Some hallucinogens come from plants but most are synthesized and manufactured. Mescaline comes from the cactus plant called peyote. Psilocybin comes from certain mushrooms often referred to as *magic mushrooms* or *shrooms* (for short). LSD (lysergic acid diethylamide, also known as *acid*) and a dissociative anaesthetic, PCP, (phencyclidine or *angel dust*) are widely available synthetic hallucinogens.

Taking LSD may make you feel several emotions simultaneously and may merge senses so that you see sounds and hear colors. LSD itself, is a clear or white, odorless, water-soluble material synthesized from lysergic acid, a compound rye fungus.

The potential of LSD for abuse is fairly high because the experiences are exciting to some people and they want to re-experience their excitement until, of course, they have a bad trip. If you value self-control, it's unlikely that you'll want to gamble in this way about having a good versus a bad trip.

If you use LSD, you may experience *flashbacks* — a repetition of earlier LSD experiences. A flashback often has an unsettling effect, because it is something that is frequently beyond your control. Flashbacks can occur later in your life and seem to be set off by past associations. A similar experience has been reported by people with post-traumatic stress where they relive their trauma. In a flashback you have to redirect your attention to the present and get out of your head. Flashbacks are a significant concern if they occur when you're driving or in other situations where distractions can result in elevated risks.

Dissociative anesthetics

Drugs such as phencyclidine (PCP) and ketamine (*Special K*) were developed as general anesthetics. They produce distortions in both sight and sound and a general feeling of detachment (you feel far away from your body). Dextromethorphan, a widely available cough suppressant, when taken in high doses, can produce effects similar to PCP and ketamine. Nitrous oxide, sometimes known as *laughing gas,* is also a member of this same category of substances.

PCP, ketamine, and dextromethorphan work by preventing a neurotransmitter, glutamate, from attaching to its receptors in the brain. Glutamate is involved in the perception of pain, responses to the environment, and memory. Although low doses of these anesthetics increase heart rate, higher doses can depress consciousness and breathing. Combining this category of substances with alcohol or other sedatives is extremely dangerous.

These dissociative anesthetics carry the risk of extreme psychological dependence. They separate your perceptions from sensations (what you feel like with heat or cold), giving you a dreamy feeling. It is difficult to move in this state, and you may experience a sense of vulnerability. In fact, you *are* vulnerable to outside dangers because of your inability to move.

Anti-anxiety and antidepressant drugs

We're living in the New Age of the Pill (no we're not referring to the birth control pill — that was the 1960s). In this new age, the pill we're talking about controls your negative emotions, such as anxiety and depression.

Antidepressants such as the selective serotonin reuptake inhibitors (SSRIs for short), including Prozac and Zoloft, are powerful drugs designed to change your negative moods.

Serotonin is a neurotransmitter. "Selective reuptake inhibitor" means the drug is designed to pick out this particular neurotransmitter, serotonin, in your brain. To inhibit the reuptake of serotonin, the drug works by taking the spot on the brain receptor where the serotonin usually goes. This means that there is more serotonin available in the synapse, and the chemical transmission of the nerve signal is enhanced.

Antidepressant drugs aren't known as drugs of abuse because they don't produce a physical dependency. They do help restore normal mood states via their effects on the neurotransmitter system of the brain. However, these effects aren't addictive.

Anti-anxiety drugs, on the other hand, do result in tolerance and dependency. They have mind-altering effects described earlier in the chapter in the sedatives/tranquilizers section. Thus, the addiction potential of anti-anxiety drugs is considerably higher.

Volatile hydrocarbons (inhalants)

Volatile hydrocarbons (inhalants) are breathable chemical vapors that can produce mind-altering effects. Several products found at home and in the workplace contain psychoactive substances that can be inhaled to get high. On the street, this activity is known as *huffing*. Inhalants fall into three main categories: solvents, gases, and nitrates.

Inhalant abuse is most typically found in young people — peaking in grades seven to nine. Initially, more females than males use inhalants. Males start using with increasing numbers later on in high school and may sustain the use well into their twenties.

Inhalants differ in makeup but work much like anesthetics. They slow down your body's functions and numb the brain. Inhaled through either your nose or mouth into the lungs, these substances cause you to experience short-term (a few minutes) intoxication.

Inhalants can be very dangerous. The primary risks are cognitive impairment, brain damage, and other neurological (nerve-related) problems. If you've been inhaling over a long period, you may eventually start losing consciousness during your inhaling. Also, huffing concentrates chemicals that can directly induce heart failure and sudden death within minutes of using (this is known as *sudden sniffing death*). This is typically associated with the abuse of butane, propane, and aerosol chemicals. Over time, the liver and kidneys can also be damaged.

Using inhalants by way of a plastic bag increases the chances of suffocation. Suffocation occurs as the substance takes the place of oxygen in your lungs, resulting in oxygen debt and leading your brain to shut down.

Solvents

Many people don't realize that solvents can be used to get intoxicated. These substances include industrial and household solvents such as paint thinners, paint removers, degreasers, dry-cleaning fluids, gasoline, and glue. Other solvents that may be abused are office supplies, including correction fluids, felt-tip marker fluids, and electronic contact cleaners (the cleaner used to clean computer keyboards and screens). These substances have addiction potential primarily because of their easy access and their powerful effects to numb the person who is trying to escape the realities of his or her life.

Gases

Gases include household and commercial products such as butane lighters, propane tanks, whipping cream aerosols, and refrigerant gases. Household aerosol propellants and associated solvents include spray paints, hair spray, deodorant sprays, and fabric protector sprays.

Medical anesthetic gases include ether, chloroform, halothane, and nitrous oxide *(laughing gas)*. Nitrous oxide is the most commonly abused of these gases and can be found in whipped cream dispensers and products used to increase octane in racing cars.

Nitrates/poppers

These substances range from the aliphatic nitrates including cyclohexyl nitrate (an ingredient found in room deodorizers), amyl nitrate (used medically), and butyl nitrate (previously used to manufacture perfumes and antifreeze but now illegal).

Nitrates act primarily to dilate blood vessels and to relax the muscles. They're often used to enhance the experience of sex or before sporting events to reduce stress. On the street, ampules of amyl nitrate and butyl nitrate are known as *poppers* or *snappers*.

Volatile hydrocarbons have a high addiction potential because people build tolerance for them over time. Psychological dependence also builds because users may start to count on the substances to avoid reality.

Recent research suggests the possibility that the abuse of nitrate inhalants may increase the risk of infection or tumor, because the body becomes less resistant to disease.

Steroids

Many men, particularly young men, want to develop bodies like bodybuilders. How do they do it? Well, steroids are synthetic substances that have a similar chemistry to the male hormone testosterone. The most common names of anabolic (muscle-building) steroids are anadrol, oxandrin, dianobol, winstol, deca-durabolin, and equipoise. The street names of steroids include *roids* and *juice*.

Testosterone is an important male sex hormone that both promotes muscle growth (the anabolic effect) and develops male sexual characteristics (the androgenic effect). So anabolic-androgenic steroids (often shortened to just anabolic steroids) are drugs that work like testosterone.

Anabolic steroids were originally developed to treat a condition known as hypogonadism, in which the male's testes don't produce enough testosterone. Steroids also have some limited legitimate medical uses for people with certain types of anemia (loss of red blood cells), and systemic lupus erythematosus. But steroid abuse has nothing to do with these conditions.

Some steroid users pop pills, but others inject the drug directly into muscles. Most users are taking doses that are 10 to 100 times larger than those that may be legitimately prescribed by physicians.

Steroids are primarily psychologically addicting because of their muscle-building effects. If you use steroids, you will probably feel stronger and gain bulk. But remember, you're putting yourself at risk for cancer, liver disease, and sex changes (shrunken testicles for males and male sex characteristics for females). These effects may be irreversible and may take years to develop.

Steroids affect your secondary sex characteristics. Males may experience shrunken testicles, the growth of breasts, and reduced sperm count. Females may grow facial hair, develop a deeper voice, and grow excessive body hair. All users are prone to acne, hair loss, tumors (usually liver tumors), and violent, angry mood swings — rampages. Scary stuff!

Chapter 3

Behavioral Addictions: Addictions Without Substances

This chapter focuses on activities that become excessive and addictive. We explain how certain emotional problems (like loneliness, depression, and anxiety) underlie behavioral addictions, driving people toward isolation, secrecy, and self-destructive actions.

Behavior refers to how you act and is scientifically studied in the field of psychology. It's observed by others and linked to your thinking (and how it is expressed in verbal behavior) and your *physiology* (bodily processes). *Behavioral addictions* refer to actions that are out of control and dominate your time and attention. Interruptions of these actions produce withdrawal symptoms similar to those experienced when withdrawing from substances.

Behavioral addictions can be as destructive as substance addictions. Some, like compulsive gambling, are associated with a significant risk to life (via suicide), but all behavioral addictions involve extremes that disrupt the lives of individuals and sometimes, the lives of entire families. Like substance abusers, behavioral addicts have preferences (preferred activities) that are linked to experiences of pleasure, excitement, and success.

Behavioral addictions take up a great deal of your time, and they also rob you of a tremendous amount of energy. More than anything, they rob you of your relationships with others. Your addictive behaviors can be so dominating that they get in the way of you relating, in a sensitive or meaningful way, to anyone else.

An *obsession* involves not being able to stop thinking about something, and a *compulsion* involves not being able to stop doing something. When a behavior becomes compulsive, you're driven to act out the behavior. You've lost control.

Some General Advice

We all act automatically, but we have control mechanisms that limit these automatic behaviors. When you have a behavioral addiction or are developing one, you find these controls oddly absent. You feel that you're going beyond what is healthy, reasonable, or normal but you just keep going, pursuing an activity to the point of disruption and ill-health.

This is not an indication of a genetic or character weakness or of an underlying problem that can't be effectively treated. However, like any other pattern of use, abuse, and addiction, behavioral addiction is more effectively treated if addressed earlier rather than later.

Try to see whether your problem behaviors are now beyond your own problem-solving abilities. Are you falling prey to your own compulsions? If you are, seek treatment *now* rather than *later.* You'll be much better off — and so will your friends and loved ones.

Compulsive Gambling

Gambling involves the betting or wagering of valuables on uncertain outcomes and takes many forms — from games of chance to skill-based activities. People have many motivations for gambling, but all involve the hope of gaining more. Gambling is sometimes a rite of passage by which people discover more about themselves and how to compete with others. It is sometimes a way of life (for people such as casino pros and escape gamblers). It can be, in its healthiest form, a way of socializing and having fun.

Pathological gambling is a progressive disorder that involves impulse-control problems. The consequences of pathological gambling are severe and may be devastating to the addicted person's family and career, but the disorder can be treated. Pathological gambling has been officially defined, in psychiatric terms, as "a persistent, recurrent maladaptive gambling behavior that disrupts personal, family, or vocational pursuits" (*DSM-IV-TR*). As with all addictions, pathological gambling has personal, familial, and neurochemical aspects. Pathological gamblers may even have a genetic vulnerability, although such complex behaviors are unlikely to be traced to one specific gene in the same way some medical conditions, like cystic fibrosis, have been.

Three phases of compulsive gambling

Dr. Robert Custer has identified three phases to a progressive gambling problem: a winning phase, a losing phase, and a desperation phase.

Winning

In the winning phase, you may experience a "big win" or a series of smaller wins that result in excess optimism. You may feel an unrealistic sense of power and control and you're excited by the prospect of more wins. ("Hey Doc, this is a sure thing. I'm betting the farm.") At the same time, you can't maintain the excitement unless you're continually involved in high-risk bets. Your bets increase, and ultimately, the increased risk puts you in a vulnerable situation where you can't afford to lose . . . and then, sure as the sun rises, you do lose.

Losing

In the losing phase, you may brag about past wins; how you had the casino or track or bookie on the ropes. But in the immediate situation, you're losing more than winning. You're more likely to gamble alone, and when not gambling, you're more likely to spend time thinking about how and when you'll gamble next. Most importantly, you're concerned with how you'll raise more money, legally or illegally. You may have a few wins that fuel the size of your bets. But the dominant pattern is that of losing. Moreover, making the next bet becomes more important than the winning of any previous bet.

As you continue to read these descriptions, you may find yourself feeling more desperate. A sense of futility may begin building. You may think "How stupid can they be?" or "I don't do that!" The emotions within you are building for a reason. Don't avoid seeing the compulsive nature of your gambling behavior. If the shoe fits, at least try it on. If our descriptions fit your experiences, be aware that your behavior may be getting progressively out of control!

The business of gambling

Many groups, from governments to native peoples to criminals are involved in the gambling business. In fact, research reveals that gambling is a $100 billion per year business in the United States. People spend more money on legal gambling than on movie tickets, recorded music, theme parks, spectator sports, and video games combined. This fact indicates how strong commercial gambling interests are — and how difficult they are to restrain.

As the losing continues, you start lying to family and friends and feeling more irritable, restless, and emotionally isolated. You start borrowing money that you're unsure about being able to repay. As your life becomes unmanageable, you may be developing some serious financial problems. Your denial of the huge financial pressures that are building may seem unbelievable to some people: You're also likely to start *chasing your losses,* trying to win back what you lost. ("Doc, I'll stop, but first I've got to get back to even.") If you don't change your pattern, however, you'll be engaging in more and more self-destructive behavior.

Desperation

The next phase, the desperation phase, involves still another marked change in your gambling behavior. You may now make bets more often than is normal, in more desperate attempts to catch up and "get even." The behavior that's now out of control is associated with deep remorse, with blaming others, and with the alienation of family and friends. You may engage in illegal activities to finance your gambling. You may experience a sense of hopelessness and think about suicide and divorce. Other addictions and emotional problems may also intensify during this phase and drag you down.

The impact of compulsive gambling

If any of the preceding descriptions fit you, you may be one of the 3 percent of adults in North America who experience a gambling problem that results in debt, family disruption, job loss, criminal activity, or suicide. There is another important statistic to keep in mind if you're a youthful gambler or a parent of one: According to researchers Dr. Henry Lesieur and Dr. Durand Jacobs, people who begin gambling as adolescents are about *three times more likely* to become problem gamblers than people who begin gambling as adults.

Examples of frauds related to compulsive gambling

Here are just a few examples of crimes committed because of compulsive gambling:

✔ The president and CEO of a company fraudulently obtained loans of more than $10 million to pay off gambling debts.

✔ The chairman of a bank passed $8 million in checks with insufficient funds to cover debts to 2 casinos.

✔ A physician borrowed over $8 million to cover gambling debts and then declared bankruptcy.

✔ A 66-year-old grandmother embezzled $4.9 million to feed her gambling habit.

An excellent review, available at www.wasc.noaa.gov/wrso/security_guide/gamble.htm, lists the prosecutions and convictions associated with gambling debts. Some of the amounts of money involved are staggering. All of the people who wound up with these huge problems went through a phase of denial. If you're unsure whether you have a gambling problem, you may want to check out this Web site and the movie *Owning Mahowny,* the true story of a bank employee who became a compulsive gambler.

It's about money

Money helps buy fantasies. When people play the lotteries, they can dream of winning money and living out fantasies. But what really happens to the people who win? Most donate to charity; some report being happy afterwards; but many stories don't have happy endings. In fact, many stories of lottery wins remind us that winning doesn't help some people. As is true for problem gamblers, winning can be the first slippery step in a downfall.

Researchers at Emory University demonstrated that working toward rewards is more stimulating to the pleasure centers in the brain than simply winning rewards. If you watch people play slot machines, you can observe this in their behavior. What dominates them is the compulsion to keep playing. They seem to be in a trancelike state. This finding can be understood in combination with the often-observed experience of numbness in casino winners. After you're in a numb state of mind, even winning loses its thrill and you wind up putting your winnings right back into play in order to recapture your excitement with more betting. You're trying to hold on to the excitement.

Ryan

Ryan B. is a 26 year old who was facing several charges of theft and forgery related to his gambling habit. He loved the rush of the casino but was equally at home at the racetrack or the poker table. He was on the lookout for *pigeons,* inexperienced people who would get into a game with him. He forgot that as one of the players at the table, he too was caught up in the game. He loved going to the action spots, from Monte Carlo to Las Vegas, more than he loved people or himself.

Ryan won and lost millions. He would be up thousands and even though he knew enough to leave, sometimes he would stay, and lose. He was in debt more than $300,000, and he started stealing from his employer to pay off his gambling debts. After serving five years for fraud, he is now a member of Gamblers' Anonymous, and as of today, remains in control.

It isn't about money

Some would argue that compulsive gambling isn't about the money. Well, then what is it about? What is the motivation for gambling? Some gamblers are sensation seekers or action gamblers. They love the stimulation and excitement. They like being the center of attention, with people admiring their risk-taking and their courage to stay in the game — no matter what the stakes.

Other gamblers are known as escape gamblers. If you're an *escape gambler,* you gamble to get away from the tedium of your every-day life.

Mary

Mary B. was a 66-year-old widow who loved to go to the casino on weekends with her seniors' group. Unlike her friends, Mary loved the casino for its calming influence, a chance to get away from her humdrum life, and, especially, to get away from the grief she typically felt on weekends.

Mary was concerned that her daughter was going to cut her off from her only form of entertainment, because she had gone a little wild and lost $ 1,500 in one weekend, "a silly mistake for a retired person."

Mary was in denial. She didn't see or accept the extent of her problem. In reality, Mary had lost over $60,000 of her life savings. She went to the casino and didn't really care if she won or lost. She only wanted to escape and "have some fun." Mary still hasn't gotten it. We are trying to help her daughter understand her mother's problem.

So, gambling may not be about the money. For compulsive gamblers, it rarely is. The thrills come from the action and the escape, among other things — these behaviors are understandable but, nonetheless, destructive.

Sex and Pornography

Sex addiction may involve one compulsive activity or several, often in a progressive process. You move from masturbatory activities, frequently involving pornography, to searching for contacts with others that are mostly related to sex and have little to do with building real relationships. If you're addicted to sex, you're likely to experience a sense of powerlessness over your behavior that transforms your life into an intensifying spiral of shame, self-hate, and loss (of relationships and jobs).

Pornography

Pornography involves viewing explicit sexual behaviors that typically include abuse, degradation, and/or aggression. There is more to pornography addiction than sex. It is a compulsive process that involves people shaming and humiliating other people.

Pornography users and addicts often find many different forms of stimulation sexually arousing and gratifying. Thus, it may be difficult to define a particular pattern of pornography use and addiction without a detailed history of the behavior involved. However, masturbation is usually a central process. Pornography addiction is similar to other behavioral addictions in that you lose control of your life and retreat from emotional intimacy. The emotional intimacy associated with sex, in particular, is often lost.

Sex addiction

Compulsive sexual behavior involves fantasy, excitement, and *satiation* (the process whereby you're no longer turned on by the same stimuli). It may be that you're always looking for that fantasized relationship. Sexual conquests are another side of the same coin, spurred on by the excitement of chasing and finally getting what was previously forbidden and dangerous. Over time, with no interest in intimacy, you become satiated and look for new stimuli and a new conquest.

Sexual addiction is about sex, not love. You have no interest in learning about another person and what he or she likes or who he or she is. Sex addiction is about the act and the independent experience of orgasm. Sex addiction is about conquest, not cooperation.

Here's a puzzle for you: Billy has been with Rachel for four years. They have made love about 1,000 times. Freddy, in the last four years, has had sex about the same number of times as Billy, but with more than 300 women. Who feels better about himself?

Billy has built a relationship with Rachel. They have memories of sexually ecstatic times and emotionally fulfilling times, and vacations in places that, for them, were exotic. They have a tradition of being there for each other and supporting each other through tough times. Freddy, despite the frequency and variety of his sexual conquests, is still alone.

Sex addicts are always looking for opportunity. "Any time, any place" is Freddy's motto. He does have some amazing stories. He feels good about them. They're his badges of honor and achievement. But when he looks at life, it's all about sex and it's not about love. Freddy has lost control and needs treatment. It's no longer about fun — he's behaving compulsively.

Love addiction

Falling in love is inevitably associated with periods where you're consumed with a relationship. Your thinking may appear obsessional. You may have trouble thinking of anything but your loved one. You can't conceive of not having him or her in your life. This belief can be anxiety provoking because it leaves you vulnerable to loss or rejection.

Fred

Fred was a vulnerable person. He was neglected as a child and felt alone, unloved by his family, and starved for affection (although he covered it up with a tough-guy act). Women could sense his little-boy vulnerability and unpredictability. Fred started to equate sex with love. He wanted to be loved, and sex was the ultimate expression of love. In this regard, he was sadly mistaken, because he would manipulate others in order to have sex, only to feel guilty and worthless when the act was over. He would leave only minutes after having sex. He was proud of his record: sex with over 200 women in three years (no need to get the calculator out, it averaged out to a date every five days). His conquests were a string of empty victories because his rage and hurt about his earlier abandonment still festered, untreated.

The process of falling in love and the obsessive nature of love addiction are often difficult to differentiate except for one critical element: Love matures over time and loses its compulsive nature, but addiction grows more and more compulsive. An increasing sense of desperation marks relationships involving love addictions.

Obsessive thinking is repetitive and centers on events and outcomes that are anxiety provoking. As an anxiety based response, it redirects your emotional pain toward something familiar and away from the more painful realities.

Love addiction is closely tied to low self-esteem, low self-confidence, and a fear of rejection and abandonment. You may behave in a dependent, needy, or even desperate way, fantasizing about the ideal relationship and worrying about what will happen if you don't have a lover in your life. If you insist on one particular person who must love you ("I'm nothing if X doesn't love me"), you're making it even harder on yourself.

Just like people who are addicted to substances or gambling, people who are addicted to sex or love are advised to go through a period of withdrawal and abstinence. The goal is to normalize relationships based on self-respect and not on obsessional thinking or compulsive behavior.

I fell in love with a fantasy

Judy, 33 years old, was an average person. She had a steady job and a good family. She loved reading articles and books on romance and knew that she would eventually find the right guy. She was always open to love, whether at work, while grocery shopping, or while doing her laundry. You just never knew when Mr. Right may show up. Judy was in a holding pattern.

When a man showed interest in Judy, she wanted to do everything "right." She knew that she should not be desperate or needy and should go slowly at first in building a relationship. The trouble was that Judy broke all her own rules. When within a relationship, she became clinging, afraid to lose her man (who didn't have a clue that he was so special). It would only get worse. Judy would behave in ways that went against her own values; she wanted constant attention and was sullen and explosive if she didn't get it. Judy's relationships were extremely intense at first and out of control with passion. She was willing to do anything. But then, like a fire starved for oxygen, the whole relationship would flame out. Judy suffered from love addiction; her real relationships could never compete with her fantasies. Judy needed treatment.

How do you normalize your reaction? During your period of abstinence, pursue some real interests and build some new skills (any
skills). See what turns you on in a nonsexual and independent
way. It may involve doing something creative (such as sculpting
or photography) or something challenging (like tennis or golf).
The goal is to develop a range of interests and activities that make
you feel good.

Computer Games and the Internet

In this section, we discuss computer gaming and other compulsive
uses of the Internet. Of course, some people regularly surf the
Internet to feed their pornography or relationship addictions, but
we don't discuss those issues here. Those situations are dominated
by sex or love addictions. The Internet is just the device by which
those addictions are pursued.

Experts disagree about what constitutes computer game and
Internet addiction. Although many behaviors are compulsive, every
compulsive behavior doesn't equal an addiction. The biggest test
of an addiction is the destructive, often antisocial nature of the
behavior. Because the Internet is often a very important way of
communicating in the 21st century, it is sometimes difficult to
judge where normal use ends and compulsion begins.

For example, relaxing by playing a game is a common stress-reliever.
But if playing that game dominates your life and excludes other
responsibilities, the behavior may be addictive.

As Ken Keyes Jr., the spiritualist, said: One test of addiction is as
follows: "Anything you tell yourself you have to have before you
are happy."

The appeal of the technology

When a new technology appears in our lives, it often promotes a
wider network of connections, new acquisitions of knowledge, and
increased convenience. You may get caught up for a time in this
new technology until you restore balance in your life. With every
interesting activity, there is some aspect of wanting to learn all you
can, often pushing yourself to the limit, before you pull back and
use the new technology in a reasonable way. For example, you may
love your new camera, because it's a sophisticated piece of technology that yields incredible images. If you spend hours with your
new camera, discovering all of its features and taking many pictures,
you aren't necessarily addicted to photography.

Popular computer games

What are some of most popular computer games that folks may be addicted to?

- ✔ Solitaire: A card game sorting into the categories of hearts, diamonds, spades, and clubs.

- ✔ The Sims: You help your characters cope with everyday life in the suburbs. There is no winning and losing. You just try to keep your Sims alive, happy, and entertained.

- ✔ City of Heroes: A multiplayer online role-playing game.

- ✔ Far Cry: A detailed action shooter combat game.

- ✔ Lord of the Realm: A medieval game of warfare and politics.

- ✔ Unreal Tournament: A gladiator game.

- ✔ Universal Combat: An epic space battle.

In contrast, addiction is a destructive and compulsive behavior pattern characterized by dependence, tolerance, and negative reactions to withdrawal. Learning something new and learning to use it as part of your life is seductive, but not addictive.

An example of computer addiction

You know you're addicted when your life is out of control. Barbara was an expert games player. She loved playing and started most afternoons before the kids came home from school. Over time, she played when the kids were home and even late into the night, long after her husband had gone to bed. Barbara interspersed her game playing by exchanging instant messages with newfound computer friends.

She liked herself during these times. She was a skilled player and liked the social contact of messaging. She preferred being on the computer to housework or spending time with her husband and gradually, preferred it to looking after her kids. Her family was frustrated. But according to Barbara, they didn't understand. Besides, her "friends" were all online.

Barbara's life started to become unmanageable. She neglected the house and kids. She was always waiting to get back online.

Computer addicts aren't particularly productive. They use the games and their contacts to live in a fantasy world.

Food Addiction

As described by Dr. Nora Volkow, psychiatrist and Director of the National Institute of Drug Abuse: "Eating is a highly reinforcing behavior just like taking illicit drugs." A recent study at the respected Brookhaven Laboratory reaffirmed this statement, demonstrating that the mere sight, smell, and taste of a favorite food, elevated the levels of dopamine (a neurochemical) in food-deprived subjects. This neurochemical is associated with experiences of pleasure and reward.

Addictive drugs increase the levels of dopamine in the brain. Some people with addictions tend to have fewer dopamine receptors than people who don't have addictions. Therefore, they may need to generate more dopamine in their systems in order to get rewarding effects. Some people who are obese also have fewer dopamine receptors. Thus, in a similar way, obese people may be trying to increase their dopamine levels by eating.

Eating too much

Obesity is a major public health problem in the Western world, having increased to epidemic proportions since the 1980s. More than 30 percent of American adults are now obese. The mechanism of obesity is simple: Obese people take in more calories than they burn up, usually on a daily basis. The reasons for this imbalance are often complex. In many cases, imbalances may be partly genetic and partly behavioral.

Binge eating is often a critical part of this behavioral pattern. Thousands of calories are consumed over a short period of time. A binge that is followed by purging, through vomiting, taking laxatives, or exercising excessively, is known as *bulimia* (for more on this, see the next section). Obesity, on the other hand, results when people fail to balance their normal need for calories with their consumption of food.

The person suffering from obesity faces a daily challenge to eat *some* food but not too much. We know that controlled drinking and drug use is hard (or impossible for some). Don't you think that controlled eating is just as hard? The dilemma is obvious. Driven to gain a sense of pleasure, a person overeats and hopes to find another way to lose weight. What else is there except exercise — which becomes increasingly difficult? Yo-yo dieting is the most likely response. Food becomes the source of constant misery. The only way out is to neutralize food emotionally and find other sources of pleasure and reward.

Eating too little

Anorexia is a condition whereby the person consumes too few calories. There are a couple of different types:

- ✔ **Restricting:** You prevent yourself from eating calories.
- ✔ **Purging:** You consume calories but get rid of them by vomiting, laxative use, or compulsive exercise.

Those suffering from anorexia often balance or overcompensate for the calories consumed by exercising excessively. Is anorexia part of food addiction? Is the avoidance or restriction of drugs or alcohol part of drug addiction? You can see that a specific symptom can't explain a complex condition.

Eating too little is a very serious state that can eventually lead to death.

Bulimia is an eating disorder characterized by a cycle of excessive consumption of foods (calories) followed by behaviors to rid the body of these calories. This cycle is the binge-purge cycle. Ultimately, the pattern of behavior leads to a number of adverse physical consequences, including dental disease (from excessive stomach acid in the mouth) or your hair falling out.

The compulsive nature of bulimia is like other compulsive behaviors (for example, drug use, sex, eating). You lose control of your life when you lose control of your behavior.

Work Addiction

Work, the backbone of our society, is the activity that takes up most of our waking hours. You may work longer and harder to accomplish more, fearing that if you don't, you'll experience feelings of inadequacy. If you suffer from work addiction, your efforts are typically reinforced (there's that term again) with praise, promotion, and financial reward. Organizations directly or indirectly support work addiction — after all, that extra work gives the corporation more bang for the buck. Employees affected by this behavioral pattern are prone to stress, personal problems, and other addictive behaviors. They're also at risk of being exploited by employers.

Do I have a problem?

Use the Work Addiction Checklist shown in Table 3-1 to help figure out whether you have a problem.

Table 3-1	The Work Addiction Checklist		
Question		**Yes**	**No**
Does the amount of time you spend working cause problems for your family or social life?			
Do you feel out of control or powerless when it comes to setting limits, going home, or leaving work?			
Do you have trouble enjoying life, preferring to work rather than play?			
Do you break promises to your family or friends regarding your work, travel schedule, and related work activities?			
Do you have difficulty dropping tasks or delegating them to others?			
Has your work pattern affected intimate relationships or recreational activities that you used to enjoy?			
When on vacation, is it difficult to relax and disengage from work, so that your time away is contaminated by work or work technology (PDA's, pagers, phone calls from the office, e-mail)?			
Has your physical health suffered because of excessive work? Have you ignored advice given by family, physicians, psychologists, or other therapists?			
Have you been surprised at how quickly you fly off the handle or lose it? Are people you care for having to give you space?			
Have you unsuccessfully attempted to cut down or stop overworking, overcommitting to others, and staying later and later at the office? For instance, you promise to change to spend more time at home, at the gym, or in a recreational activity but don't do it.			

If you answered yes to three or more of these items, you may be work addicted. Consider seeking a professional opinion.

How work addiction starts

Work addiction (like all addictions) starts because what you're doing feels good! Some people love to work — in part because they like to accomplish tasks and because they like the positive feedback. These two sources of reinforcement, the internal and the external, are powerful. Throw in the very likely financial incentive for achievements, and you're on the path. What helps people avoid the pitfalls of work addiction?

People with Type A personalities (very common in the executive suite) may appear to be following the work addiction pattern. They are at some risk but should be okay if they do the following:

- ✔ Set healthy boundaries when needed (or when asked to by a loved one).

- ✔ Remain in control of work tasks.

- ✔ Stop working when you experience negative consequences.

- ✔ Accept, instead of deny, your actions and responsibilities.

- ✔ Genuinely retain your modesty and humility and define yourself by who you are rather than what you do.

The hard part of work addiction is that it is sometimes very difficult to distinguish it from the pure, simple dedication to doing a good job. The esteem you earn with hard work is also very reinforcing. ("You're the best! No one else can do what you do! You are so dedicated. You came in over the weekend, wow! We'd be nowhere without you.") The key question is whether you see it yourself. If so, then it's time to take a forced vacation, despite the needs of other people and their rooting you on to more and more work.

Kicking the habit when everyone is asking for more

So here's the real kicker! Other people, including co-workers, bosses, and sadly, even family, start to get used to your work addiction. They like the money; they like the productivity; they like you carrying the ball. This is a blueprint for resentment, however — yours. You may find yourself suddenly out of gas, and immersed in feelings of fatigue and irritability. You feel lousy because you've lost perspective on how much rest, relaxation, and diversion you need to be a truly healthy human being and, over the long-term, an effective contributor to your workplace. It may be strange to take time off but you need to — you need to experience a retreat from work.

You need to withdraw. Don't expect others to reward you for this — they may prefer you to keep on working, because you're helping them just by your good performance. Despite all of this — you need some time off. Take some.

Other behavioral addictions

This chapter has focused on the most common behavioral addictions, but keep in mind that any behavior can become addictive. The distinguishing feature is whether that behavior starts to dominate your life in an unhealthy way.

Chapter 5 describes how to recognize whether you're addicted. Many behaviors or activities can become addictive, some of which are actually healthy in smaller doses. For example, you can get addicted to exercise — or to a particular group activity or mission. You can become addicted to collecting any number of things. The list of potential behavioral addictions is endless. If you're reading this book, you may already have some concerns about certain habits. Take a good clear look — behavioral addictions are quite common and diverse, and, fortunately, treatable.

Chapter 4

Dancing with the Tiger: The Risks of Experimenting

*W*e want to be clear — everyone experiments. Whether it's a beer, a hit of cocaine, or gambling, you're trying out something that could, under certain conditions, ruin you. That's why we offer the image of dancing with a tiger. You face excitement and thrills, but also danger. This chapter explores how much danger.

We're all a bit dulled about the danger because the wrong message is sent by the media's coverage of substance use in famous people. What's the message? That excesses are okay in using drugs, alcohol, gambling, and so on.

In this chapter, we cover the different addictive substances and activities you may run into at raves, parties, and casinos, and we explore the power of peer pressure. Most importantly, throughout this chapter, we explore that slippery slope that connects experimentation with addiction.

We're not *against* experimentation. It's a fact of life. But there are risks and there are illusions of safety induced by the substances, themselves, as well as by the environments where addictive behaviors take place.

The excitement you gain from addictive substances and behaviors lowers inhibitions. This leads to artificial feelings of freedom and elation. Over time, these desirable feelings cause you to slip into dependencies that have made people, as strong or stronger than you, act in ways that have been very destructive.

Going with the Flow: Peer Pressure and Other Influences

The influence of your friends is very powerful. Peer pressure can be extremely hard to resist. Psychological research has shown peer pressure influences people to change correct answers to incorrect answers, even when they're certain they know the right answer — just because everyone else in a group has given the incorrect answer! Psychologist Stanley Milgram showed us that even abhorrent acts, like torturing another person, can be encouraged by peer pressure.

On the other hand, peer pressure is also a force for good. All it takes for peers to change the direction of their support is for one person to take a stand. Just one! The principle holds true for people of all ages in peer pressure situations.

Peer pressure works for good and for not-so-good. If peers are pursuing healthy activities, you're likely to follow their lead. Teenagers are often watching out for each other's best interests. They often generate positive peer pressure by urging each other into working harder at school, training at sports, and developing skills in activities like dance and music. They want their friends to be successful. Others may take an interest in maintaining the environment and in taking part in community services. In time, teens may convince friends to do the same, and communities benefit as a result.

Relationships with parents and caregivers also have a profound effect on personal choices and coping behaviors later in life. The influence of peers in experimentation is also significant. Reputation in adolescents and young adults is a very persistent concern. One way to gain a reputation (good or bad) is to engage in higher-risk behavior.

You will decide which potentially addictive behaviors you will try and which ones you won't. Just be aware that to make your own choice, you must consider how much you're being influenced by peers. When in doubt, assume your friends are having a big influence on you.

Partying and party drugs

Let's party! When you answer that invitation, you get into party-mode and expect to have fun, meet new people, and be attractive. You want to relax, let go, and get down. These expectations begin to define how you'll feel and behave until late in the evening. How much will the partying involve addictive substances? What substances will be used? These aren't simple questions — but they do define the situation. After something is offered, it's much harder to turn down. It's easier to stay away from those who will likely offer you tempting and dangerously addictive substances.

Club drugs (such as Ecstasy, GHB, Rohypnol, ketamine, methamphetamine, and LSD) are now generally available at raves, dance clubs, and bars. Sooner or later, if you go to one of these venues, you'll be offered drugs. So it makes sense to think ahead about what your answer is going to be.

Using club drugs can cause serious health problems and, in some cases, death. If used in combination with alcohol, these drugs are even more dangerous. As an example, dehydration is a significant side effect of Ecstasy use. Organ damage from dehydration is one long-term health-related complication from using Ecstasy. There are others dangers, of course, the most serious being overdose or an inability to tolerate the drug. You're unique, and therefore you have unique responses to substances. What is tolerated well by someone else can be dangerous for you.

Hooking up

One of the emerging social phenomena in the 21st century is *hooking up,* sexual involvement through casual contacts. Teens and young adults (both heterosexual and gay) who get into no-commitment casual sex are also exposed to high-risk substance use. The two go hand-in-hand because substances are used to break down the natural inhibitions involved when people approach each other with the goal of becoming intimate.

"I didn't know what I was doing"

Illegal actions undertaken as a result of substance abuse or other altered states often leave a person vulnerable. Using diminished capacity (that is, "I didn't know what I was doing" or "I didn't know what was going on") as the explanation for actions that harm others or pose threats to society is increasingly unrealistic. Chances are, you'll be held responsible for your actions even if you were under the influence.

Many illegal and unwise acts are typically linked to addictive behavior. We review them from two perspectives: risks and consequences.

What influences your behavior?

Which of these behaviors do you believe are under the major influence of: a) your friends or peers, b) the media, or c) advertising?

✔ Drinking alcohol at parties

✔ Buying clothes

✔ The type of music you like

✔ The words you use to describe stuff you like

✔ Using cannabis/marijuana

✔ How you describe people who are outside your group

✔ Whether you will push the limits in terms of sexual behavior

✔ Your confidence in getting away with something risky

If you answered friends and peers more often than either the media or advertising, you're like most people. Media and targeted advertising have a significant effect, but your friends are the major influence on your behavior.

Rebellion and experimentation

The more rebellious you are, the more likely you are to experiment with substances and behaviors that are high-risk. Although you may expect negative reactions from parents or establishment-type people, you probably expect, and gain, respect and support from peers.

Thus, punishments for your rebelliousness don't have much influence on your behavior. Being the high-risk rebel has a certain influence on peers. It's impressive. But beware of being pushed into especially dangerous and foolhardy risks. Some of these foolish risks can include substance use as well as sex and criminality.

The Risks of Experimentation and Addiction

Not only can experimentation lead to addiction, but it can also lead to other risks associated with addictive substances and behaviors. Many of these relate to your own health, but some relate to the health of other people, including your loved ones.

Drinking, drugging, and driving

Is there anyone who doesn't understand the risks of using drugs and alcohol while driving? Apparently so, because in North America the statistics about impaired driving are still staggering. According to data from the U.S. National Highway Traffic Safety Administration (NHTSA), 17,400 people were killed in alcohol-related crashes in 2002 — an average of one every half-hour. These deaths constituted approximately 41 percent of the 42,815 total traffic fatalities in 2002.

Not all crashes result in fatalities. In the United States, 500,000 people are injured every year from motor vehicle crashes involving alcohol. In all, there are approximately 3.2 million injuries from motor vehicle crashes every year.

Driving under the influence of mind-altering drugs other than alcohol may also be an important cause of traffic crashes. The major risks of acute cannabis use show some parallels with the acute risks of alcohol intoxication. Both drugs produce psychomotor and cognitive impairment, especially of memory and planning.

A study conducted in the United States illustrated some of the concerns about drug use and driving. Drivers were stopped for careless or reckless driving (speeding, driving on the wrong side of the road, driving at high speed through red lights or stop signs, passing dangerously). Those who had no obvious alcohol use (smell of alcohol on breath, denied alcohol use) were taken to a special van where field urine tests were conducted. Fifty-nine percent of those tested (mostly men in their late teens to early thirties) tested positive for marijuana or cocaine.

Unsafe sexual behavior

Sex is one of the most basic human behaviors. Unfortunately, the drive to reproduce is associated with risks — like sexually transmitted diseases, unwanted pregnancy, fetal abnormalities, and plain, old, ordinary embarrassment.

People who suffer from substance abuse and addiction are more likely than others to have unsafe sex. As a result, it is wise to know some of the most common sexually transmitted diseases and how to identify early signs and symptoms. With the exception of the chronic infections such as HIV and herpes, most of these diseases can be cured.

According to the World Health Organization, at least 250 million new cases of sexually transmitted diseases occur every year world-wide. Included are 120 million cases of trichomoniasis (an easily treatable infection), 50 million cases of genital Chlamydia (also a bacterial infection that is curable), 30 million cases of genital papillomavirus (which is implicated in cervical cancer), 25 million cases of gonorrhea, 20 million cases of genital herpes, 3.5 million cases of syphilis, 2 million cases of chancroid (a bacterial infection that causes ulcers), and approximately 2 million new cases of HIV.

The difficulty with sexuality, of course, is knowing whether, how, and when to stop. It takes discipline, but the discipline requires experience. It helps to know what you can tolerate, and what you can't.

Appetitive behaviors such as eating, drinking, and sex all require control of the tendency to overindulge.

The sex trade

Sex and drugs: This relationship intersects at many different levels. For example, many people in the sex trade also have problems with substance abuse and addiction. Some may even engage in the sex trade to support their habits.

Research shows that sex trade workers are particularly vulnerable to drug addiction. Their drug of choice is usually crack cocaine. Drug use may be a way of coping with the act of prostitution, or prostitution may be a way of supporting a drug habit. An estimated 70 percent of women involved in street prostitution eventually become drug addicted.

The influx of crack cocaine has been devastating to women involved in prostitution. The lowest cost for drugs on the streets somehow typically stays close to the lowest cost for sex. In the 1970s, for example, heroin was the drug of choice. A hit of heroin cost about $20, and the lowest cost for sex on the streets equaled $20. Today, the drug of choice is crack cocaine. It can be purchased for as low as $5. In order to compete in today's prostitution market, women have to work more, for less, and often under higher-risk circumstances. Working more means more client contact, which increases the risk of customer-related violence and transmission of sexually transmitted diseases.

Crime

Contrary to popular views, most people with an addiction aren't hardened criminals. But they are likely to resort to minor crimes to feed their habit. Most of these crimes don't involve violence. As you can imagine, if you're living a life of addiction, it becomes difficult to hold a job. If you don't have a job, you have to find other ways to support your habit. One of the sad effects of addiction is criminal activity.

About three-quarters of all prisoners in the United States may be characterized as being involved with alcohol or drug use during the time leading up to their arrest. Some highlights from 1997 data:

- Fifty-seven percent of state prisoners and 45 percent of federal prisoners reported in 1997 that they had used drugs in the month before their offenses.

- Thirty-three percent of state and 22 percent of federal prisoners said they committed their current offense while under the influence of drugs.

- About one in six (16 percent) of both state and federal inmates said in 1997 they committed their offenses to get money for drugs.

- Fifteen percent of both state and federal inmates said they had received drug abuse treatment during their current prison terms.

- Twenty-one percent of state prisoners and over 60 percent of federal prisoners were in prison for drug law violations.

Feeding the habit

With drugs, you rarely get what you pay for! Based on data from the United Nations, the retail price of a gram of heroin is roughly US$125 in Europe and US$300 in the United States. And as the drug moves through the distribution system, there's a tendency to cut down the actual proportion of drug you receive (powder, pill). So when you pay $40 for a gram of heroin, only a fraction of the gram you buy actually is pure heroin, and the rest consists of added substances (fillers).

What does it cost to feed an alcohol or drug habit? What does it cost to maintain a gambling, sex, shopping, or other behavioral addiction? It varies greatly from person to person, but over time the costs go up, either to keep the buzz or to fight the withdrawal.

Tolerance increases over time with drug use and behavioral addictions. This means that the cost of an addictive behavior also increases over time.

Impulsive crimes under the influence

Mind-altering chemicals typically disinhibit you, sometimes to the point of impulsive behavior. With behavioral addictions, the intense urge to engage or the accumulated debt from engaging in the behavior (for instance, gambling debts) may induce you to resort to crimes such as embezzlement and other types of fraud (typically stealing from friends and family) to feed the addiction or to pay off debts.

Anger and aggression

Driving seems to bring out the worst in some people as does waiting in lines. But some people have trouble controlling their anger all the time. Uncontrolled aggression is frightening to others and even to the person experiencing it. You can imagine how the problem is magnified when the hostile person has been using drugs or alcohol: The goal is often to get even and make the other person pay.

Many drugs reduce inhibitions and result in the expression of raw emotion. In addition, many drugs will disinhibit a person to the point of overreacting to small frustrations.

You can't always judge anger by outward behavior. Two people can feel anger with the same intensity but handle it differently. One may show anger outwardly by shouting, cursing, even acting aggressively. The other may handle anger by holding it in. How angry you are depends on both the intensity you feel and how often you feel it. Typically, anger is assessed by asking you to rate the frequency with which you experience different degrees of anger. Try completing the anger scale in Table 4-1 to get an idea of how you might score on an anger assessment scale.

Table 4-1		Anger Assessment		
How Often Do You Feel?	*Rarely*	*Some of the Time*	*Most of the Time*	*All of the Time*
Irritable				
Impatient				
Angry				
Annoyed				

How Often Do You Feel?	Rarely	Some of the Time	Most of the Time	All of the Time
Short-tempered				
Fuming				
Livid				
Cross				
Furious				
Enraged				

If you checked off a high frequency rating with most items, then you probably have trouble handling anger, especially when taking an addictive substance.

Ask yourself if the angry feelings in Table 4-1 were typical of you even before you started to use addictive substances or engage in addictive behaviors. If your answer is no, then it's likely that your anger is a consequence of your addiction.

Child abuse and neglect

Parental drug and alcohol abuse and addiction are linked to an increased likelihood of child abuse and neglect. Research on this topic is fraught with difficulties because it is hard to definitively determine which of the many factors may be responsible for the child abuse or neglect. Keeping in mind the inherent challenges in studying this topic, research surveys appear to implicate alcohol and illegal drug use as potential factors in either causing or exacerbating the abuse/neglect. And not only does alcohol and drug use appear to increase the likelihood that parents will abuse or neglect their children, but substance use appears to increase the frequency of the episodes of child abuse or neglect within a family.

Health risks

"This won't happen to me. I'm usually more fortunate than others." If this is how you think about your health risks, then you're like the majority of people. The most common response to potential risks is a feeling of unrealistic optimism. The truth is that generally your health risks are the same as the majority of people of your age and gender. So what are the risks when it comes to addictions?

Below are a few facts about the health risks associated with using addictive substances and engaging in addictive behaviors:

- ✔ If you use injectable drugs and share needles with others, you risk exposure to infections such as HIV and Hepatitis C.

- ✔ If you're a sex or love addict and have sex with multiple partners, you're at risk for sexually transmitted disease (for example HIV) if you don't practice safe sex.

- ✔ Because most street drugs aren't pure and you don't neces-sarily know what has been mixed with them, you run the risk of overdose and possibly death from ingesting the substance. In some cases, the substances added to the drug increase the drug's potency or speed of absorption into your body.

- ✔ If you're a gambler, you're at elevated risk for depression and suicide compared with the general population.

- ✔ Individuals with a substance addiction are also at a higher risk of suicide than the general population.

- ✔ Long-term use of alcohol is associated with damage to multiple organs, most commonly your liver and brain cells.

- ✔ If you're a pregnant woman who drinks alcohol or takes addictive drugs, you risk the health of the baby you're carry-ing. Health risks to your baby include learning disabilities, hyperactivity, inability to manage anger, poor judgment, and delayed growth. Certain substances will actually result in your baby being born with addictions (for example, narcotics).

- ✔ Overdoses of amphetamines (stimulants), barbiturates (tranquilizers), alcohol, inhalants (for example solvents, gases, and nitrates), and narcotics can cause death.

- ✔ Risks of drugs and alcohol abuse are progressive — the longer you abuse these substances, the greater the health damage.

The bottom line is that both experimentation and long-term abuse can cause serious health problems including death. (In Chapter 5, we discuss the effects of substance use on the brain, and in Chapter 10, we go over the risks associated with acute substance withdrawal.)

The Costs of Addiction to Families

The degree of distress experienced by families affected by addic-tion is usually underestimated. In all normal situations, families try to take care of each other, especially in times of illness. What hap-pens when you refuse your family's help, and then appear to go out of your way to upset them? Most people in this situation will try even harder to get the result they want — and most family members want their loved one to stop the drinking or using. It's one of life's ironies that the harder the family members try to help you, the worse your problem sometimes seems to get.

The blame game

In the early stages, the family, especially the person closest to you, doesn't want to believe what is happening to you. We discuss the family's responses to addiction more in Chapter 18.

Some very normal personalized beliefs come into play for your loved one, including the following:

- ✔ If I were a better wife (or husband, son, daughter, mother), you would love me enough to stop drinking or using.

- ✔ As a parent, I must have done something wrong to make you feel so bad that you have to take these drugs.

- ✔ I need to work harder to make sure you love me, and then you'll stop, and everything will be okay.

Believing they're to blame, the family members begin to bend over backward to make things better for you and to keep the family functioning. Meanwhile, you tend to blame someone for your need to drink or use and you likely pick on those nearest you, your family. No one can talk about what's really happening — after all you may get angry or you may leave.

Communication begins to break down, and the vicious circle goes around and around, with all players locked into their own very private pain.

The consequences to you and your family

The addiction problem of a family member can lead to all sorts of harmful consequences:

- ✔ **Socially:** Through embarrassment and shame, families decline invitations, stop inviting friends to their home, and start to ignore friends and hobbies. The family becomes gradually more and more isolated — unable to tell anyone what's happening.

- ✔ **Psychologically:** When family members have been lied to many times, they find themselves furiously searching for evidence to support their suspicions.

✓ **Emotionally:** Living with you and your addiction is like being on a roller coaster. The family members feel angry, frustrated, helpless, confused, hopeless, desperate, guilty, and ashamed.

✓ **Physically:** The stress of living in a chronic state of chaos, being on edge all the time (constantly worrying as to what your next phone call will bring and what they'll find when they open the door to your room) eventually takes a toll. Family members of addicts have more than the average prevalence of anxiety, depression, headaches, migraines, digestive disorders, and heart problems. It's not unusual to find close family members of addicts admitting to feeling periodically suicidal.

In short, the family becomes so focused on your behavior that they're distracted from all but essential matters. The family develops its way of coping; the family becomes so hooked on helping you that contemplating no longer helping you is as difficult for them as it is for you to stop drinking or using. A huge fear of making changes builds up, and this eventually becomes counterproductive for you and for them.

Part II
Taking Those First Steps

The 5th Wave   By Rich Tennant

"I've tried Ayurveda, meditation, and aromatherapy but nothing seems to work. I'm still feeling nauseous and disoriented all day."

In this part . . .

We help you assess your risk of becoming addicted and how close you are to being addicted right now. We explain how your body and mind become addicted and give you information on the various biological tests used to detect addictive substances in your body. We help you assess your readiness for treatment, and we help you detect the triggers for your addictive behaviors and develop strategies to neutralize these triggers. We review the many types of treatments now available for addictions, and we provide information so that you can select a treatment that is best suited to your needs.

Chapter 5

Recognizing Addiction in Yourself and Others

As healthcare providers, we work hard to help addicted people recover their lives. In many cases, we work hard to help their loved ones recover as well. Why, you may ask, would people risk their lives, jobs, and relationships to take drugs — and to act in ways that are so self-destructive?

Scientists and caregivers have struggled with this question for decades. We don't have all the answers, but we've come a long way, and the bottom line is this: Substances or activities that feel good in the beginning can later become the darkest and most destructive aspects of your life. Of course, not every activity is a basis for addiction, but the ones that feel very good in the beginning can become very deadly in the end.

After you're caught in the cycle of addiction, addiction dominates your very being. How can something that once felt so good hurt so much?

Plainly stated, nobody wants trouble — you start using drugs because you want to feel good. You wonder whether some magic bullet, activated in your bloodstream, will do the trick. The substance may be an illegal drug, a drug prescribed by your doctor, or an over-the-counter medication. It may not even be a substance, but rather a self-destructive activity like gambling or overeating. In this chapter, we discuss how you get addicted, what drugs and activities are most addictive, and how to know when you or someone else crosses the lines from use — to abuse — to addiction.

Am I at Risk?

In trying to determine whether you're addicted, you must first look at your risk of addiction. Knowing your risk can help you decide how you will approach certain substances and activities. It can help you monitor or evaluate your behavior when you engage in activities known to be addictive. To assess your addiction risk, make yourself aware of the following:

- ✓ **Your family history.** Substance abuse and addictive behaviors tend to run in families. If you know that a parent or another relative became dependent on drugs or alcohol, you're at greater risk of abusing. The same kind of family risk applies to behavioral addictions, like gambling, overeating, and sexual addiction. (See the section "Genetics: Addiction Across Generations," later in this chapter.)

- ✓ **Your willingness to experiment with different drugs.** If you consider yourself a "risk-taker," you're at greater risk of experimenting with addictive behaviors and substances.

- ✓ **Your mental state.** If you're anxious, depressed, and angry for weeks at a time, you're more likely to escape reality through drug use or different addictive behaviors to try to feel better.

- ✓ **Your choice of drugs (some are more addicting than others).** If you gravitate to the more powerfully addictive drugs (such as morphine, cocaine, and nicotine), you're at greater risk for addiction. We discuss these drugs in greater detail in Chapter 2.

- ✓ **Your support system of family and friends.** If you have little social support and often feel lonely, you're also at greater risk. You may turn to drugs or other kinds of addictive behaviors to counteract feelings of loneliness.

You need only one of these risk factors to be at-risk for developing an addiction problem. When considering all these factors, slow down and think about your life and how you're dealing with the challenges you face. The time you have to think about yourself is precious. Think carefully about what stressors you're facing and how you may be using something, either an addictive substance or behavior, to avoid some of these stressors.

Taking a hard, honest look at your daily stresses and feelings is often difficult. This type of honesty is especially difficult for people who are addicted or becoming addicted. Getting in touch with and expressing feelings can be difficult. Bluntly put, drugs or addictive activities often numb your feelings.

Start by picking an issue to focus on. Then spend five minutes think-ing about everything related to that issue. For example, evaluate your mental state. How have you been feeling the past few days? You may have a tough time determining how you've been feeling, so pick one emotion from the following: mad, sad, glad, or afraid.

How've you been feeling for the past few weeks? For the past few months? Think about how you've dealt with your feelings. Have a piece of paper handy to make notes about what you remember. Then look to see what patterns emerge. Do you turn to a particular activity or substance to get through rough spots? Do you celebrate by performing a particular activity or taking a drug? If you have addictive tendencies, you'll see some patterns.

No definitive biological tests exist to determine who is at risk for addiction and who isn't. Nevertheless, you can still find consider-able scientific literature on the risk factors of addiction. (A great Web site with information on the latest research findings on addic-tions is www.drugabuse.gov.) Many scientists are struggling to find how to detect a person's vulnerability to addiction. New discoveries emerge all the time.

Genetics: Addiction Across Generations

Most of us know our birth parents, grandparents, and other rela-tives. If you don't know your birth family, understanding your addiction risk is more difficult. We inherit our *genes* (the codes of life that turn on and off under different conditions) from our birth parents — half from Mom and half from Dad. Although scientists don't completely understand how genes operate, they do know that genes interact with environmental factors (stress, diet, exer-cise). For example, a gene that helps people handle cold weather is found in many people in northern climates. Some genes are *triggered* (or turned on) only under certain conditions, and using drugs may be one of these conditions. Although you're born with your genetic risk for addiction, you're responsible for it, and with effort, you can influence it. Read the following sections to figure out whether you may have a genetic risk.

Determining who's susceptible

To understand your genetic risk, chart out your family tree by first listing your parents, brothers, sisters, and all relatives related to you by birth. Put a circle around any relative who suffers from substance abuse or who has an addictive behavior like gambling. If you have more than one relative who is addicted to drugs or who engages in a self-destructive, addictive behavior, you may carry this risk yourself. The more circles on your family tree, the higher your risk. By the way, the *addictive tendency* runs in families, but the substance or self-destructive behavior involved may differ from one family member to another.

In addition to the risk associated with a family history of substance abuse or addiction, other family characteristics put you at risk for developing a substance or nonsubstance abuse problem. So far, we know that you're at increased risk of addiction if any of the following characteristics are true of you:

- ✔ You are aggressive by nature.

- ✔ You have a personal history of attention deficit disorder (ADD) or attention deficit hyperactivity disorder (ADHD).

- ✔ You have a family history of depression.

Asking relatives about their personal medical histories can set off emotions and stressful reactions. Proceed cautiously and start by telling your relative why you're asking and what you hope to achieve. Remember that not everyone who has a family risk will become addicted. Be respectful and matter-of-fact in your questioning. Above all, try not to be judgmental about the answers you get.

Applying your family history

When facing your vulnerabilities, honesty is important. Obviously, if your family history is loaded with addicts, you need to be very careful about using and experimenting with drugs. In some cases, using certain drugs may place your health at especially high risk. Sometimes, addiction comes down to being hypersensitive to a specific molecule in the drug.

People differ in their sensitivity to some drugs and knowing your family history may reveal a pattern of hypersensitivity that runs in your family. If a family member was sensitive to a particular drug, you may have the same reaction. And if some of the relatives with addictions have overcome them, your family history may also yield clues to what treatments or interventions may work for you. It never hurts to hear another person's story, especially stories from family members who have overcome addictions.

How a Body Gets Addicted

The interaction between the mind and the body can't be separated, and addiction has both mental and physical components. For example, the mind is so powerful that simply thinking about getting high can result in bodily changes (a faster heart rate and increased sweating). Your body can ache and scream out for a specific drug just because your mind is picturing you taking the drug.

From the mind out

If you find yourself craving a drug or an activity (gambling, binge eating) and can't get your mind on anything else, you may be psychologically addicted. If you're willing to risk losing your family, friends, and work in order to engage in your addictive behavior, then you're addicted.

When your mind is preoccupied with getting the next high, your addiction has taken hold and is exerting a powerful mental influence. On the other hand, powerful mental experiences can trigger addictions. You can crave a high to distract yourself from a difficult-to-heal emotional wound. Emotional pain is often difficult to describe. No one likes being emotionally vulnerable. You can hurt emotionally when depressed, anxious, angry, shamed, guilty, or just plain sick. You're especially tempted to turn to substance use and abuse when you're just tired of feeling down. (Flip to Chapter 15 to find out how negative moods can act as triggers for substance use and how to resist these triggers.)

Being addicted also brings on certain kinds of mental anguish. In the early stages of addiction, sometimes all you can think about is when and how to get the next fix. Your mind searches for the quickest way to get back to normal, to get back to feeling good. You may even dream about getting loaded or engaging in addictive behavior — nothing is more important to you. This search becomes more desperate when you use substances to numb the emotional pain in your life. You may be using substances or engaging in high-risk activities because you can't bear to think of doing anything else. When this is the case, you can be sure that you're *psychologically addicted.*

From the body in

If you find yourself needing more and more of the substance or activity to reach the same high, or if you experience physical anguish when you're without it, then you're *physically addicted.*

In your brain are biochemicals called *neurotransmitters*. Some help activate various systems of the body, whereas others inhibit certain systems. The neurotransmitters that play a role in addictions are listed in Table 5-1. (Note that this table isn't exhaustive.)

Table 5-1	Neurotransmitters and Their Triggers
Neurotransmitter	*Addictive Substances Believed to Affect It*
Dopamine	Opiates, stimulants (cocaine, amphetamines, nicotine), Ecstasy, possibly cannabis
GABA	Alcohol, benzodiazepines
Serotonin	LSD, Ecstasy and its derivatives MDA (Adam) and MDEA (Eve), opiates
Glutamate	Solvents, alcohol
Norepinephrine	Opiates

In addition to neurotransmitters, your body's *opioid system* also plays a role in increasing your susceptibility to addiction. Studies of the heritability of addictions suggest that neurotransmitter and opioid genes may increase susceptibility to substances like drugs and alcohol, as well as to self-destructive behaviors like gambling.

Addictive substances such as alcohol, amphetamines, and opiates directly affect neurotransmitters and opioids in your brain, in some cases delivering a pleasurable high, in other cases producing a sense of calm or an emotional closeness with others. Initially, small amounts of the drug get you high, but over time, you need more and more of the drug to produce the same effect. This process is called *tolerance.* As you build up tolerance to the drug, the more of the drug you need. Now here's the kicker — at some point in your history of using, if you don't put the drug into your system (and hence your brain), your body starts screaming. Now you've developed a *dependence* on the drug. It physically hurts if you don't have the drug. You feel sick all over — your head, your stomach, your muscles, your bones. You simply must have the drug to function. Your addiction has become a physical one.

When we think of addiction to alcohol and drugs, it's easy to see how a person could build up tolerance. What about the behavioral addictions? How do behaviors escalate to addictive levels?

When you take part in addictive behaviors, you're usually in states of high arousal. Tolerance refers to the fact that it takes riskier and riskier actions to get your arousal up to that high level. For gambling, increasing your risk is often achieved by raising the stakes. For sexual addictions, increasing your risk means having sex that involves greater danger. For eating, increasing your risk may involve eating more food, different types, or more forbidden foods. For computer games, increasing your risk may involve using more violent, explicit games or simply spending more hours playing games where others are competitors.

Interestingly, not only do certain drugs affect neurotransmitters, but behaviors associated with using the substance may, over time, come to affect neurotransmitters. For example, just seeing a syringe may stimulate a rise in dopamine levels because of the learned association between syringes and heroin injection. Addictive behaviors like gambling also appear to be associated with dysfunction in certain neurotransmitters.

What drugs are the most addictive?

What two substances do you think most people become dependent on? Are you ready for a surprise? You may think the most addicting drugs are illegal. It's true that many illegal drugs are addicting. But legal drugs are also very addicting — in some cases even more addicting.

The most addicting drug for humans is nicotine. Yes, nicotine . . . that legal substance that adults purchase and use nearly everywhere. Nicotine is most commonly delivered to your bloodstream by smoking tobacco or chewing it. Although rates vary by age, gender, state, and culture, about 25 percent of North Americans are addicted to nicotine. Young people are clearly the most vulnerable to picking up the *habit* (which really means the addiction).

The second most addicting drug is caffeine. Caffeine is found in many different products but is most commonly accessed by drinking beverages such as coffee, tea, soda, and energy drinks. About 70 percent of all soft drinks contain this legal stimulant. Caffeine can also easily be obtained in pill form. Over-the-counter pain medications such as Anacin, Excedrin, and Midol contain caffeine. Many food and drink products contain caffeine, and you can even buy caffeinated water!

Think about how your mind focuses on getting that first cup of coffee or tea in the morning. Surveys report that 40 to 70 percent of people who have tried to reduce their intake of caffeine experience withdrawal symptoms. You may not notice withdrawal until you have been off caffeine for at least two days, so if you consume caffeine daily, you may not even know that you're addicted.

In reviewing Table 5-2, keep in mind that the samples of people being considered are "all people who were studied and who were found to use the particular substance." Also, the samples only include people who actually use the drug for a period of time (say 3 months of smoking 10 cigarettes per day). So 32 percent of people (approximately one third of the sample) who use nicotine for a period of time become dependent.

Table 5-2 Percentage of People Who Become Dependent on a Drug after a Period of Use

Substance	Percentage
Nicotine	32%
Caffeine	30%
Heroin	25%
Cocaine	17%
Alcohol	15%
Marijuana	9%

How quickly you become addicted depends upon how addictive the substance is and how physically and mentally vulnerable you are when using it. For example, depending on your physical and mental vulnerabilities, you may become addicted to nicotine after smoking one or two cigarettes a day. On the other hand, it may take you three months of smoking ten or more cigarettes a day to become physically dependent.

Waking Up to Your Own Addiction

One of the most difficult things to face is the realization that you're addicted. For our purposes in this section, we use the term *addict* to describe anyone who is addicted. Addict is a label most people hate to apply to themselves. However, a certain reality hits home when it's used accurately. By confronting this reality, we can reduce the stigma associated with addiction (as can be seen with caffeine and nicotine, a good proportion of people are addicted to something).

When you're trying to come to terms with your own addiction, the first question to ask yourself is: "Is my life out of control because of my drug or alcohol use?" The same question can be asked of a nonsubstance-related addiction like gambling, overeating, or sexual addiction.

You're an addict when a substance (or an activity, as we will see later in this chapter) dominates your thinking to the point that you "gotta do it now." You think about the substance or activity first and all other aspects of your life (like your family or job) afterward. Your addiction trumps all other important events or needs. You may miss your kid's games, your best friend's wedding, your dinner plans, or intimate time with a loved one. You're determined (as in highly driven and motivated) to use that substance or to do that activity. There is no choosing. You're on a track but you've lost control of the steering. You're caught in the web of addiction.

Starting with self-observation

Completing a written test can give you a good indication of whether you've given control of your life to a substance or an activity. But first, get honest with yourself. Take a real look, a hard look, at your behavior. Don't waste time and energy on self-deception.

In the world of drugs, sophisticated tests have been developed that tell scientists, in fine detail, whether you have taken a drug and how much of that drug is in your blood stream. (The tests don't reveal the extent to which the drug is affecting your brain chemistry.) No tests, however, can tell you if you're addicted. Everyone experiences drugs in a different way — some people have enormous tolerance for drugs, and others have very little tolerance at all.

If your experiences resemble the three following descriptions, you don't really need another test — you may as well admit that you're an addict:

- ✔ Your drug-seeking behavior (for example, contacting your sources, going to places where you can score drugs, checking out the odds lines for sporting events) increases.

- ✔ Your main reason for living becomes using.

- ✔ You lose touch with important aspects of your life (like family, friends, job) because of your drug use.

Drug tests

The amount of time it takes for a drug to show up in your system depends on four factors:

✔ The amount and frequency of substance use

✔ How quickly the substance gets absorbed into your body

✔ How long after absorption trace elements of the substance, called *metabolites,* linger in your system

✔ How efficient your system is at *excreting,* or removing, foreign elements from your body

Metabolites are stored in the fatty cells of your body for different lengths of time and can cause you to fail a drug test many weeks or even months after your last drug use. The slower your body metabolizes the substances, the longer the drug can be detected in your system. A slower metabolism can be the result of low body weight, old age, poor health, and shorter length of time using the substance.

The five ways of testing for chemical drug substances in your system are:

✔ Urine test: Most common, most affordable, level of accuracy similar to blood test

✔ Hair follicle test: Most accurate, most expensive, can detect toxins consumed five days to six months or more prior

✔ Blood test: Somewhat common and affordable, level of accuracy similar to urine test

✔ Saliva test: Least common, generally less accurate than the other tests, can only detect toxins consumed three to four days prior

✔ Breathalyzer test: Alcohol consumption can be tested through a Breathalyzer

Taking a quick self-assessment

If you suspect you're addicted to something, be it alcohol, drugs, or a nonsubstance behavior like gambling or computer games, ask yourself the following questions:

✔ **Is my life out of control because of my _____ use?** (Fill in the blank with the substance or activity you think you may be addicted to.)

✔ **Do I think about my preferred substance or activity first and other aspects of my life (family, job) second?**

✔ **Do I use my preferred substance or do my preferred activity almost every day?**

✔ **Do I fail to do what is normally expected of me because of _____?** (Fill in the blank with the substance or activity you think you may be addicted to.)

✔ **Do I risk my personal safety (or even worse, the safety of my loved ones) to get drugs, alcohol, or to engage in my preferred activity?**

✔ **Does my body crave the experience associated with the substance or the activity so strongly that I feel I must have it?**

A "yes" response to any of these questions suggests addiction. Also, the more "yes" responses you give, the more severely you're addicted.

Breaking down the types of addictions

Addictions can take many forms (including substances and non-substances). We discuss these forms, one-by-one, in the following sections; we hope you'll recognize whether your experimentation with a substance or behavior has crossed the line into addiction. For more details on each of these substance and nonsubstance addictions, flip back to Chapters 2 and 3. And for information on treatment options for the addictions outlined below, look at the chapters in Part III of this book.

Alcohol

Drinking alcohol has become the only way you can feel normal. You may have a drink early in the day to stop feeling lousy ("the hair of the dog"). You may also drink secretly, often alone, and if you haven't had a drink, you may be thinking about how to get your next drink. If you don't have a drink, you feel irritable and discontented. You hate it when family and friends interfere with your drinking. You may find yourself saying things like "It's my life, not yours," and "I don't care what you say."

The *CAGE* test is one of the best-known screening tools to determine whether you have a problem with alcohol. Ask yourself four questions:

✔ **C:** Have you ever felt you ought to **Cut Down** on your drinking?

✔ **A:** Have you ever felt **Annoyed** by someone criticizing your drinking?

✔ **G:** Have you ever felt bad or **Guilty** about your drinking?

✔ **E:** Have you ever had a drink first thing in the morning **(Eye-Opener)** to steady your nerves and get rid of a hangover?

Ask these same questions to see if drug use is a problem. The first three questions are also relevant for behavioral addictions such as gambling and sexual addictions.

Street drugs

You feel irritable, agitated, and nervous or jumpy on a daily basis. If you crave street drugs (cocaine, heroin, PCP, mushrooms, LSD), your first question of the day is "How do I get today's supply?" You have a reliable "source" to get your drugs from, but dealers you don't even know may approach you. You may not be forced to scour the streets for your drugs because some dealers may come right to your door. If you decide to risk personal safety (or even worse, the safety of your loved ones), to get drugs, that's another indication that you're addicted.

If your body screams out for the drug and you want to do whatever it takes to calm it down, you're addicted. Interestingly, you may feel better as soon as you purchase the drug and before you even use it! How do you explain this reaction? You know relief is on the way.

Prescription drugs

If you "doctor shop" or have multiple physicians prescribing the same drugs, you may be addicted. Prescription medicines like anti-anxiety drugs, antidepressants, sleeping pills, and pain medications may create a dependency leading to addiction. The hallmark of any drug addiction is an increased tolerance and dependency on the drug.

Physicians are experts in prescribing medicines to cure disease or to ease pain and illness. But they may not be experts in addiction. Some physicians are more likely than others to give patients a prescription for their sleep, behavioral, or emotional problems. Be aware that your physician could be inadvertently overprescribing your medication.

Gambling

You get an adrenalin boost when you gamble. Your heart races, you breathe faster, your blood pressure rises, and you sweat. Gambling is arousing — the thrill of winning, the threat of losing. If you're in a casino, the level of noise is purposely kept high to keep you aroused. You get a *kick,* a stimulant effect, from gambling that is very much like a drug effect. Over time, you get a sick and tired feeling like any other addict — you're gambling to exist and no longer gambling for fun.

Winning isn't as important as being in the game. If you're a compulsive gambler, you hate being on the sidelines and are easily drawn back into playing. You often demonstrate an impulsiveness that drives you to risk everything. The pattern is familiar: When you're losing, you bet more and more money trying to get even; when you're winning, you bet carelessly until the game ends.

You know you have a problem with gambling if the next game is always on your mind. Family, friends, and responsibilities all fade into the background. Every dollar is held so you can play. Winnings only help prolong the agony and the emptiness.

You'll do anything to get money to gamble: cash in family savings, empty bank accounts, and, in some desperate cases, steal from your employer.

Gamblers come in two types: *action gamblers,* the thrill-seekers who love the action (and usually the attention that goes with it), and *escape gamblers* who love to get away from life and escape into fantasy.

Computer games

Isn't it amazing how computers can dominate your life? This is another case where technology is used to generate a fantasy world. You can be a great warrior, a supreme commander, or a mystical sorcerer in computer games — all with none of the messy consequences of real life. Furthermore, computers are everywhere, in cars, offices, telephones. In most instances, you may view computers as helpers that make your life easier. Sometimes, though, computers can dominate your attention to the point that nothing else matters to you. You're lost in a world of limited reality — a computer world.

Here are some signs of a computer game addiction: you're a person who feels lonely; you may also feel anxious around people and paradoxically, feel most comfortable with strangers than people you know socially. Computer games have become a way to tune out troubles and experience pleasurable highs. You live for computer games, know all of the latest releases and perhaps you even contribute to hint sheets on improving computer games. The other activities in your daily life fade in comparison to the time and effort you put into computer games. You play to the point of neglecting important social, vocational, and personal responsibilities.

You know you have a problem if you play computer games to the point that your schoolwork or other work is put aside and chores are forgotten. If this profile fits, you may be on a track where the train is out of control. The game dominates your life. You're a game addict.

Eating

An eating addict rarely enjoys food. Instead, you eat to forget — to numb your feelings with a near constant flow of calories. Food relieves you from the boredom or pain of life. Food serves as the treat, the compulsion, and the reason to get up in the morning. Activities are planned around eating, and over time, the mirror becomes the enemy, the one sign of your empty feelings inside. The agony of this experience can't be overstated. Like all addictions, the addiction to food can dominate your life.

When telling the difference between normal and possible addiction-level eating behaviors, you need to consider several dimensions:

- ✔ **The quantity of food consumed:** If you consistently take in more calories than your body can burn off in a day and the quantity of food consumed is excessive, your eating behavior is likely serving another purpose, such as eating to relieve boredom or stress.

- ✔ **The types of food chosen:** You crave high-fat foods for the calming effect they produce. You turn to certain types of foods to make you feel better.

- ✔ **The ability to stop eating when you choose to:** You're unable to control yourself and stop eating when you know that you should.

 The average recommended caloric intake for adult men and women is between 2,200 and 2,800 calories a day.

 Binge eating is characterized by eating a quantity of food larger than what most people would eat within a similar time period. Binge eating also features a lack of control over how much and what is eaten.

Addiction to food, as you may have guessed, isn't really about food. If you eat a loved food compulsively, (perhaps even storing up an extra supply) then before long, the pleasure and enjoyment fade away. This fading effect is termed *satiation* and means that foods you may have once craved or loved no longer appeal to you. If you're a binge eater, then you may have experienced satiation in eating certain foods, but you eat them regardless of the satiation. In fact, you may be mystified by why you can't stop eating them when they no longer taste good to you.

Fetish behavior

Fetishes (behaviors that are associated with sexual relief and orgasm) are common and having one doesn't mean that you have a sexual addiction. However, you may behave compulsively in looking for fetish actions to arouse yourself. If this compulsive behavior gets out of control, fetishes become more closely associated with sexual addiction. Similarly, you may be turned on by the possibility of getting caught and thus engage in sexual behavior that is inappropriate (in public places or in situations where someone else may see you). This behavior isn't an addiction until it gets out of control, with serious consequences instead of just the embarrassment of getting caught.

Are you food addicted? The key to the answer is asking yourself if your eating is out of control, if other people have annoyed you by commenting on your eating, and if you feel guilty about your eating behavior.

Sex

Sex addiction is especially painful because, when healthy, sexual acts are ways of becoming intimate and loving. When unhealthy, this remarkable vehicle for intimacy makes a U-turn, and sex becomes antisocial, trust destroying, and isolating.

If you're addicted to sex, you probably don't perceive yourself as a worthwhile person. You may not believe other people really care for you or wish to meet your emotional and sexual needs. Most importantly, you feel that people won't accept you if they really know you. So you can only get your emotional and sexual needs in situations that are partially or totally secret from friends and family.

You substitute sex for true intimacy. Sex makes your isolated life bearable. Being a sex addict doesn't mean that you appear unsuccessful or undesirable to others. In fact, you may very well be unusually attractive or magnetic and, thus, better able to persuade others to engage in your addiction.

You may find yourself in a cycle of sexual addiction that begins with *preoccupation,* a mental state so dominant that it's virtually a trance. You're obsessed with thoughts of sex and the search for sexual stimulation. You progress to *ritualization,* an individualized set of routines that precedes sexual behavior. You move through the cycle to *compulsive sexuality,* the sexual act that, no matter how unhealthy, risky, and shameful, must happen. You can't control or stop it. In the last part of the cycle, instead of feelings of satisfaction and contentment, you experience depression and despair centered around your compulsion and the degradation of the sexual act.

Everything else is risked and devalued next to a potent, transitory "hit" of immediate sexuality. As with other addictions, the drive for sexual experiences comes to dominate your life.

Work

Work addiction often accompanies other forms of addiction, like alcoholism, drugs, addictions, sex, and gambling. If you're addicted to work, you may see it as a retreat from painful emotional circumstances, like a failing marriage or the death of an offspring. Or you may find that only when working do you feel secure and free of constant anxieties about losing your job or your company going belly-up. Whatever your reasons for overworking, you're likely suffering work addiction if you're compelled, from within yourself, to work incessantly.

Work comes to dominate your life. Family responsibilities, your health, and personal obligations are all forgotten or neglected. You isolate yourself from your family. Relationships with co-workers replace the more challenging intimacies that may occur away from work. Family and friends voice concerns or annoyance at your excessive work habits. You may feel guilty, but you feel powerless to reduce your work time.

Work addiction is very tricky for many people to acknowledge because it is, for the most part, socially rewarded. The clue to uncovering work addiction is that despite your outward achievements, inwardly you feel personally degraded by your drive to work. Any sense of achievement or accomplishment feels short-lived and empty.

Perceiving Addiction in a Loved One

Perhaps one of the most unbelievable stories of recent years is how the two young men responsible for the Columbine High School shootings in 1998 were able to stockpile a virtual armory of weapons in their bedroom closets, while living in a close-knit American town like Littleton, Colorado. Even more surprising is that the parents of these unfortunate young people were conscientious and highly involved in their children's lives.

This painful story is also a powerful example of how much parents of troubled youth and families of troubled adults can deny their loved ones' problems. The tendency to deny, rather than recognize, becomes more understandable when we examine the complications of intervening with a loved one in trouble.

The example described in "Case study: Jack and his daughter" reveals the slow and painful journey from denial to discovery regarding a loved one's addiction.

Case study: Jack and his daughter

Jack had two daughters. His youngest daughter worked full-time in a job that she enjoyed. Over time, Jack began to feel puzzled by changes he noticed in her. She started to arrive late to family gatherings. Sometimes, she would miss family functions and provide no clear explanation for her absence.

She began to socialize with a new group of friends, and Jack received telephone calls from her old friends asking him if he knew how they might contact her. Jack was concerned, but when he asked his daughter about why she wasn't seeing her old friends, she said that she simply didn't enjoy their company anymore. She said that when the "old group" got together, her friends were only interested in talking amongst themselves. She reported feeling "left out" and lonely when with them. She also told Jack that she wanted to break up with her long-term boyfriend because she didn't feel she loved him anymore. Jack also noticed that his daughter seemed to be getting ill more frequently than usual. She admitted to missing a lot of days of work due to illness.

In time, Jack noticed that she was complaining more and more about work. In fact, she appeared generally more irritable and emotional. When she eventually quit her job, Jack was very surprised because she had always been a very conscientious and hard-working person. Soon she couldn't afford to pay for an apartment so she asked Jack if she could move in with him until she was able to get another job. He welcomed her but he became increasingly more puzzled and frustrated with her behavior. She stayed up most of the night and slept until the late afternoon. Uncharacteristically, she would sometimes lie to him. Finally, her old boyfriend called because he was worried and wanted to let Jack know that his daughter needed help because she was dependent on drugs. When Jack confronted his daughter about her drug use, she admitted to experimenting with drugs but denied that it was a problem. She said that she appreciated his support and caring but that he shouldn't worry.

Recognizing the warning signs

In Chapter 18, we talk about how to deal with a loved one who has an addiction. But you have to recognize the problem before you're able to deal with it. What follows is a checklist of the signs that your loved one has a substance addiction or is engaging in a self-destructive addictive behavior. Answer yes or no to the following questions.

Does your loved one:

- ✔ Turn up late for functions or dates?

- ✔ No longer follow through on his or her commitments?

- ✔ Have more trouble with illness than usual?

- ✔ Have more problems at work than usual?

- ✔ Appear to be withdrawing from intimate contacts?

- ✔ Have unexplained absences from or inconsistencies in his or her usual schedule?

- ✔ Appear to have a new set of friends who he or she is highly involved with but who you don't get to meet?

- ✔ Have major financial fluctuations (like carrying more or considerably less money than usual)?

- ✔ Have lapses of concentration or memory?

- ✔ Stay up later at night and sleep in more during the day?

- ✔ Have more trouble than usual getting it together in the morning?

- ✔ Appear surprisingly secretive about specific aspects of his or her life?

Although this checklist can't diagnose an addiction in a loved one, the more "yes" answers you produce, the greater the chances are that your loved one is suffering from an addiction.

In addition to the signs in the checklist, keep in mind that people are often addicted to more than one substance or behavior. A problem gambler is more likely than the average person to have a problem with alcohol or a sexual addiction. Alcohol helps to calm them down initially so they don't get too excited. In addition, many gamblers like all types of action. Thus, noticing one form of addiction in a loved one is a warning sign that he or she may have other addictions as well.

Keep in mind, however, that any of the warning signs mentioned can be signs of an addiction in someone no matter what his or her age. The following list highlights the kinds of addictions most common to specific age groups. We also give you some tips specific to noticing addiction problems with the various people in your life:

- **A child:** The type of substance abused is likely to be different for adolescents who may still be living at home. If adolescents start experimenting with drugs, they usually start with alcohol and nicotine and then move on to "party" drugs like Ecstasy and marijuana. An adolescent with an addiction problem may start to socialize with a new set of friends that you never get to meet. He may have more trouble than usual getting going in the morning or may stay up late into the night and sleep a lot during the day. He may have become more secretive than usual.

- **A parent:** The choice of substance is more likely to be alcohol or prescription drugs. Also, behavioral addictions are more likely to occur in adults. You notice the parent drinking alcohol daily, usually to the point where she appears high or intoxicated, and she even drinks when alone. She has trouble fulfilling usual daily responsibilities such as preparing meals, going to work, and attending social functions. An addiction to prescription drugs is harder to detect than alcohol addiction. Some of the signs to watch out for with prescription drugs are memory and communication problems and trouble waking up in the morning.

- **A friend:** The choice of addictive substance or behavior may vary depending on the person's age. Keep in mind that if your friend is an adult, he can have any of the addictions mentioned in this book. With teenagers, on the other hand, the choice of substance is usually alcohol, nicotine, and party drugs. As a friend, you may well notice an addiction problem more easily and more quickly than you would notice an addiction in a family member, because friends tend to confide in each other more freely. You may also be one of first people in the addict's social network to notice his withdrawal from his usual social contacts.

- **A spouse:** The choice of addiction in a spouse can be any of the addictions that we discuss in this book. It can be very hard to recognize addiction in a spouse because you yourself may be caught up in denial and in a web of codependency. By codependency, we don't necessarily mean that you have an addiction like your spouse, although this is always possible. Rather we mean that you start to behave in ways that you think may "cure" your spouse's addiction problem but that paradoxically serve to facilitate and support the addiction. An example may be trying to protect your spouse from the negative consequences of his or her addiction by paying for debts or lying about illegal actions. In Chapter 18, we talk more about codependency and how to break out of it.

✔ **An elderly family member:** Sometimes, the elderly relapse to a previous addiction because they feel lonely and isolated as more and more members of their social network die or move away. So don't be deceived by age — addictions occur across every age group.

✔ **An ill loved one:** An ill loved one is likely somewhat limited by his or her illness and so may have limited access to certain substances or less ability to engage in some of the addictive behaviors. Sick people *are* at risk for addictions to prescription drugs, over-the-counter painkillers, and alcohol.

✔ **A co-worker:** You may not be able to detect your colleague's type of substance or behavioral addiction, but telltale signs you may notice at work include: a sudden deterioration in her work behavior such that she turns up to work late, appears poorly rested, misses more work due to illnesses, and perhaps starts stealing money at work.

Chapter 6

Assessing Your Readiness: Do You Need Help Now?

In This Chapter

▶ Being a client

▶ Knowing your options

▶ Deciding which treatment is right for you

▶ Choosing when to start

*W*hy now? You may struggle with this question. It combines with the other question: If not now, when?

Admitting that you're addicted is difficult. It is especially difficult, because there are no clear-cut absolutes that convince you of the need for medical attention, such as a tumor or a heart attack. On the contrary, making your decision often involves weighing the pros and cons of *getting help* against the pros and cons of *staying addicted.* The tipping point, that final convincing link, may be as heartbreaking as your child's tears or as terror inducing as facing time in jail or a threat to your life.

The best time to enter treatment is when you're ready to make a sincere effort to change. Clinicians can help you list your whys and help you find the emotional momentum needed for the first step. But only you can get to that crucial point of saying, "Now!"

Understanding Your Role as the Client

Families, friends, and employers often want you to stop your addictive behavior. At times, they may seem to want it more than you do. But you're the real client. You'll be doing all the hard work in treatment. You'll be looking in the mirror and being brutally honest with yourself. The level of commitment that you need may come from positive motivations or from feeling sick and tired of your addicted life and of being afraid of losing what is most important to you.

Your decisions will move you forward or derail recovery and slip you back into the cycle of addiction. The more you realistically review treatment options and consequences, the more likely you are to make good decisions. The critical consequences of your decisions will be discussed later in the chapter.

Who is the client? You are. The simple goals of treatment are to stop addictive behavior and restore harmony in your life. Only you can learn how to stop and turn it around, and rebuild your life.

The institution paying the treatment bills isn't the client. Nor are the family, friends, and employers who invest in the outcome. Although they may have suffered major losses, emotionally and otherwise, they aren't the clients. *Only you are.* In this chapter, we help you review treatment characteristics to find the types of treatment that best suit your personal characteristics. We also help you assess whether you're ready to seek treatment at this time.

Family members are often the first to confront you about getting help. There is a good chance your addictive behaviors now dominate your contacts with your family. Addictions can readily destroy family relationships, so it's important to get expert advice as soon as possible about treatment options and choices.

Assessing the Options

One of the oldest medical guidelines is *primum non nocere* meaning *first, do no harm.* In addiction, the major consideration in reducing harm focuses on stopping the addictive behavior. If you're addicted, you may consciously or unconsciously burn bridges with family and friends, meanwhile seeking out people who share or support your addiction. You may place undue reliance on the support you get from others in the addictive subculture and find yourself surprisingly hostile to anyone who interferes with your addiction, including family members. You may behave in ways that frustrate them and, ultimately, reject their positive efforts.

So when we think of the potential harm of treatment (for instance, that treatment could be too harsh or strict), we compare it to the reality of the destruction of addiction that we, as professionals, know only too well. If you're at the point of considering treatment, you're likely aware of the harm your addiction is causing you and your family.

Avoiding hopelessness

Treatments can harm you when they inadvertently result in your developing a sense of hopelessness. This occurs most often when you don't accept the fact that addiction is a chronic, relapsing disorder. The reality is that addicted people have slips and make mistakes, and some of the mistakes result in relapses.

If you conclude that you have tried it all, that you have failed treatment (however defined), and that nothing works, then the treatments you have tried *have failed you.* You're not alone if you wonder how hard it will be to give up your addiction. Unfortunately, the reality is that quitting is never easy. After all, the decision to quit would be faster and easier, if quitting were easier. If you expect quitting to be too easy, you're likely to see yourself as a loser if you relapse. If you expect it to be tougher, then you're not *as disappointed* in yourself after a relapse. In other areas of medicine, in cancer care, diabetes care, asthma care, and depression care, clinicians accept relapses as a reality. In addiction, we do the same — although we remain grateful for each day that the addiction doesn't dominate your life.

Hopelessness is that mental state where you think that future success is impossible because your problem or illness can't be beaten. You feel like giving up, quitting life because all you see is a never-ending cycle of pain and hurt and defeat. Hopelessness is, of course, strongly linked with suicidal behavior. You can see how it might induce you to give up entirely. The up side is that hopelessness can be effectively treated when given the immediate attention it deserves.

From a clinician's perspective, it's important to understand that compliance with treatment is the number one problem in all of addiction medicine. If you don't comply with treatment advice, then you significantly increase your risk for relapse and for reestablishing the addictive behavior.

Choosing what's right for you

There is no perfect treatment, no perfect doctors, and no perfect patients. You need to keep reminding yourself of this when you're looking for the best treatment options. Don't get caught up with searching for the "perfect" treatment, the one that can't fail. The best treatment entails a combined effort from several disciplines that results in a termination of addictive behavior and maintenance of that termination over the long-term. As you may already have discovered, the goal of maintaining your quit effort is harder to attain than the goal of stopping. Each is difficult — but it's important to remember that stopping is only the beginning. Maintaining that stop is an entirely different matter.

Matching Your Characteristics to Treatment Options

Before reviewing the details of different types of treatments (these are described in Part III of this book), we want to inform you about particular client and problem characteristics that may help you narrow your choices of treatment options.

Client characteristics

Addiction spares no group, race, religion, economic class, gender, age, sexual orientation, level of success, level of celebrity, or family structure. Nevertheless, research suggests your personal characteristics are important to the choice of treatment. One size certainly doesn't fit all. The initial goal of any treatment, especially addiction treatment, is to *stay in* treatment. Dropping out is common and reflects the tremendous pull addiction has on you. Treatment is designed to help you stop your addictive behavior and control the urges and cravings that could drive you back to it.

The process of matching a client to a treatment has been the focus of much research. In general, the most important aspect to consider is your readiness and motivation for change. Before we get there though, we review other client characteristics that influence what help you need and where and when to get it.

Demographics

Considerable research has focused on your demographics. *Demographics* are characteristics about people that help classify them into specific social groups. For example, demographics include your age, gender, race, nationality, religion, height, weight, and so on. How are demographics relevant when assessing your treatment options? First, certain special interest programs and clinicians focus on specific demographic groups (for example females versus males). Plus, it may be helpful to get into a treatment setting knowing that you're going to spend a good deal of time with other people who do or don't share similar demographics. How much difference are you willing to tolerate? Will it matter to you whether people are richer or poorer, better educated or less educated, of different ethnic backgrounds or from a similar ethnicity? These are good basic questions to ask. You may find it more comfortable to go through treatment with others who have similar demographic characteristics to your own.

Ultimately, your treatment options may be decided by what is available and affordable. Although demographics are important to consider if you have choices in treatment options, ultimately, the most important consideration is what's available to you when you're ready to start treatment.

Age and extent of addiction

If you're addicted, you're at a certain age and stage of addiction. For example, if you're younger, you may be experimenting with drugs and subject to the intense peer pressures associated with early use. If you're older, you're more likely to be isolated in your addiction and involved in seeking out strangers to support your addictive behavior. Your stage of addiction refers to the process of addiction that may start with a minor problem and wind up with you living your life on the very rough edge.

The extent of risk-taking, how on the edge you are, is always an important variable to understand and assess. For example, reflect on whether you're at the stage where you're taking few precautions and adopting an *anything goes* attitude. Or perhaps you're more cautious and you're trying to keep the risks at a manageable level. You may not be prepared to change your risk level, but even thinking about it is a step in the right direction.

If you're at the point where you're continually risking more and more to feed your addiction, the sooner you get help, the better. You're likely at high risk of doing permanent harm to your body and your life. See Chapter 4 to find out more about the risks and consequences related to addiction problems. If you're at the stage of experimenting with an addictive behavior, but don't think you're totally hooked yet, you still may want to get help soon. It can be easier to quit an addiction if you're not physically dependent or if your social life doesn't revolve around the addictive behavior. Get help before your drug or behavioral experimentation causes you permanent physical harm.

The term *development* refers to how people and situations progress, but it can have many different meanings, which we want to be clear about here. *Development* refers to a process of change that follows a predictable, predetermined course. For example, children develop rapidly in their early years. Addictive behavior may also develop rapidly at some times and stabilize and change little at other times. We sometimes refer to the metaphor of cheese left in a refrigerator for a long period *(aging)*. The cheese eventually develops into a moldy mass that looks nothing like it did originally (it has entered a new stage of development). Similarly, the addicted person may develop into someone very different as the addiction extends and intensifies.

The dual diagnosis factor

Clinicians refer to you as having a *dual diagnosis* if you have a mental health condition or another health problem in addition to your addiction. In healthcare, clinicians use diagnoses to classify signs (observed behaviors, appearances, test results) and symptoms (reported problems, such as sleeplessness and agitated feelings) in combination with other variables such as time (when the condition started) and context. The diagnosis also includes events such as trauma and exposure to infectious agents.

Dual diagnosis is more common than you may imagine. According to a report published by the *Journal of the American Medical Association:*

✔ Thirty-seven percent of alcohol abusers and 53 percent of drug abusers also have at least one serious mental illness.

✔ Of all people diagnosed as mentally ill, 29 percent abuse either alcohol or drugs.

✔ These mental health conditions are more likely to be associated with addiction problems: depressive disorders, bipolar disorder (having episodes of mania and depression), anxiety disorders, and other disorders like personality disorders and schizophrenia.

Table 6-1 shows the percentage of people with a substance abuse addiction who have one of these mental health conditions. As you can see, there is an increased likelihood of an addiction if you have one of these mental health problems. Another way of thinking about these percentages is that they represent the increased risk of you having an addiction if you have this particular mental health problem. The comparison group is people who don't have a mental health problem.

Table 6-1   Risk of Substance Abuse Addiction in People with a Psychiatric (Mental Health) Diagnosis

Mental Health Problem	Increased Risk for Substance Abuse (% of people who also have substance abuse)
Antisocial personality disorder	15.5%
Manic episode	14.5%
Schizophrenia	10.1%
Major depressive episode	4.1%
Obsessive-compulsive disorder	3.4%
Phobias	2.4%

What came first, and does it matter?

With addiction problems, you may not be able to figure out what came first. Sometimes, children with significant mental health problems fall into drug experimentation in early adolescence and sometimes, children with other health problems (for example, cancer, heart disease, diabetes, asthma) delay experimentation, because they're *already* taking drugs and know the dangers of drug mixing.

If you're a person with a dual diagnosis, however, you present additional challenges to your doctor. His first rule, again, is to make sure that you're safe. If you've been using mind-altering substances, you may have neglected taking important medications. Depending on how preoccupied you are with your addiction, you may be temporarily incapable of discerning whether you missed taking medications. Some drugs (for instance, methamphetamine) produce a temporary psychosis that can be very frightening. The temporary psychosis must be treated before you're exposed to other treatments.

Addiction treatment, unfortunately, can be slow and laborious. It isn't a matter of "just saying no" despite your yearnings for such simple solutions. Having another diagnosis complicates matters, because the clinician must focus on shorter-term goals. After personal safety and normal brain function are re-established, the focus is, once again, on terminating the addictive behavior. In the case of substances, it means getting clean and sober; for behavioral addictions, it means stopping the compelling activity. In all cases, it means moving toward healthy behaviors and healthier relationships.

Using the problem list to decide on treatment

If you have a dual diagnosis, one of the questions you may be asking is: Which problem should I get help with first? This is an important question that may influence your chances of treating your addiction problem effectively.

Addiction problems typically occur within the context of other life problems. Sometimes, these problems precede the addiction problem, but others undoubtedly stem from the addiction problem. Not all problems can be solved. However, the insoluble problems may give way to processes (for instance, divorce, legal appeals, bankruptcy) that serve to cut your losses and secure a base of hope for the future.

Table 6-2 shows a list of some of the problems that clients have reported at the time they entered an addiction treatment program. This list isn't exhaustive, but it illustrates that an addiction problem is often one of many problems that must be resolved. In deciding whether this is the time to seek help for your addiction problem, it may be necessary to review all the possible problems you're dealing with and determine which can be put aside in order to deal with your addiction problem. You also must decide which of these problems need to be dealt with prior to tackling the addiction problem. There may also be some problems that you can deal with *while* undergoing treatment for the addiction.

Table 6-2 List of Problems Clients Have Reported at the Time They Entered An Addiction Treatment Program

An addiction problem other than the primary one he/she sought treatment for
Serious financial debts
Marital issues
Chronic health problem (for example, HIV, AIDS, cardiac, liver disease, head injury)
Trouble with the law
Mental health problem
Restraining orders regarding contact with one's children or partner
Unemployment

Attitudes of clinicians and caregivers

Caregivers can get caught up in hoping that the simple passage of time will be the ultimate cure. Even if sayings like "He'll grow out of it," "It's a stage she's going through," or "All kids get into trouble" are true, these attitudes put the caregivers into the passive stance of waiting for something to happen. In treatment, the passive wait-and-see approach isn't likely to succeed.

Clinicians, on the other hand, often take a confronting stance — a no-nonsense attitude — early on in treatment. This attitude achieves three major goals: It clearly identifies who is the client (it's you, not your parents, spouse, kids, or boss); it confronts the typical denial ("Really doc, I don't know what the big deal is. So what, if I <fill in the addictive behavior> a lot?"); and it deals with the sense of entitlement that you may demonstrate ("Do you know who I am? Don't tell me what to do! You don't know what you're talking about.").

We have often heard that helpers in the addictions business are hardened, no-nonsense types. This attitude toward addicted persons and their families is learned from both training and experience. It isn't mean or cynical, but it confronts the reality that in addiction treatment, actions speak louder than words.

Treatment characteristics

Treatment means intervening in and changing a person's life using psychological, pharmacological, and social methods. Many treatment options exist. These are described in more detail in Part III of this book. Here we describe some of the general characteristics of treatments that may be helpful for you to know about when deciding on the best treatment option for you. The major treatment characteristics can be classified under four categories:

- ✔ **Setting:** Setting characteristics include inpatient (or residential) versus outpatient (or ambulatory) treatment facilities, community facilities (churches, schools, and community centers) that offer self-help or peer treatment programs, and virtual settings that enable you to access help via the telephone or Internet.

- ✔ **Modality:** Treatment modalities come in many varieties, including the *treatment team approach* consisting of a physician, counselors, nurses, social workers, psychologists; self-help treatment approaches; individual counseling based on a specific treatment model (for instance, psychodynamic therapy, interpersonal therapy, cognitive-behavioral therapy, family therapy); group therapy; and pharmacology.

Psychopharmacology is a field of addictive medicine in which physicians use medical drugs to help people with their symptoms, their cravings, and their behavior problems. The pharmacological methods for treating drug and alcohol dependence are described in Chapter 10.

✔ **Providers:** These are different categories of clinicians and nonclinicians who provide addiction treatment. The sponsors in twelve-step programs guide people through the process of recovery, supporting them every step of the way. Addiction counselors, physicians (some are addiction specialists), psychologists, social workers, nutritionists, exercise therapists, and others help you manage your addictive behavior and related problems. Each different provider works within one or more modalities, meanwhile bringing his or her own attitudes and orientations to the process of treatment.

✔ **Duration:** Finally, the duration of treatment is an important consideration. This is an extremely controversial area because of the recurrent nature of addiction, the relative lack of research, and the wide range of expert opinion.

The treatment options that are described in Part III of this book vary with respect to these four categories. In considering your treatment options, decide whether you have any preferences with respect to the setting in which the treatment is provided, the treatment modalities available to you, the kind(s) of treatment providers you will have access to, and the duration of your treatment.

Making a treatment choice

Okay, you realize that you're ready to choose a treatment. This can be a frightening time, and you may feel very vulnerable. Try to find some experienced guidance and be prepared to discover that whatever sounds easy, isn't easy. Think about the goals of stopping the addictive behavior and finding a new life. Here are some pointers to guide decision-making about treatment:

✔ Make a list of your personal characteristics and your current problems. Remember that your personal characteristics are those that could influence the types of treatment facilities or approaches that fit with your demographics (for example, your gender). For help with thinking of your current problems refer back to Table 6-2. The problems to list are those that need to be dealt with before or when dealing with your addiction problem. Put this list in front of you. Now write out or discuss your reasons for treatment with a highly trustworthy individual. Be brutally honest. Hold nothing back.

✔ Think about the duration of treatment you want.

Expect it to take longer than you want. Beware of beat-the-clock promises. We're not ignoring the fact that a single interview with an experienced helper can make a huge difference in your life and that you certainly want to stop using and to detox as soon as possible. But it is the long-term result that makes the difference. Always look to your long-term freedom from addiction.

✔ Consider the person whom you will trust to give you the best advice. It doesn't have to be a professional; in our experience the advice of someone who has been there is very helpful. That person will give you hope that the addiction can be beaten. Listen for the detailed explanation of what worked and imagine that you're in the same or a similar situation. If the advice fits your situation and you think it's right, you're on track.

✔ Consider your level of psychological-mindedness. This is a concept that concerns your willingness to think about who you are as well as what you're doing. Psychological-mindedness is the ability to see relationships among thoughts, feelings, and actions in order to discover the meaning and causes of experiences and behavior. It is also the ability to recognize psychological and interpersonal problems and to use psychological constructs to imagine the causes of symptoms and behavior. If you see yourself as a psychologically-minded person, then psychotherapy may be especially appealing as a treatment modality.

You don't need to be highly psychologically-minded to benefit from psychotherapy. However, you probably should be at least *somewhat* open to exploring feelings and thoughts to benefit from psychotherapy.

Deciding When to Start

So what's right for you? Start slowly, with the question "Is it time for me to quit?" If the answer is yes, get help. Do it now.

If the answer is no, accept it. You're not quite ready. However, whether your response is yes or no, make sure your decision is well thought out. Consider what you have to lose or gain by seeking treatment.

Cost-benefit analysis of seeking help

The cost-benefit analysis is a useful exercise for any major life decision. In this case, the decision is whether to get help for your addiction. Table 6-3 illustrates a list of potential costs (cons) and benefits (pros). Use this table as a template for drawing up your own table of pros and cons for treatment.

List the costs (cons) and benefits (pros) of not seeking treatment as well as the costs (cons) and benefits (pros) of seeking treatment.

Table 6-3   Cost-Benefit Analysis of Seeking Treatment

Impact Area	Pros of Staying Addicted	Cons of Staying Addicted	Pros of Getting Treatment	Cons of Getting Treatment
Health	None	Damage (for example, liver damage)	Detox will help	None
Family	Continuing to get along with my wife who also has this addiction	My family is losing faith in me	Help my relationship with my family	None
Finance	None	Get into further financial trouble, maybe ruin	Savings from money no longer spent on the addiction	Expense associated with getting help

Now take it to the next step and see how ready you are to seek treatment at this time.

Self-assessing your readiness for change now

One way of understanding how close or far away you are from seeking help for addiction is to track the *stage of change* you're in. Two researchers, Dr. James Prochaska and Dr. Carlos DiClemente, pioneered studies of people who successfully made major changes in health behaviors such as addictive behaviors and found that they typically went through six stages.

The following statements will help you determine which one of these stages of readiness you fit into. Pick the one statement that best describes how you feel about seeking treatment at this time. Use a pencil to circle this statement. After time or after reading more of this book, redo this analysis to see whether you have moved any closer to seeking treatment.

Here are the statements:

- ✔ **I am not even seriously thinking about seeking treatment for help with changing my addiction.** This stage of change is called *precontemplation*. Even if you're not ready to stop your addiction, it is important to mitigate as many of the risks associated with your addiction as possible. (Chapter 4 tells you more about these risks.)

- ✔ **I am seriously considering and debating whether a change is necessary and positive for me now.** This stage is called *contemplation*. It's marked by ambivalence about change. You may have as many reasons for seeking treatment as you do for not seeking treatment at this time. You may also feel uncertain that you have what it takes to stop the addictive behavior, even if you got treatment. A place to start may be to begin to mitigate the risks associated with your addiction (see Chapter 4) and to review how large the problem of addiction is for you (see Chapter 5).

- ✔ **I feel resolved to seek treatment and I have even started to consider my options for treatment.** This stage is called *preparation*. You are actively seeking out treatment. You may even have started to cut back on your addictive behavior. You feel determined to try to tackle the addiction, even if you're not 100 percent certain that you can do it. (You may find it helpful to read Chapter 8 of this book and review other relevant chapters in Part III.)

- ✔ **I am in a treatment program for overcoming my addiction.** This stage is called *action*. In this stage, make sure that you're getting all of the treatments you need in order to overcome your addiction and recover successfully. (For pointers, review the chapters in Part III of this book and read Chapter 15.)

- ✔ **I have kicked my addiction.** Although it depends somewhat on how long you have quit, this stage is called *maintenance*. In maintenance, you need to protect yourself from relapse. (For tips on how to do this, read Chapter 15.)

If none of these statements apply to you because you have recently relapsed, don't feel alone. It is extremely rare to quit for good on the first, second, or even third quit attempt. However, every quit attempt does teach you about what you have to do differently the next time to make the next quit attempt the successful one.

When is it too late, hopeless, and time to say, "Forget about it"? Never! We have seen incredible recoveries. We have seen a person leaving the street to go into intensive care and then on to a liver transplant list. That person smiled for the first time in years and expressed amazement that he could actually sense his senses (in this case the smell and taste of apple pie). Tears rolled down his face, and his human spirit was rekindled. Never give up. Addictive behaviors are changeable. People recover. Never say never!

Chapter 7

Quitting: Easy to Say, Hard to Do

- -

In This Chapter

▶ Stopping addictive behavior

▶ Understanding your triggers

▶ Becoming willing to change

▶ Discovering factors that can help or hinder quitting

- -

*W*hen you begin your journey of quitting, you use the best available knowledge — the information you most trust — and you use it to find a unique path to success. Your path is unique no matter how much you feel you're following the usual, conventional methods. It's unique because you, and only you, make the difference. After it's all done, you'll be able to write a how-to manual of quitting, based solely on your experience. It will describe what worked for *you.*

Starting recovery usually requires a leap that's preceded by a good deal of thinking, talking, and consideration. Then a person goes through a struggle in which his or her personal strengths and motivations become crucial factors. At this point, practical strategies aimed at stimulus control become very important — strategies such as staying far away from situations that tempt you back into addiction while exposing yourself to healthy situations and satisfactions.

Although every quit effort does exhibit basic similarities, the most important points of your program are those that work uniquely well for you. In this chapter, we give you some pointers to help you figure out what may work.

Successful Quitting

Although many paths can lead to a successful quit, there really is only one definition. *Successful quitting* is staying free of addiction — no matter how long. If that length of time is one day, one month, or the rest of your life, you've had a success. In other words, during any period of time you remain addiction-free, you learn something about how to stay free. All of those lessons can accumulate — they can heap up to help you reach longer and more satisfying periods of freedom from addiction.

Defining the quit goal will make you choose between abstaining from the addictive behavior versus controlling the addictive behavior. *Abstinence* means that the quit goal is absolute quitting (I will never use alcohol again; I will never gamble again). *Controlling* the addictive behavior means that the person still engages in the behavior — but in a controlled versus an addicted way (I will not binge eat; I will not engage in compulsive sexual behavior). You must decide which is best: abstinence or control. Get good advice before deciding.

Some people with addictions have to be abstinent because just starting the behavior ("one drink or just one puff") breaks their resolve and starts them back down the slippery slope to relapse. Some addictive behavior has to be controlled because abstinence is impossible or unrealistic (for example, you can't stop eating). Other addictive behaviors (like compulsive sex) are best managed by a long period of abstinence followed by a gradual return to normal behavior.

The phrase from the Paul Simon song that goes "There must be 50 ways to leave your lover" captures the essence of quitting. There are many methods. It's impossible to carefully consider each one before you leap into your own unique quit attempt. At some point during your review of them, you feel you have enough information and then you leap. After you leap, persistence is the key to success. Stay focused and keep moving toward your goal, even though you'll hit bumps and stalls — and possibly relapses along the way. A smooth journey isn't necessarily the golden road to success, as long as you learn about yourself and what works with each bump.

Becoming Aware of Your Triggers

Triggers for addictive behavior are the stimuli preceding the addictive behavior that become associated with the addiction. Most addictive behaviors are *classically conditioned,* which means that one stimulus (like the sound of a bell) becomes associated with another stimulus (like food) to produce an automatic response (salivation). Over time, the bell ringing, by itself, can bring about salivation. The Premack Principle describes how behaviors that happen prior to a self-rewarding behavior tend to increase. As is true with classical conditioning, the person responds to more than just the addictive substance or activity — he or she responds to all of the stimuli that become associated with the addictive substance or activity.

You can't always reduce the power of triggers. But you can reduce how often you're exposed to your triggers. In a way, it's simple physics. You keep the matches away from the firewood, and you keep the heads of the matches away from the striking surface that can ignite them. In time, with concerted and consistent efforts at stimulus control, your addiction triggers lose their power. But even after years of abstinence, their power can sneak back to surprise you. In this section, we review the different types of triggers you may face.

External triggers

Do you feel like engaging in your addictive behavior when with certain people? Does visiting certain places increase your urge to engage in your addictive behavior? Does the time of day or the sounds of certain songs increase your urge? If you answered, "yes" to any of these questions, your urges to engage in your addictive behavior are being influenced by external triggers.

A surprising variety of external events in your immediate environment can trigger a response that pushes you to behave addictively. For example, seeing someone give you a "hungry look" may set off a sex addiction. Alcohol use may be stimulated by TV commercials, or just by being near a liquor store or bar. An external trigger is something in the outside world that sets off the urge or craving that brings on addictive behavior.

In particular, you may not realize that people can serve as external triggers. Just being with friends or acquaintances who are into an addictive behavior (like gambling) can powerfully increase your urges to gamble.

Internal triggers

And what about internal triggers — inner stimuli that drive you to drink, shoot up, snort, or engage in the compulsive behavior characterizing a behavioral addiction. Your internal trigger often takes one of two forms. It may be a low mood that feels crushing and intolerable, or it may be a high that drives you to disregard regular considerations and throw caution to the wind.

The challenge in learning about internal triggers is that sometimes they're linked to particular relationships. Some people have a special influence in undermining the natural positive moods you experience, inadvertently convincing you that only with drugs or alcohol or gambling can you get something positive from life.

Combination triggers

External triggers often combine with internal triggers, and when this happens, you veer closer to addiction. You can be more susceptible to your external triggers because your internal triggers quietly drive you in the direction of greater risk. In fact, you rarely wind up in a high-risk area (for your addiction) by accident. Usually an internal trigger is working in ways that may be operating below your radar screen and outside your usual levels of awareness.

To avoid this, you must figure out how to actively steer your life, especially in keeping yourself on the paths that maintain sobriety. As soon as you feel directionless, it can be a signal that you're headed for trouble, driven by an internal trigger of which you're only partly aware. If you suspect this is the case, take action before it's too late. Remember that when the stronger conditioned responses or habits take hold, you will pass surprisingly close to a cliff. You can find yourself driven by inner and outer forces that are temporarily stronger than your capacity to resist. Going over the cliff represents falling under the influence of the powerful reactions that cause relapse.

If you ever doubt the power of triggers, pay attention for one day to how many times you're exposed to cues, mostly commercial cues, that encourage you to eat or drink or have sex with someone. You face hundreds (if not thousands) of these stimuli. Most are connected with fundamental urges or cravings. How do you think companies sell products? For example, beer commercials often target males from 25 to 35 years of age. The commercials link sex (usually sexy females) and beer, while emphasizing the camaraderie of friends (joking around, laughing). The same message is conveyed over and over again — everything goes better when you have a beer.

Think of other associations (coffee and donuts; gambling and luxury). The commercial marketing machine won't let up if you're fighting an addiction. You will always face a stream of images, voices, sounds, and text designed to link one of your basic urges to a product that is skillfully placed in your unconscious and conscious mind. The product placement influences you to later reach for some change or some dollar bills to buy it.

Time as a trigger

Time is a very specific cue for addictive behavior. We get pro-grammed to eat meals at a certain time of day — and the 5 p.m. round of drinks is a well-known ritual. Later in the addiction process, the song "It must be 5 o'clock somewhere" reflects the attitude that the time cues give way to the internal addiction trig-gers. In some cases, the weekend is the trigger to relax, let go, and indulge in your addiction.

Your identity as a trigger

Another type of stimulus control is that which counters the per-suasive attempts of suppliers. Suppliers of addictive substances and activities often treat you with deference, being especially solic-itous and respectful, meanwhile looking for that gleam in your eye that signals you're hooked on another sale.

The ease of availability as a trigger

Triggers remind us of the surprising accessibility to addictive substances and environments. Cigarettes, for example, are widely available, with alcohol nearly as available. Prescription drugs are harder to get (although if you're an addict, you can find a way to get them fairly easily). The increased availability of slot machines and other games of chance are clearly tempting for compulsive gam-blers. Online betting and pornography are immediately accessible — only a few mouse clicks away. With Internet technology, it will be easier and easier to make a "connection" around any one of several behavioral addictions.

Magical thinking

Amidst all of the temptations of everyday life, you must remember that quitting begins with deciding that you're ready and with com-mitting yourself to stopping for one day. To maintain the quit beyond one day, you must discover how to control urges, cravings, and symptoms of withdrawal. Unfortunately, people with addictions often exhibit *magical thinking* in managing their behaviors. Often, a core magical belief is that change is just going to happen one day. This is like believing you're going to get hit with a bolt of lightning. It *could* happen, but the probability is very, very low.

We use the term *magical thinking* for thoughts based on wishful thinking or fantasy. Sometimes these wishful thoughts are laced with a grain of truth, which makes them even more seductive. If part of the thought is true, you won't have a hard time believing that all of the thought is true. For example, people often use New Years as the best time to resolve to give up a bad behavior, or to make a positive change in life. Resolving to do something does help strengthen your commitment for change. However, thinking that New Years is an especially good time to make such a resolution is magical thinking. The best time to make a change depends on the individual. It depends on what's going on in your life and whether you have really resolved your decision to change (see Chapter 6 for guidance in assessing your readiness for change).

Magical thinking is common and forms the base for superstitions and hopes for a miracle. We all need hope, and how we achieve that state of mind depends on personal experience. We're not opposing spirituality and related beliefs here. We're just challenging the various beliefs people have in magical cures for addiction.

There are, of course, as many triggers as there are people and addictions. Everyone's triggers are slightly different and ultimately unique. We have just covered some of them — you may have some that are considerably different than those we've covered. Review your life carefully and try to understand your triggers. Try to especially focus on the ways they seem similar to those experienced by others, and the ways they seem unique to you as an individual.

Increasing Your Motivation to Change

Motivation is elusive. You will find many ads touting increased motivation as an answer to addictive behavior. For example, one claim was "You can easily quit smoking and drinking. You can find the self-respect you deserve." As you will discover, the initial quit isn't as difficult as sustaining and maintaining the quit.

What follows are some ways to increase your motivation:

- **Give yourself incentives.** Give yourself special rewards that are meaningful to you even though they may not be interesting or meaningful to anyone else. Desire is always motivating. You just have to appeal to your healthier desires.

- **Love.** Realize that perhaps the greatest boost to your motivation is the experience of loving. When you feel yourself weakening or need a boost, deliberately bring to mind one of your loved ones — one of the people in your life whose trust and faith mean a great deal to you. Sometimes, the greatest boost to your will lies outside of yourself — in the people who mean the most.

✔ **Relax.** Consider the view that sometimes, strangely enough, the most direct route to experiencing motivation involves simply releasing and letting go of struggle. Often, this means finding a nonaddictive way to thoroughly relax. Getting a deep muscle massage is good. Or you can try practicing meditation or yoga. Or you may be the kind of person who responds to taking off into pleasant, natural environments that represent, for you, a retreat from stressful surroundings.

✔ **Talk to yourself.** Resort to the simple method of self-talk, be it silent self-talk or the use of actual verbal utterances (if you're going to talk loudly, try it when you're alone). In self-talk, you're anchoring your thoughts and emotions to your voice, be it a silent inner voice or your regular speech. You're mobilizing the same forces that you mobilize when you cheer for favorite athletic teams or athletes. You're simply making yourself the object of your own cheering section. It may sound a bit simplistic and even hokey, but if you need to increase your motivation, you don't have time for standoffish sophistication. You need more because you feel you'll be in trouble if you don't have it. Don't hold back from trying something new — try it and see whether it works.

Factors That Affect Your Ability to Quit

When we, as clinicians, review the reasons why clients relapse, we learn about the real factors that influence addictive behavior. Although such factors vary for each individual, quitting is easier and more probable if you pick a time when the events in your life permit or support a good quit attempt. Of course, the opposite is also true. Some events in your life can make it hard to muster the focus and the motivation to quit at this particular time. The emotional upheavals caused by big life changes can be these types of events.

Don't be fooled, however, into thinking that changing your geography or your job or your relationships will help if you're not committed, in other ways, to changing your addicted behavior. When addicts go on the road, it can stimulate addictive behavior and excitement to new heights. As soon as you arrive in the new location, you may find yourself checking it out for the connections you can make.

The quit attempt must be a very active attempt. You must act to get it started and you must act to sustain it. Whenever it looks easy and you feel you can just passively linger, consider whether something is wrong. A passive approach is very likely to lead back to addiction. As long as you're deliberately moving in the right direction, you can be assured that you're moving away from trouble and temptation. As long as you're actively moving in the right direction, you are actively weakening the forces of addiction while strengthening yourself.

Geographical change

The geographical cure is a popular method of controlling addictive behavior. Moving is a very significant change that alters the stresses on your system and heightens a sense of hope and excitement. Moving can be the fresh start that many people want in their lives. We have heard people in the depths of their addiction say many times, "I'm going to get out of here, move, and leave my troubles behind."

It can be a good idea to leave your geographic situation for a period of time to discover something new. This is the thinking behind university professors taking sabbaticals. Several companies have similar leave policies that ensure their employees maintain a creative edge and avoid burn out.

It may be necessary for you to leave your home or your job for a period of time to get treatment for addiction. We discuss residential treatments in Chapter 9.

The geographic cure is very tempting because it's a routine that many people with addiction already follow. When people build their lives around their addictions, stealing time to feed the addictive behavior, they get into more and more troubles. When they think about quitting, they often think of all of the troublesome situations they want to avoid. Moving on seems attractive because there is just so much to fix in the place where you are. At a certain point in the quit attempt, a break from your immediate environment can be just the thing to stir you into action. Sometimes this is the best way, or the only way, to take that first important, definitive step.

A change of job

Job stress is often a significant contributor to addictive behavior. The familiar pattern is to blame one's job and the related stressors for addictive behavior. This is often a valid point, by the way. Some people who become addicted first get work addicted: Their jobs become so intense that they end up with little time to engage in normal leisure and quality time activities with intimates. Under such conditions, they have the understandable desire to pack highly pleasurable activities into their few free moments — particularly at the odd or unpredictable hours when their jobs simmer down. At those times, they often want to "live it up" to prove that all the work and tension is worth it. Thus work stress can increase your risk for addiction in two ways. First, because you're working long hours, addictive behaviors may become the quick and easy way to relax. Second, because you're struggling during those long hours, you want to celebrate the major and minor successes with the intake of celebratory substances (drink, food, drug) or activities (gambling).

If this profile fits you, a change in job may be helpful. Perhaps you're ready to embrace more balance. You need time to cultivate relationships with those you love. Keep in mind that love is the all-important element in boosting your motivation.

A frequent pattern leading to addictive behavior starts with the attitude "you deserve it," which is actually a variant of "poor me." You think that you have to decompress and find a way to relax, and what better or quicker way than with drugs and alcohol. A psychological dependency readily develops from this mindset.

New relationships

People who are quitting their addictive behavior need to change some (and perhaps, many) relationships. You want to find people who have interests that aren't related to your addictive behavior. Finding friends who have no interest in your addiction and instead have a considerable interest in you as a person, is refreshing and healthy.

Patterns of risk taking and social relationships develop early. You may love the action, the rush, the being cool, the rebellion. It defines you and influences your socializing. Perhaps you find yourself frequently experimenting and taking risks as a way of experiencing the spice of life. Although this willingness to experiment and take risks can be very positive when exercised in the right ways, it can also be a pattern that you need to modify if you are to make a sustained effort and have sustained success with quitting. The key to a sustained quit may be a balance of experiences and a balanced set of relationships with other people, in contrast to the excitement of extremes.

Codependency with a partner

The proximity of a live-in partner or spouse is a powerful factor that influences quit attempts. You will have stronger times and weaker times with respect to sustaining a quit, and being exposed to the wrong temptation during a weak moment can push you over the top.

If you're in a serious and committed relationship where your partner supports your addictive behavior, we say there is a problem of codependency. *Codependency* was the term initially used to reflect situations where people in relationships with addicts acted in ways that denied the problem and thus supported the addiction. It has now come to represent the type of relationship where your *autonomy,* or independence, is discouraged or considered threatening to your partner.

The same forces are at work in either or both definitions. One partner denies a problem in the other partner (be it addictive or otherwise), because she's anxious about rocking the boat.

This pattern of refusing to honestly observe and communicate can, of course, be present when neither partner is addicted. In most cases, refraining from honest communication occurs around a problem area in the relationship. In other words, it occurs in the same area where honest dialogue would be anxiety provoking were it to occur. Communication is anxiety provoking, because it reveals truths about the relationship that indicate definite needs for change — in either individual or in both partners. The partners fear the change, so it seems easier to deny the problem and avoid the truth.

A recovering partner

Partners who are recovering together can be incredibly helpful to one another and can find a much more meaningful and connected experience — with the addiction out of the way. The mutual support of recovery can be a tremendous strength in the relationship. Relationships depend on open communication, honesty, and trust.

However, the situation can be very tricky because partners may progress at different rates in freeing themselves of addiction. The partner who is ahead can feel lonely — or angry that the partner who is behind isn't living up to his or her commitment. On the other hand, as we have said before, the partner who is engaged in more risky activity can exert a major negative influence on the willpower of the partner who is struggling and, for the time being, succeeding in recovering.

Part III

Examining
Treatment
Approaches

"I realize the diagnosis is serious and raises many
questions, but let's try to address them in order.
We'll look at various treatment options, make a list
of the best clinics to consider, and then determine
what color ribbon you should be wearing."

In this part . . .

*W*e explain several treatment approaches in detail, including residential treatment, psychotherapy, and detoxification. We specifically review the advantages and disadvantages of twelve-step programs. To help you select a treatment approach, we review the seven different views of addiction that guide treatment, and we provide case stories of people's experiences in treatment. We also provide information on alternative treatment approaches for addictions, and we discuss how different treatment approaches are combined for maximum benefit.

Chapter 8

Treatment Choices

In This Chapter

▶ Looking at different perspectives on addiction

▶ Understanding how combination treatments work

*W*hich treatment approach resonates with you has a lot to do with the beliefs and attitudes you have about yourself, the world, and your future. These make up your mindset, influencing what and how you learn, the kinds of information that prompt you to take action, and the kinds of actions you're most likely to try out.

To help decide what treatment you go with, ask yourself whether you're open to new ideas and activities or conservative and inclined toward conventional methods. The next most critical question has to do with how much medicine you're willing to take. You may be willing to take anti-addiction drugs to see if they benefit you. On the other hand, you may feel that you've had enough drugs and that the less drug treatment you receive, the better.

This chapter describes the most common treatment options to help you make educated decisions about treatment. It also tells you about combined treatments and why and when it's best to use a combination strategy.

Different Viewpoints on Addiction

In this chapter, we assume that you will choose your own treatment and provide you with important information on which to base your decisions. Depending on your mindset, one or more of the following perspectives on addiction and treatment may appeal to you. We discuss current perspectives on how your personal characteristics may make you a good match for certain treatments in Chapter 9.

The moral dimension

Experimentation with mind-altering drugs has taken place in every age of recorded history. Throughout the ages, it has been normal to use some form of drug or alcohol to celebrate, to reduce anxiety, to soothe pain, to raise spirits, or to cultivate spirituality. Addictive behaviors emerged and became more frequent as we developed the technologies to refine these intoxicants and make them potent stimulators of pleasure centers in the brain.

The moral dimension enters into addiction because addicts can sacrifice almost anything to feed and sustain addictions. How much is this a moral problem? How much are these actions under the control of the individual addict and therefore, a matter of conscious, immoral choices? We know that addictive behavior involves many choices, and the responsibility for these choices, even the bad choices, rests squarely on your shoulders. Nevertheless, other factors are at play, ranging from genetic risks to psychological vulnerabilities.

Twelve-step programs are often seen as moral treatments because they assume a consciously willed aspect to addictive behavior. They also generally acknowledge that a great deal of addicted behavior is beyond one's control. That is why twelve-step programs place emphasis on appealing to a higher power: The higher power assists you in gaining more control.

An unfortunately consistent part of interpretations of the moral perspective is the assumption that humans are weak by nature. Therefore, if you engage in addicting behaviors, you're an especially weak person and, to balance this weakness, must appeal to other sources of strength, including your faith. You may even believe in a higher power that will forgive past weaknesses (sins).

Many treatments were once based on these fundamental beliefs and involved purification or purging rituals. However, the more modern twelve-step programs have evolved away from this perspective of weak character and now include some emphasis on the disease model. These developments are covered in Chapter 12.

These types of questions are debatable — a good case can be made for addiction involving moral problems, but a good case can also be made for the opposite perspective — that addiction is a disease that undermines any and all choices, especially with greater quantities or lengths of use.

The disease perspective

The notion that addiction is a disease arose because addiction's destructive effects resemble those of other physical and mental illnesses. Most diseases escalate from mild forms to moderate or severe forms. During the mild forms, symptoms are often and unfortunately confused with negative behaviors. For example, the fatigue accompanying illness can be seen as laziness, or the confusion associated with neurological illness can be viewed as lack of attention.

After an illness is properly diagnosed, you can often trace back such behavioral changes to the milder forms of illness that caused them. Addictions are similar. After an addiction is severe and properly identified, people can look back and recognize its milder forms during which life was more in control, even though control was slipping away.

Briefly put, the disease perspective, in its pure form, bypasses moral questions and defines the problem as a disease that undermines and eliminates much, if not most, responsible decision-making. Being under the influence of an addiction is seen as similar to having contracted an infectious illness that affects brain function.

The moral and disease perspectives aren't mutually exclusive. For example, if you're aware of some addictive tendencies and patterns in yourself or your family, you may consider it a moral obligation to deal with these tendencies, especially when still in the mild or moderate stages of addiction. (If you're not sure whether your behavior constitutes an addiction problem, read Chapter 5 and use our guidelines to observe yourself and decide.)

What is known from the disease perspective is that addictive patterns, left to run their course, become progressively more severe, leaving you with less control to direct your life in a positive way.

Act when you have more room to move and when more of your personal life remains salvageable. The longer you wait to get help and the more addicted you get, the harder it will be to turn your situation around, and the more your life will be destroyed by addiction.

The pharmacological perspective

The pharmacological perspective, really a subtype of the disease perspective, proposes that addictions result from chronic insufficiencies of certain biochemicals in your brain. Rather than addictive substances being used to overcome insufficiencies, appropriate psychoactive medications, such as antidepressants, are prescribed and used. The pharmacological perspective, like the disease perspective, isn't opposed to the other viewpoints mentioned. You can read about pharmacological treatment options in Chapter 10.

Thinking your way free: The cognitive-behavioral perspective

This perspective differs from other approaches to addiction in that the insufficiency leading to addiction is seen as originating in your thinking. In other words, distortions of thinking and communicating are seen as forming the basis of your addiction. The key beliefs concern relying on things (substances) for enjoyment because you believe satisfactions can't be found in sober relationships with others. Simply put, you have little or no confidence in finding satisfaction with another person unless substance use is involved. This perspective doesn't stray far from everyday perspectives — most people develop patterns of relying on something for consolation when disappointed or dissatisfied with other people.

Another central point is that rather than focusing on transforming negative situations when they occur, one tends to retreat into using substances to avoid confronting problems and to forget about them. Instead of learning from problems, the person turns to substance use and addiction.

The good news of the cognitive-behavioral perspective concerns the power of clear and healthy thinking. Not only can we resolve problems and find satisfactions, we can understand and resolve the thinking patterns from which addictive tendencies originate.

Addictions as a bad habit: The learning models

The learning perspective on addiction has similarities to the cognitive perspective; however it emphasizes the many levels of learning involved. At the most basic level is conditioning, where you're *conditioned* to react to certain situations with specific physiological and psychological responses. Some of your conditioned responses are *subcortical,* meaning they influence behavior by bypassing your thinking apparatus altogether.

Subcortical areas of the brain are those areas that control the basic survival needs of the body. These areas regulate emotional, physiological, and behavioral responses to threat stimuli as well as to reward stimuli. The cortical areas of your brain are where thinking, planning, and judging take place.

Subcortical responses can be very powerful and influential because they seem to stem from the core of your experience and aren't immediately modified by changing how you think. You can see how the learning model combines with the pharmacological model because some drugs, especially during detoxification, serve to quell the subcortically conditioned responses, the ones that make you feel you'll jump out of your skin. The right drugs, at the right time, support stability and keep your focus on positive progress, instead of devoting enormous amounts of energy to resisting impulses.

As can be seen in conditioning, habits form surprisingly quickly and can be difficult to change after they're conditioned.

Habits are typically formed slowly and systematically through repeated behaviors and reinforcements that occur day by day. The power of reinforcement helps us understand how both rewards and punishments affect behavior. Behavior can be reinforced by reward and punishment or through interrupting experiences that you don't like.

 Behaviors (drinking, drug-taking) can be reinforced by both the relief associated with terminating an aversive response (anxiety) and by the pleasant feelings associated with positive stimuli (social support).

If you use a substance that temporarily distances you from problems, you can readily progress to habitual use because it stops the irritation and pain associated with your problems. The more times you experience a reinforced behavior and the more deeply engrained that behavior becomes, the more you rely on it to feel normal and stable. Substance use can insidiously and gradually progress to abuse, and on to an addiction. You can actually be unaware of just how far you've progressed down the road to addiction until you are, by all objective standards, severely addicted. This type of progression is what is meant by a *slippery slope*. You slip slowly at first and then gain momentum, as the slide becomes a steeper and steeper downhill decline.

The psychodynamic perspective

The psychodynamic view of addiction originates from the views of the great Sigmund Freud. According to the psychodynamic view, addiction problems stem from core difficulties or deficits in the *ego,* the executive of your personality.

From this perspective, the primary deficit related to addiction is your inability to manage or regulate emotions, resulting in the experiential extremes of psychic numbing and emotional flooding. Overwhelmed by the alternation of inner emptiness and unmanageably powerful emotions, you choose to retreat from the real world into a world of drug-induced psychic states. From the psychodynamic view, there is no accident about which substances you abuse — you select certain substances to numb, calm, sedate, excite, sexualize, or narcotize. Whatever the specific effects sought, what's desired is retreat from the real world. How you perceive the world as threatening and frightening dictates which substances you use to drown out or eliminate fears and which substances you use to retreat from reality.

Naturally, this retreat requires dependency on others, which points to another major ego problem. With extreme dependency needs, you manipulate people around you to provide care and support. Although you may be alienating immediate intimates, these violations of family and friends are all part of an attempt to be taken care of by them. Meanwhile you, with the help of chosen substances, regress to infantlike or childlike states. This regression characterizes a basic fantasy — that of life without real consequences.

Around these basic problems, the psychodynamic model suggests further difficulties in the frequent use of personality defenses like denial, projection, and minimization of conflict. It certainly is true for many people with addiction problems that denial is a frequent method of avoiding reality, as is *projective identification* (a way of identifying with the status of other people without really getting to know them in depth). Both of these methods combine in the magical attempt to minimize conflict, wherever and whenever possible.

Regardless of the explanations, a key issue in the psychodynamic treatment of addictions is how treatment proceeds and how the treatment process can lead to recovery. Psychodynamic treatment can take place in both individual and group therapy formats where, for the most part, addiction is seen as a result of ego problems, not as the cause of them. Resolving ego problems involves tracing them back to core events and issues, many of which initially surfaced during childhood and adolescence. Overall, the therapist takes a compassionate position — that your tendency to use substances to escape results from emotional victimizations during childhood. These boil down to situations that were inescapable and emotionally injuring and have since echoed in the development of defenses designed to avoid reinjury. However, this avoidance actually leads to addictive behaviors, and these addictive behaviors cause injury to you in the current time frame, as well as to your intimates and family members.

If you have a distinct feeling that you use or abuse substances because of traumatic past experiences or emotional injuries, and are willing to honestly explore and relive your past in order to heal yourself, psychodynamic treatment may just be the best match for you.

The biopsychosocial perspective

The biopsychosocial perspective combines all of the other perspectives, emphasizing the important impact of social support and contact. In other words, this perspective links purely biological influences (vulnerabilities and changes in your brain chemistry), with psychological (as in the cognitive-behavioral and learning models) and social dimensions (certain social environments increase the likelihood that you will engage in addictive behaviors).

Few current-day scientists dispute the value of the biopsychosocial perspective, because of the strong consensus that all of these pieces of the puzzle ultimately link together. The question is where and how linkage occurs and how useful knowing each link is to delivering and finding effective treatment. Answers derived from the biopsychosocial model are useful in guiding the selection of a comprehensive treatment plan that addresses all components of your addiction problem.

You probably didn't set out wanting to become addicted when you first started to engage in the addictive behavior. But at some point, your addiction took over. What was at one time under control becomes controlling. That switch point can be hard to define. But you're bound to understand it better when you review all three dimensions — the biological comfort and pleasure that seems to automatically follow use, the psychological dependency that gradually bends your life so that real life has less and less to offer, and finally the social dimension where everyone who doesn't support or know about your use seems to misunderstand you and treat you with less and less respect. Put all these dimensions together, and they form a downward spiral that can seem nearly impossible to turn around. We emphasize *nearly* impossible because although it's difficult, all the dimensions mentioned above can be used strategically in recovery.

The best combination for treatment combines excellent physical care and conditioning (including proper drug treatment) with serious, sincere counseling and behavior change programs, supported by people who care about you and your recovery.

Combination Treatments

Now that we've reviewed the basic viewpoints underlying treatment, we get down to the all-important details of real applications so that you can make a good choice for yourself. When you approach the bumps-and-grinds of real treatment, you want to feel you're in the right place — that you're with people you trust. You want to believe that all the pain you experience will ultimately be worth it.

If you read more about the specifics of different treatment approaches in the other chapters of Part III, you'll discover that most treatment approaches are based on a combination of addiction perspectives. However, there are significant differences in what is emphasized and how much it is emphasized, and these differences truly affect the inner experience one has as well as the social experiences that are required, promoted, or facilitated.

Twelve-step programs, cognitive-behavioral, and learning programs (all discussed later in this chapter) can be undertaken in individual and group formats and in residential communities that emphasize intensive approaches to restructuring your beliefs, your behaviors, and your life. Twelve-step and cognitive-behavioral methods and pharmacological approaches aren't mutually exclusive. You may be changing your addictive behaviors because you feel a higher power is guiding you, or you may be changing them because it simply makes good sense to you — it hardly matters as long as you're making progress toward a productive, loving, and nonaddicted lifestyle. Still, these different kinds of emphases are driven by different kinds of enthusiasm and experience — some of which are going to be more appealing to you than others. Respect your own sense of what you resonate with.

The twelve-step treatments and other variants of the AA model

Although some people feel twelve-step programs and other variants of the AA model follow a heavy moral agenda, the twelve-step approach actually combines moral re-education with a cognitive-behavioral perspective and a hefty dose of social support (also known as social reinforcement). Twelve-step programs are realistically based in the disease, pharmacological, cognitive-behavioral, and learning models.

The moral dimension of twelve step is related to seeing the strength to overcome addiction ultimately deriving from a higher power — a presumably divine source of inspiration. This reliance relates to your declaration that you have no control over alcohol (or other substances). This declaration is essential because you're replacing the substance and its central position in your life with rededication to a higher power.

The higher power need not be associated with a particular faith or religion. The higher power could even be something *within,* an inner strength and intelligence you find during your battle with addictive tendencies. Nonetheless, *higher* refers to a more moral and uplifted outlook that is discovered only after complete abstinence from alcohol and other drugs is achieved. Higher can also refer to a clearer outlook you find after addressing and modifying the dysfunctional and distorted thinking that led you to the addictive process.

You can learn more about the twelve-step program in Chapter 11 and other variants of this approach such as therapeutic communities in Chapter 9. These programs have a number of advantages to offer you, including the following:

- ✔ They welcome everyone who wants help.

- ✔ They're surprisingly plentiful in many communities.

- ✔ Meetings and programs are held in neutral locations such as churches and community centers.

- ✔ Attending these meetings can be very helpful because an immediate connection can be made to others engaged in the same struggle of becoming free of addiction.

- ✔ They combine mutual aid with self-help, because emphasis is placed on each member helping others get well and stay well.

By helping others progress, you progress further yourself — and the process recycles, so that each helped person eventually helps another person.

If you're a person who thrives on first-hand contact, a twelve-step program may be a very good match, because you can engage in social support (receiving and giving) several times a week or even several times in the course of a single day. The peer support process, made up of *oldtimers* who have used the system successfully in the past and *newtimers* who are just breaking out of addiction (and may be still using) often works brilliantly. The oldtimers are reminded by newtimers that their success can be disrupted by a slip from sobriety, and newtimers get to see and model themselves after living, breathing examples of success.

But you may find a certain degree of inflexibility and automatism within twelve-step programs. It may feel like you're expected to become a mindless adherent of their philosophy. The structure of the meetings may also be a challenge. For more on the negative side of twelve-step programs, see Chapter 11.

Treatments based on cognitive behavioral, psychodynamic, and learning methods

If you don't feel at home with twelve-step models, programs that seem less spiritually and morally focused may be more appealing. For example, you may feel decidedly uncomfortable with the assumption of a single higher power and prefer dealing with the more practical perspective of simply improving your life and your relationships.

If this more practical focus appeals to you, the cognitive-behavioral and learning programs may be better matches.

 Whether it is a twelve-step program, a therapeutic community, or a variant of either, most treatment programs address the behavioral and psychological aspects of an addiction. Thus, the differences among these programs aren't based so much on what is left out but rather on what elements receive more emphasis.

The cognitive-behavioral model approach to treatment

The basic point in the cognitive-behavioral programs is that different thoughts and images enter your mind. Some of these thoughts and images are healthier than others. The unhealthy ones are those that drive you back to addictive behavior. You have the ability to tell the difference and to emphasize your most *functional, healthy* thoughts. The term "cognitive" in the cognitive-behavioral model refers to these kinds of healthy thoughts. From this perspective, your behavior is under the influence of your thoughts. In other words, the way you think about something determines how you act.

Accordingly, your behavior can be determined by healthy thinking, rather than by thinking that is flawed, distorted, and characterized by pessimism and hopelessness. An example of this type of thinking is "I can't believe that I had a drink — I'm hopeless. I may as well get hammered now." Your counselor or therapist provides you very clear and practical tools for modifying your dysfunctional cognitions and for tracing how different cognitions influence and are influenced by different relationships in your life. Your counselor will also teach you how you can challenge your negative thinking and change your behavior and your feelings.

Then, having gained important insights about what changes are needed in your life (whether they're changes in your thoughts or in the behaviors that follow certain thoughts), you can go about skillfully changing your life for the better.

In terms of addictions, these methods are often used to find the key cognitions that drive you to use those substances that get you to the highs that inevitably lead to harms. You're confronted (frequently) with your own disbelief about being able to find healthy, nonaddictive highs that involve honest, caring, reciprocal relationships with others and don't require the associated use of substances.

Working on cognitive change also involves working on behavioral change.

Cognitive-behavioral treatments also include strategies to help you change your behaviors. The target behaviors can be those linked to the cognitions you're trying to change, or they can be behaviors that help you directly control the addictive behavior. Below are examples of both:

✔ Targeting a behavior that is linked with changing your cognitions can be sitting down to talk to a friend or family member who has done something to hurt you rather than automatically assuming that the hurt was intentional.

✔ Targeting a behavior that can help control the addictive behavior may be taking fewer sips of a drink so as to make it last longer or even taking up an exercise program to help relieve tension rather than self-medicating yourself with the addictive substance or behavior.

The psychodynamic approach to treatment

The psychodynamic model focuses on the core conflicts and deficits that people with addiction have. The most prominent issue concerns dependency, an excessive need to be cared for by others. Sometimes, this neediness comes from past experiences of neglect. In the extreme, the person with addiction stops caring for basic needs and has to relearn these skills. The two other core issues are emotion management (learning how to identify, understand and express your feelings) and understanding and improving self-concept (what you think about yourself).

If you struggle with these issues, you may get into relationships that bail you out. Therapy, as we discuss in Chapter 9, helps you to confront these issues and develop new ways to manage the conflict.

To deal with painful addiction-related issues and associated feelings, you *can* find a supportive and safe counseling relationship. Within this relationship, you can gradually learn about, and take responsibility for, the emotionally corrective actions that lead to a healthier approach to resolving problems.

The learning model approach to treatment

The learning model approach helps you analyze your addictive behavior from the perspective of how it is rewarding and reinforcing for you. You can read more about learning model approaches to treatment in Chapter 9.

The term *reinforcing* refers to the needs that addictive behaviors fulfill for you. For example, you may be using alcohol and drugs to relax, to enjoy a moment of pleasure, or to socialize more easily. Engaging in the addictive behavior is reinforced by the relief or pleasure experienced by fulfilling these particular needs.

Humans learn quickly. If a substance relieves pain or helps you get some sleep, taking the substance is reinforced, and the substance will be used repeatedly to obtain these rewarding effects. Your ability to learn is getting you into addictive difficulties.

The focus of treatment is on finding healthier alternatives for meeting these needs instead of resorting to addictive behavior. The following list presents some of the functions an addictive behavior may be serving:

- ✔ Helps you relax
- ✔ Creates a means of socializing
- ✔ Lifts up your mood
- ✔ Helps you feel powerful and in control
- ✔ Helps you feel loved
- ✔ Helps you sleep
- ✔ Is energizing
- ✔ Eases pain
- ✔ Combats boredom

Chapter 9

Reviewing Inpatient and Outpatient Treatment Options

*T*ypically, your search for help first involves turning to a trusted advisor (your doctor, teacher, insurance agent, pastor, or anyone else you trust). Although addiction is a familiar topic, you may need to reach beyond this most trusted person to get expert treatment advice. Finding good advice can be surprisingly difficult.

The major obstacle is internal. The *stigma* (shame) you feel (about addiction) stops you from undertaking the thorough searching you need to do. The experience of stigma is powerful. It makes you feel defensive and ashamed. You may see yourself as a loser. The pain of admitting a need for help may feel worse than the pain of staying addicted.

But rather than letting shame and fear dominate, remember that you've become caught up in this illness. It certainly wasn't your intent to develop an addiction problem. Other people have other illnesses; you have this one. Nobody goes through life without getting ill sometimes, and it's hard to say, ultimately, which illness is the worst. It's also hard to say how much any one illness results from someone's own doing.

The bottom line of illness is that our bodies and minds are temporarily out of control. The only thing that helps is gaining more control. If you need help, the strongest, most effective, and most dignified thing you can do is to get the right kind of help.

Another simple reason for the difficulty in finding the right care is that addiction services aren't usually well-publicized. To help you find some addiction services, we've listed most of the easy-access entries to care in Chapter 21. A tremendous network of recovering people who welcome questions and offer advice is available through twelve-step programs. In addition, the American Society of Addiction Medicine is dedicated to educating physicians and improving treatments. Although the society is making progress, professional knowledge regarding addictions is still too often elementary and problematic.

In this chapter, we discuss how to obtain professional services (including intervention services) and outpatient care, and we help you decide what to do if inpatient care is necessary.

Interventions: Breaking Through Denial and Fear

Your family often no longer knows what to do. Their lives have been turned upside down. They're worried sick. Every waking moment becomes weighed down with serious concerns. You may have promised many times to end your addiction and get help. As they look back, the explanations for the hours lost, the money gone, and the emotional trauma, are now clearer. These losses are the many sad faces of addiction. You're not yet ready to stop — you may only be capable of empty promises and guilt-ridden apologies. What can they do? What can *you* do?

When you seek professional help, you and your family are scared. You may be more frightened than ever before. Your secrets will be exposed. You may find yourself willing to do anything at this point to avoid getting help. Lying (best with a straight face and indignation) is typical. You may promise anything to take the pressure off. If that doesn't work, you lash back: "What right do you have to tell me what to do? If you don't stop questioning me, our relationship is over." The fear and hostility may be palpable.

The situation is intolerable. Something has to give. Your family may consider the services of a professional interventionist at this point.

I'm afraid to get help

Molly was desperate for help. She had grown up in a small town with a loving, middle-class family. She wanted to be a high school teacher. Still, at 23 years of age, she was filled with self-doubt and confusion. In high school, she had been very sociable. She loved to dance and party. She experimented with alcohol and smoking. One night after a dance, she got involved sexually with her date. One thing led to another, and she "got a bad rep as one of the school sluts." She couldn't wait to move out of town to attend teachers' college to get a fresh start. Then the unbelievable happened: She went to a party at college, got loaded, and got casually involved in sex. The cycle started all over again. Boys asked her out, but they only wanted "one thing." No one took her seriously. She was so ashamed. She felt too ashamed to talk to her girlfriends or her family. She "knew" that she was "bad" and badly flawed. How could such a rotten person ever be a teacher? She hated herself and saw no hope for change.

When she did go out socially, she felt unworthy. To dull the emotional pain, she drank. Drinking seemed to help. She could forget her insecurities. Alcohol became a way of soothing her pain.

Molly was caught up in a vicious cycle. She felt too ashamed to ask for help. She felt alone and empty. Drinking became her solution and her problem. She couldn't bring herself to ask for the kind of help that she really needed.

Family members will find no easy ways to guide you into care. You're in a cycle of denial and fear, fueled by shame, resentment, and deep inner pain. You feel so alone that you become hardened to the emotional outbursts and rage of loved ones. Professional help is strongly recommended if you're at this point.

How an intervention works

An intervention is an objective, caring, nonjudgmental process. You're confronted with the reality of your actions by those adversely affected. The objective is to motivate you to accept help. Although your family is definitely involved, a professional interventionist guides the process.

The first formal interventions used the Johnson method, which was developed by a priest named Vernon Johnson and two friends, Wheelock and Irene Whitney. The Johnson method started as a challenge to the idea that you couldn't be helped until you hit bottom — a point in life where family, job, finances, or a combination of them is lost. The purpose of any intervention method is to help you confront your denial of problems and your fear of change, and to help you get into care.

An interventionist's experience

Dan Cronin of AIR, LLC is an experienced interventionist. He sent us this description of a recent case.

I received a call from a father who told me that his daughter, April, age 20, spent most of her time in a drug-haze hanging out with people who "don't give a damn about her." He didn't know what to do but he wanted to do something. Her mother was a wreck, and her brother and sister couldn't understand her. He wanted to arrange for treatment, but hadn't spoken to his daughter in three weeks. He deeply regretted the last contact where he called her "every name I could think of" while pleading with her to stop. The call to me was a call for help.

My approach: The first job is to ensure the safety of patient and the participants. April was in danger. She was in a situation where she was at risk for assault, including rape. Her father's first inclination was to charge in, but that approach rarely works and generally increases the risk because April would likely rebel against her father's take-charge attitude. I decided to go in gradually, using contacts in the area and make a direct approach to April. After ensuring the addicted person's safety, protecting his or her dignity is uppermost in my mind. I give people a chance to refocus their lives. April was in "escape mode." She didn't really care what happened to her, but she reacted when I spoke about her brother's worry. Actually, she started to cry and said she missed him. This was an opening — the motivation for change. I use my experience (which spans the entertainment and sports businesses), my understanding of the resources available in communities and nationally, and my openness to the process. April was willing to go to a small (six-bed) treatment facility where she would get intensive therapy along with twelve-step work. Every intervention is different, because every person is different. The commonality is the addictive process, which doesn't get better with time. I care about my clients and their families and stay in touch with them through the early stages of treatment.

The interventionist is trained to communicate supportively, helping you accept your need for help and educating you and your family about addiction. She provides a link to treatment, ensuring that the right treatment center is found and contacted and that background preparation for your entry is completed. You're invited to a meeting but you may not be told much about the purpose of the meeting. At the meeting, which is carefully planned and structured, concerned persons express love and caring while describing, in behavioral terms, how you're affecting them. They express their wishes and needs for you to enter treatment.

Concerned persons need to state concerns clearly, without lapsing into accusations and anger. One simple skill is to communicate with an "I" message versus a "you" message. For example, "I feel sad" versus "You make me feel sad." Describing behavior versus voicing feelings, opinions, and judgments is a learned skill. It is based on making references to the actions that are clearly observable, like those that could be captured on video or audiotape, for example.

During the intervention, the realistic consequences of not entering treatment are described, matter-of-factly. The consequences may include separation or divorce, the refusal of adult children to attend family functions, job loss, and loss of friendships. Other people can't control *your* decisions and behavior. They can only control *their* responses to your decisions and behavior.

The intervention process often exposes weaknesses in the family system. Families who have long suffered from a member's addictive behavior may be angry and punitive. Or they may be numbed into temporary or chronic states of no longer caring about what happens to you. Conversely, they may fear reprisals for breaking your secrets and the codes of silence that have helped you maintain your addictive behavior. The denial of problems and disbelief in the potential for change often add up to turning a blind eye to your addictive behavior. The interventionist has to balance the goal (getting you into treatment) with the complex communications of family members who may have old and new issues to settle.

However, an intervention isn't the time for a complete course of family therapy. Family therapy meetings can and should occur after the addicted person is established in treatment.

Most interventionists and experienced clinicians are specialists in helping you move past your denial and increasing your motivation for treatment. To achieve this goal, they use a motivational interview.

The motivational interview has become one of the more powerful interventions to help you. Such an interview is conducted by a trained professional and is designed to help you go beyond your guilt, fear, and anger to participate in healthy decision-making. The interventionist helps you consider your decisions practically, in terms of what you stand to gain by change and what you stand to lose by change — and what you gain and lose by not changing. The goal is to help you make an informed decision about treatment.

Intervention principles

There are ten general principles that influence the decision to intervene and that guide the intervention process. These are:

- ✔ Your behavior is causing significant damage in your life.
- ✔ Denial is preventing you from fully appreciating the damage the addiction is doing to you and your life.

✓ You're unlikely to seek help on your own.

✓ The people involved with you can change the environment by changing the enabling system — making it more likely that you will seek help.

✓ The sense of genuine concern and understanding conveyed by the interventionist is one of the most important factors in influencing you to seek help.

✓ Anger and punitive measures have no place in interventions, because they increase your defenses, making it less likely you'll seek help.

✓ The consequences for not going into treatment should not be designed to punish but rather to protect your health and well-being.

✓ You require an initial period of intensive treatment such as a 28-day residential program or an intensive outpatient program to address your denial.

✓ The intervention may be useful even if you aren't likely to go to treatment.

✓ The intervention isn't a confrontation. Rather, it is a well-organized expression of genuine concern for you, given a chronic and serious addiction problem.

Choosing an interventionist

The standards guiding the choice of an interventionist are clear. Adapting the Johnson Institute guidelines, we recommend the following. Choose an interventionist who:

✓ Uses generally acceptable criteria and procedures for assessing problems of dependency and addiction.

✓ Demonstrates the necessary ability (knowledge, skill, and attitude) for assessing the physical, emotional, motivational, and mental capacities of concerned persons to carry out an intervention.

✓ Commits to the principle that the goal of the intervention, first and foremost, is to secure help for the addicted person.

✓ Commits to the principle that pre-intervention counseling is short-term and time-limited and shouldn't be prolonged to an extent that causes help for the addicted person to be postponed.

✓ Ensures that during the intervention, statements by concerned persons to the addicted person are not shaming or

> demeaning but are caring and respectful, describing specific facts, behaviors, and feelings.
>
> ✔ Treats all people in the intervention process with care and concern, and works to preserve the dignity and self-respect of the addicted person.
>
> ✔ Commits to helping families by directing all family members involved in the intervention into their own process of recovery.

Interventionists may not even need to bring all of the concerned persons together in a single gathering. Sometimes, the intervention-ist just meets with the addict privately and informs her about her family's concern and their interest in stopping the enabling process.

Residential Versus Outpatient Care: Deciding What's Best for Your Needs

Intensive outpatient care may be attractive because you don't have to leave your job, family, and friends. On the other hand, residential care provides a secure environment that focuses exclu-sively on recovery. The challenge is to match your needs with the treatment setting.

Getting help for problems in the other areas of your life, aside from reduction of use or abstinence, makes it more likely that you'll be successful at managing the addiction problem.

Getting treatment for three specific problem areas is particularly important in helping you overcome your addiction problem. These three problem areas are: employment, family relations, and psy-chological problems.

If you get individual treatment for problems in these three areas, you're more likely to stay in addiction treatment longer, complete the addiction treatment, and achieve a better six-month outcome (meaning less alcohol and drug use than someone who doesn't get help for problems in these three areas).

Outpatient Treatment

There are many different types of outpatient care, ranging from group therapy to individual counseling to long-term psychotherapy, and from behavioral self-control training to psychopharmacological interventions. Because more people seek help for mental health treatment than for addiction treatment, mental health professionals are learning to ask about and effectively treat addictive behavior. (Review our section on *dual diagnoses,* those other conditions that complicate treatment for your addictive behavior, in Chapter 6. Dual diagnosis issues also influence the type of care needed.)

Disrespect of a person because he has a particular illness has the effect of putting up barriers to that person getting help. The stigma of mental health problems, however, is gradually decreasing as new treatments are developed and the media becomes more sophisticated about covering these developments. The main issue is to see people as *suffering* from a mental illness, not as *consumed* by it. More than 20 percent of Americans experience a mental disorder every year.

Psychotherapy

Psychotherapy is a formal, confidential, professional relationship within which you explore difficult and often painful emotions and experiences. These may include feelings of guilt, anxiety, and depression, and experiences of trauma and loss. Psychotherapy is a process that allows you to gain an increased capacity for choice, through which you can become more autonomous, effective, and self-determined. There are many different types of psychotherapy (see Chapter 8). The key consideration for you is that the therapist, no matter what her method, must have considerable experience with addictions.

Ask your potential therapist explicitly "How much experience do you have in treating people with addiction? What methods do you use? Is there scientific evidence supporting the treatment you employ for my type of addiction? What are the risks, if any, of the treatment that you recommend?"

Controlled drinking

The goal of treatment is important. Many addiction treatments have the goal of abstinence or total avoidance of the addictive behavior. Other addiction treatments have the goal of controlled use. Controlled drinking, for example, takes the goal of moderate, problem-free drinking. The goal for moderate drinking was proposed in the 1960s. Moderate drinking involves drinking below levels that incur significant health risks. These levels are based on medical guidelines and vary depending on your background health status. The controlled drinking approach involves relearning how to manage your consumption. This approach can be applied to any substance (although we know of no proposals for controlled heroin or cocaine use).

How controlled drinking works

Many different outpatient treatments encourage moderate or controlled drinking, but we'll focus on the example of Behavioral Self-Control training. Below are some of the strategies used in Behavioral Self-Control training:

- ✔ **Self-monitoring** of your drinking so that you map when, where, and with whom you drink.

- ✔ **Functional analysis** of your drinking so that you can determine all of the ways that alcohol serves and influences you (for example, "Helps me relax. Helps me dull pain. Helps me to socialize.")

- ✔ **Goal setting** so that you know your limits.

- ✔ **Learning alternative** ways of meeting the needs that alcohol has been serving. (Use exercise as a means of relaxing. Find healthier pain management strategies. Alternate alcoholic and nonalcoholic beverages when socializing and take small sips and fewer sips of alcohol to make a drink last longer.)

Is controlled drinking for you?

A number of factors go into determining whether a controlled drinking or a controlled substance use approach is a treatment solution for you. It depends on the severity of your addiction problem, how much you're using the substance, your health status, and other health and addiction problems — and sometimes on a trial-and-error basis.

Definitions of moderate drinking vary, but generally, these definitions classify moderate drinking as not exceeding more than 4 to 12 drinks a week, or no more than 1 drink a day for women, or 2 drinks a day for men. Generally, a drink is considered to be 12 ounces of regular beer, 5 ounces of wine, or 1.5 ounces of 80-proof distilled spirits.

This treatment is an option for you only if your drinking problem is considered as mildly to moderately severe.

Risk reduction

Risk reduction is a widely applied term that refers to procedures designed to help people cut down on the risks associated with addiction. Risk reduction is sometimes also known as harm reduction. Risk can be increased or decreased by the lifestyle choices you make, or the environments that you live and work in. Risk reduction applies to many diseases such as heart disease, HIV, and diabetes.

Addiction can increase your risk for HIV and other sexually transmitted diseases. When on a "run," your judgment is impaired, and you may get involved with multiple partners and unsafe sex. These kinds of risks are described in Chapter 4.

Some of the most common risk reduction strategies include:

- ✔ **Reduction of risky drug use:** This approach involves distributing needles and syringes so that you don't have to share needles and syringes with addicts who may have infectious diseases. Sometimes, the injection setting may be provided so that you can use your preferred drug safely.

- ✔ **Reduction of morbidity and mortality:** The focus is on helping you, no matter what your circumstances are, to reduce the health and mortality risks associated with engaging in your addictive behavior. This is achieved by the changed attitude of health and social services toward addiction disorders.

- ✔ **Opiate maintenance:** This method refers to giving the addicted person an opiate (methadone) under medical conditions (see Chapter 10).

- ✔ **Reduction of social harm:** This strategy involves decriminalization and the creation of settings where a drug use lifestyle is tolerated as long as it doesn't influence the surrounding society.

In the United States, the most common risk reduction strategies are opiate maintenance and the reduction of morbidity/mortality risk. The other strategies are more common in Canada and Europe.

Some tips on seeking outpatient professional help

You must consider a number of things when choosing a therapist. The most important consideration relates to whom you feel confident in and comfortable with. Who do you click with? Apart from credentials, fee structures, and therapeutic models, the personality characteristics of your therapist can affect how comfortable and confident you feel.

Don't hesitate to shop around for the therapist who you feel comfortable and confident working with.

Therapist or counselor?

Credentials and experience are important and sometimes complex because counselors come from many different backgrounds. In the addictions area, many recovering people want to help, want to tell their stories, and want to encourage newcomers. These activities are often best left to the self-help and twelve-step meetings with stable structures and long-standing traditions of helping. Professional care requires credentials, experience, and supervision. Make sure that your counselor is licensed to provide treatment. If he isn't licensed, he should have an explicit supervisory relationship with a licensed practitioner.

Credentials

Your therapist should have credentials from an established and recognized group. She should have special training in addiction. The credentialing authority should have clear procedures so that you can read about how your therapist was registered and how to lodge a complaint, if that becomes necessary.

The therapeutic relationship

The therapeutic relationship in individual therapy involves three key aspects:

- ✔ **Bond:** The bond is based on your emotional and empathic connection with the therapist. Does he seem to understand you? Does she seem to respond to your feelings and emotions in ways that help you? This connection can be based on your similarities (gender, cultural background, religious beliefs) but is more basically related to your ability to communicate openly and honestly with each other.

- ✔ **Therapeutic goal:** Many therapists work hard to define the goals of therapy early in the relationship. Specific goals are often preferable to general goals. "Feeling better" as a goal, for example, is quite different from "being able to resist urges in specific situations." You may not feel better *while* you're engaged in resisting, but you'll probably feel better *after* you've successfully resisted. You can see how important it is to be very specific in how you define goals.

- ✔ **Therapeutic tasks:** You may have expectations of the therapist such as how much he communicates and explains, and how much or little structure he provides. Some therapists actively assign tasks for you to do as homework. You may be given exercises that enable you to practice your newly developing skills outside of the therapy office. Other therapists may expect you to free associate and report on recent dreams and fantasies.

The tasks focused on differ widely across different types of therapy. All tasks, however, play an important part in how you judge the therapeutic relationship and how comfortable and motivated you are within the therapeutic relationship.

Typically you'll know if the therapy and your therapist will help you after three to four sessions. By then, you can judge the bond, goal, and tasks of therapy. You'll know more about your problems and how they're being addressed, but you'll also have to take a leap of faith in your therapist. Always try to get personal references from other people if that is possible.

Residential or Inpatient Treatment

Given the media attention paid to figures in the entertainment industry, the 28-day rehabilitation (rehab) program is well-known to the public. What isn't well-known is what goes on behind the closed doors of these programs. Before entering the rehabilitation setting, you'll probably have to be detoxified of alcohol and drugs and cleared medically. (See Chapter 10 for the procedures of detoxification and the medical risks.) Entering rehab is a big step; a pivotal step in your life.

The stages of inpatient treatment

Regardless of the treatment model, when you enter treatment for an addiction you will likely progress through three stages:

- ✔ **Stage one represents the induction and early treatment phase.** You learn about the treatment community rules, expectations, and procedures. This is an important phase, because you build trust with the treatment team and your fellow members. During this time, you assess your treatment needs and set goals for what you want to change in order to support your recovery from addiction. You acquire a deeper and fuller understanding of the nature of your addiction and, hopefully, commit to the recovery process.

- ✔ **Stage two represents the active treatment and rehabilitation phase.** You focus on changing your attitudes and behaviors toward yourself, your addiction, and others. You also focus on taking responsibility for your actions and their consequences. During this stage, you may focus on developing new skills — for instance, acquiring further education and vocational training. You may also undergo interventions to help with health, psychological, family, and work problems.

✔ **Stage three represents the time of re-entry into life outside the treatment community.** Post-residential aftercare interventions may include individual and family counseling and vocational and educational guidance. Often, aftercare includes linking up with self-help groups that can support your recovery process.

It's voluntary

Laws across states and countries differ, but in general, most inpatient treatment is provided voluntarily, which means that you're attending because you want to and you're free to leave at any time. If you leave before the treatment team recommends discharge, you've left "against medical advice."

The rules of rehab

Every setting has a unique set of expectations for clients and their families. The rules or expectations from the Renaissance Institute of Boca Raton, Florida, a well-known residential center, are listed below. These expectations evolve from the treatment facility's fundamental philosophy of human nature and addictions:

✔ "We consistently ask the patient to take responsibility for whatever is happening in his/her life."

This is based on the belief that you must accept that the choices (made consciously or unconsciously) you make in responding to life events are entirely your own, and these choices bring about consequences that you create.

✔ "You must earn before receiving, whether it's emotional support, financial support, spiritual support, or physical support."

This expectation is based on the belief that addiction is sustained by the unconscious fantasy of life without consequences. Recovery is the acceptance of the position that you aren't entitled to support nor are you pardoned for all of the logical consequences of your actions.

✔ "We ask patients to assume adult responsibilities while in treatment, including working and homemaking for themselves and others."

This expectation is based on the belief that being an addict is akin to being a child in that you have limited control and you're dependent. Recovery, on the other hand, means moving away from the childlike being to becoming an adult with the usual responsibilities of adulthood.

✔ "We ask patients to do unto themselves and others as they would have others do unto them."

This expectation is based on the belief that by helping yourself and others, you can reverse the effects of previous dysfunctional relationships. You can change the past or how you experience the past, by changing your current behavior to others.

Although at first you may think the rules or expectations of rehab seem too simple or are demeaning, look for an understanding of the philosophy underlying these rules. The philosophy is intended to guide you to a position of strength, autonomy, compassion, and control.

How long is long enough?

Professionals believe that you often leave treatment prematurely because of perceived pressures from work and family, or from the structure of the treatment center. Insurance coverage may also be a factor limiting the length of treatment that will be approved for payment.

A period of residential care from 28 days to 90 days is often recommended by addiction treatment providers. Another critical success factor in our experience is the aftercare period up to one year of postresidential treatment. Your aftercare plan is an important key to recovery.

Aftercare

The period after you leave rehabilitation is crucially important to your recovery. This is when you're challenged to apply your new behavior in your routine environments. Aftercare has different aspects, but the goal is clear: Return to your life and live without your addictive behavior — *no matter what happens.*

Fear of the real world

You may have lived so long in the counter-culture supporting your addictive behavior that returning to the real world will be very challenging. You may have to face the music at home or work. You have questions to answer and routines to establish.

Telephone counseling

Contact with the treatment center is sometimes maintained via telephone sessions. These sessions reinforce lessons about managing urges and avoiding risky situations where the probability of relapse is high. And most importantly, the sessions teach you how to maintain contact with supportive people. The well-known saying in this regard is "If you don't want to slip, stay out of slippery places." Whether you call a counselor, a twelve-step sponsor, or a recovering friend, the key is to make the call.

The Minnesota Model

In the 1940s in the United States, the alcoholic's treatment choices were severely limited. Addiction was viewed as a moral weakness, and the medical community wasn't sure what to do about it. In Center City, Minnesota, the Hazelden therapeutic community was developed out of a guesthouse for alcoholic men.

This historic development had a treatment program based on five simple expectations:

- ✔ Behave responsibly

- ✔ Attend lectures on the Twelve Steps of Alcoholics Anonymous

- ✔ Talk with other patients

- ✔ Make your bed

- ✔ Stay sober

The model started with a focus on men, in accord with the social attitudes of the times. Now, women are also active participants in both public life and in treatment programs. Addictive behavior cuts across gender lines. Women's unique health issues are being considered in addiction treatment today.

What was revolutionary was the fact that the treatment of alcoholism moved from custodial care (often in despicable conditions) to a setting where people were treated with dignity and respect. Equally stunning for the time was the observation that by telling your story and listening to others, you could help each other.

The rules, simple as they may seem, addressed the fact that as an addict you can be secretive, self-centered, and resentful. You're often isolated from others and suspicious of attempts to tell you what to do.

The benefits of residential care include: an opportunity to learn life skills from others; a time to focus specifically on getting help; a time to bring your life into order by dealing with medical, financial, employment, legal, family and psychological problems; and an opportunity to break from dysfunctional patterns of behavior and risky situations.

Relapse Prevention

Addiction is a chronic, relapsing disorder. *Relapse* is defined as a return to addictive behavior after a period of abstinence, given a client goal of abstinence. Dr. Alan Marlatt presented a revolutionary approach to the treatment of addiction in his book on relapse prevention. The revolution was based on the observation that "relapse is part of recovery." The first step is to discover what triggers a relapse and then work on how to prevent these triggers from precipitating the relapse. The statistics on relapse are staggering. For example, about 90 percent of alcoholics will experience at least one relapse over the four-year period following treatment. Given the likelihood of relapse, treatments have increasingly started to train you in relapse prevention. An important part of this involves identifying triggers for substance use or addictive behavior. These methods are detailed in Chapter 16.

Bill Moyers, a famous TV interviewer, has said that many people, himself included, have the idea that addicts choose to light up, shoot up, or drink, so the negative consequences are their own fault. "I hope that people come to a new definition [of addiction], and they realize that the addict may relapse, just as a person in remission with cancer can have a new onslaught," Moyers said. "It's a chronic problem, and people have to stay in therapy." More than 80 percent of those who get treatment will have at least one relapse.

"If your child comes to you for help, get informed, and don't panic. Don't scold or punish," Moyers said. "If your daughter came to you and said she had breast cancer, you would work out a way to have it treated. The same goes for addiction." In our view, Mr. Moyers has made a critically important point: Our culture needs to destigmatize addiction problems as much as possible.

Therapeutic communities and sober living

Dr. Maxwell Jones developed the therapeutic community concept in the early 1950s. These communities are structured in different ways, but provide the clean and sober environment and structured living that can be very helpful. Dr. Jones's view was that therapy should be a continuous process. To achieve this goal, he created an atmosphere where you could interact informally with medical and nursing staff. Dr. Jones wrote plays to help clients to tell their stories as part of an intensive therapy experience.

In a therapeutic community, people with addiction make a long-term commitment to contribute to the community while they work on their sobriety. Unlike a residential (inpatient) option, the therapeutic community is based on self-help versus getting treatment. The residential programs are usually expected to last one to three months (typically one month) while the therapeutic community membership lasts for many months (or years).

How therapeutic communities work

Therapeutic communities are drug-free residential settings that are sometimes referred to as *sober-living centers*. They're located in a wide variety of settings, including former camps and ranches and within residential communities. They have also been set up in jails, prisons, and shelters. The number of members admitted to a therapeutic community depends upon its residential capacity, but most accommodate 40 to 80 members.

The treatment model is hierarchical in that you progress through stages that reflect increased levels of personal and social responsibility. A fundamental principle of therapeutic communities is *mutual self-help:* You have a partial responsibility for the recovery of your peers, and this responsibility is considered to be an important aspect of your own treatment. Accordingly, a strong emphasis is placed on learning from each other, so members interact in structured and unstructured ways to influence attitudes, perceptions, and behaviors associated with drug use. Fellow members know the ins and outs of the abuse culture and are credible sources of change.

Activities in the therapeutic community are structured to help counter your characteristically disordered life on the outside. A focus of therapy is teaching life skills — including planning skills, goal setting, and accountability. Therapeutic communities focus on teaching *right living* (learning to be responsible for self and others and learning to behave to others as you want others to behave toward you) and *acting as if* (behaving as you aspire to be rather than as you have been).

The providers of treatment come from a variety of backgrounds and credentials. Many are licensed professionals such as physicians, social workers, nurses, and psychologists. Veterans of addiction treatment programs also form part of the treatment staff. Having struggled with addiction and recovery, they provide an experienced, informed, and compassionate model of recovery.

A focus on rehabilitation

Because of your addiction, you may have a poor history of social functioning, poor education or vocational skills, and few positive community and family ties. Recovery equates to rehabilitation — you must relearn or re-establish healthy functioning. You may never have had a functional lifestyle, and the therapeutic community may be your first exposure to orderly living. In this case, recovery may involve learning, for the first time, the behavioral skills, attitudes, values, and responsibilities that are associated with socialized living.

How effective are therapeutic communities?

The U.S. National Institute on Drug Abuse (NIDA) conducts studies to advance scientific knowledge on the outcomes of drug abuse treatment. These studies collected baseline data from over 65,000 individuals admitted to publicly funded treatment agencies. They included a sample of therapeutic community programs and other types of programs (methadone maintenance, outpatient drug-free, short-term inpatient, and detoxification programs). Data were collected at admission, during treatment, and in a series of follow-ups that focused on outcomes that occurred 12 months and longer after treatment.

Members of therapeutic communities reported several positive outcomes. Those members who successfully completed treatment exhibited lower levels of cocaine, heroin, and alcohol use; less criminal behavior; less unemployment; and fewer symptoms of depression than they had before treatment.

Who obtains treatment from a therapeutic community?

In considering whether a therapeutic community is a treatment option for you, it may be helpful to know that often members of therapeutic communities have other severe problems, such as multiple addictions, involvement with the criminal justice system, lack of social support, and mental health difficulties (depression, anxiety, post-traumatic stress disorder, and antisocial and other personality disorders). Therapeutic communities are open to you so long as you're willing to follow the specific rules of the community. The rules are there to help you develop self-control and responsibility and, ultimately, to overcome addiction. Personal privileges, disciplinary sanctions, security, and surveillance are enforced to protect you and to ensure that community life remains orderly and productive.

How long should you stay in treatment in a therapeutic community?

Therapeutic communities have no predetermined length of optimal treatment. The length of time best for you depends on your pace of change. The goal of stable, sober living is the key. If you stay to completion of treatment, you're most likely to achieve the best outcomes. However, even if you do drop out, you'll likely still receive some benefit from the experience. Research indicates that, on average, if you complete at least 90 days of treatment, you're likely to achieve significantly better outcomes over the next year than if you'd left earlier.

If you have other serious problems (multiple addictions, criminal involvement, mental health disorders, and poor employment history), being in treatment for at least 90 days or even longer is especially important for achieving a good outcome. Research suggests that you're likely to double your chances of a good treatment outcome (reduced substance abuse or abstinence) if you remain in a therapeutic community for 90 days or more compared to others being treated on an outpatient basis.

Unfortunately, many therapeutic communities have a high dropout rate. Although the dropout data isn't clear, it appears that about one third of dropouts seek readmission at a later date. Research is underway to determine whether certain characteristics of therapeutic communities can be changed to decrease the rates of members dropping out.

Some client characteristics influence your chances of sticking it out in a therapeutic community. For example, characteristics associated with dropping out of therapeutic communities prematurely include having family and friends who also abuse substances or are involved in crime. Factors associated with staying longer in treatment include being pressured by the courts or legal system to enroll in treatment, having your employer demand that re-employment be conditional on your seeking and sustaining addiction treatment, and your family providing inducements (sanctions or enticements) for you to stay in treatment.

Probably the most important characteristic about you that will determine whether you stay in treatment is motivation. Another important characteristic is your level of self-esteem. The more confident you are about yourself, the harder you tend to try to overcome your addiction problem. You can get treatment for strengthening self-esteem and for increasing motivation.

Traditionally, stays in therapeutic communities have varied from 18 to 24 months. Recently, however, funding restrictions have forced many therapeutic communities to significantly reduce stays to 12 months or less or to develop alternatives to the traditional residential model such as work-treatment arrangements.

Andrew's Choice: A True Story of Getting into Treatment and Achieving Success

Andrew was on the winning track. He was smart, good looking, and connected. In the financial markets, he was a whiz kid; he could make a deal happen. His employers trusted him. However, Andrew, at age 35, was living a lie. Secretly, he had increased his drug use to the point that every day was a mixture of uppers and downers. His judgments were clouded, and he made decisions on impulse. Andrew knew he was in desperate shape, and he decided to act. He called a friend for help and within a day he was on his way to rehab. The first section is Andrew's story of entering rehab.

The second section follows Andrew's description of one of his days in rehab. Andrew became a person committed to recovery and to helping others. Andrew has been in recovery for two years. As of today, he remains clean and sober.

How things began

It was 11 a.m. as my plane touched down. The hash I had swallowed the night before to calm my nerves was still going strong, but I knew they would be waiting just outside the gate. I grabbed my carry-on and got off the plane. The long tunnel to the terminal didn't appear to have any light at the end of it, but I continued down its path. I was going to make this change; it was time. I emerged through the entryway to see my name in big, black, bold letters held high above a man's head. I quickly looked the other way and decided that it would be easier to make a change after a few quick beers. I walked past the two men and proceeded to the airport bar. It was like any bar I had been to; rows upon rows of liquor neatly placed behind the bar in front of a mirror, with cigarette smoke gently caressing my nostrils and tempting me to light up. At that moment, I felt a tap on my shoulder. "Are you Andrew?" I was asked. By the stunned look on my face, they knew they had their man. Off to the facility I went.

The drive over wasn't too bad. The two guys that picked me up had both been there for ten weeks, and as part of the treatment process they were to show me the ropes just as someone had shown them. I waited into the busy lobby with my luggage for my intake assessment. A rather enthusiastic staff member called me to her office, as if I were a little kid going to camp for the first time, and proceeded to ask me about my drug and alcohol history. Some time later, after realizing I had had blackouts from my drinking, and acid trips do count as hallucinations, and smoking rock cocaine is the same as crack, I was to go for a blood test. No trick questions there, I thought. The needle didn't hurt; I actually got a rush from it. The nurse drew blood, looked at it, and chuckled. "I always get amused by the color of your blood when you guys check in," she said. What was wrong with the color of my blood I thought? "It's supposed to be red, not black," she said as if she was able to read my thoughts. I hope they all can't read minds here, I thought.

Next I was to meet my House group. These were the other men I would be living with. Sixteen of us. The ones who had been there for some time were obvious, but some had come just days before me. They showed me my room, which I shared with another guy. I can't sleep in a single bed, I thought, and I should have brought my own pillow. Two to a room, two rooms to a unit, four units to a house, I was told as if I was to be given a test tomorrow.

I unpacked and was called for dinner. We cooked our own. Food vouchers were given to each unit, and we were to shop for our own food, too. I had not shopped for food in months. After dinner, we had a house meeting, and everyone introduced himself. We had lawyers, businessmen, students, and the unemployed; all suffering from alcohol or drug abuse. I didn't say much. I was exhausted. I was asleep before my head hit the pillow. Where was my pick-me-up? I hadn't been to bed this early since preschool — a slight change already.

One day in rehab

My alarm goes off at 7:45 a.m. I'm still not used to getting up at this ungodly hour. They suggest I either pray or meditate in the morning, but I still fight this one. I'm going to do it my way for a while longer. I make my bed so I don't get any demerit points, and then I go to the kitchen to make breakfast. The guys who have been here for some time are already up. They've showered, had breakfast, and are reading or chatting outside. I obviously don't fit in yet. I have a banana, a shower, and brush my teeth before heading off to the campus, which is a funny thing to call a licensed mental institution. We are called "clients" not "patients," but we all meander over like students trudging off to class. Everyone gathers in a large circle for role call. Afterward, a client who will be leaving later this week reflects upon the changes she has made during her stay and then plays some music of her choice. It's usually pretty interesting to see what people choose. Next comes a presentation by someone who has been here and has been able to write down his story. How he started using, whom he hurt, how he has tried to stop in the past, the trouble he got in, effects on work, and so on. The more you hear, the more you start to realize you aren't as unique as you once thought. Some people share their feelings or make comments afterward, but if you're the presenter, a weight is lifted.

Usually, we quickly check the board to see if we have to do a random urine test today. Next, we break into groups of about ten with our primary therapist. Our primary therapist gives each of us feedback on our progress so far. At the beginning, it's usually "Try harder, stop fighting the system," or "You need to share more in this group." From here, we go off to group therapy. This is with a different therapist and a different group of people, made up of men and women. In here, we talk about the way we feel, what is bothering us, or anything else we want to talk about. We're told not to comment on anyone's sharing other than how it makes us feel or how we've had a similar feeling from some other experience. We're not to degrade, make fun of, or try to save any other client. Sometimes, it gets pretty uncomfortable, but a lot of good comes out of this group. After this, we go to lunch.

In the afternoon, we're required to go to an education class where we learn about the effects of drugs and alcohol on our brains. This class is usually pretty fun because we all think we're experts in the field. After that, we sometimes have a spiritual discussion, not from the Bible, but just about spirituality. Or sometimes we're assigned to a special group that deals strictly with a particular issue. Some people have had some pretty traumatic experiences from their using, and they find it easier to talk with only those who have had similar experiences. Some have other issues that need to be discussed, and some just need more time.

Some days, our house group gets together to talk about what's going on in our living area. These meetings can get pretty heated, especially if some guys don't get along. Other days, we're given free time and can do as we please. We have to travel in groups of three at all times, but we're able to go to a gym or for coffee as long as we're back for dinner. Afterward, we're usually required to attend a twelve-step meeting of our choice and then make it back to the Institution by curfew and a nighttime roll call for our house unit. We can stay up as late as we want, watch TV, or call our loved ones — as long as we keep it to one call a day for no longer than 15 minutes. If we do break one of the rules, we're supposed to tell our primary therapist about it. The place has lots of rules. What is even harder is that we're supposed to report on other clients for breaking rules. The idea is that you're helping them to stay the course. This takes some time to buy into. If you don't report on someone and it comes out you knew, you usually end up in more trouble than he does.

Before bed, you're supposed to reflect upon your day and see where you could improve. The longer you're there, the more serious you start taking stuff because what you start to notice is that those who do what is suggested do change. And isn't that why I came here in the first place?

Chapter 10

Treating Physical Dependence

- -

In This Chapter

▶ Finding out how your body reacts to drugs and endorphins

▶ Demystifying the detoxification process

▶ Explaining treatment

▶ Identifying medications that may help

▶ Considering the advantages of methadone treatment

- -

*W*e discuss different drugs in Chapter 2 and the process of physical dependence in Chapter 5. In this chapter, we face the challenges of *detoxification,* getting rid of the drug and restoring the normal bodily processes. We describe how the body reacts to different drugs and how your body rids itself of these chemicals.

This chapter is probably going to be of greatest interest if you're battling a drug or alcohol addiction. We discuss treatments for the acute drug and alcohol withdrawal effects associated with overcoming physical dependence.

It is extremely important that you understand the medical aspects of these processes. There can be considerable risks related to detoxification. In several critical areas, for example with sedative-hypnotics, the withdrawal process may be life threatening. Also, if you have a severe dependence on alcohol, you must be withdrawn gradually to avoid delirium tremens. Such a detoxification must occur under medical supervision.

Delirium tremens can occur upon abrupt alcohol withdrawal. The symptoms can be life threatening and require emergency medical treatment. Symptoms may include tremors, irritability, sleep disturbance, nausea, vomiting, hallucinations, confusion, delusions, severe agitation, and seizures. Other physical symptoms include increased heart rate, blood pressure, and temperature. Symptoms can be severe enough to lead to cardiovascular collapse (that is, cardiac arrest).

We should mention that behavioral addictions (such as gambling or sex) don't result in the same kinds of changes in your brain chemistry as those that cause physical dependence. They do cause psychological dependence, as we describe in Chapter 5. Although changes in brain chemistry (changes in the opiate and neurotransmitter systems of your brain) do occur with behavioral addictions, these changes aren't so severe as to cause a physical dependence requiring medically supervised detox.

Understanding Your Body's Reactions to Drugs

People take drugs to alter their brain chemistry to get a certain effect. Over time, the continued use of alcohol and other drugs induces adaptive changes in your brain cells, brain chemistry, and neural functioning. These changes result in drug tolerance and physical dependence.

For example, alcohol generally reduces anxiety and causes *sedation* (sleepiness). Over time, the brain adapts, requiring you to consume more alcohol to get the desired effect (this is *drug tolerance*). After prolonged use, specific brain cells adapt so that they don't function normally unless they have been given their daily dose of alcohol (this is *physical dependence*). If, for whatever reason, you don't consume alcohol, these very same brain cells rebel and produce symptoms such as anxiety, insomnia, hallucinations, and seizures (this is drug *withdrawal*). Large quantities of alcohol can produce sleep, coma, and even death by respiratory depression. At these quantities, clinicians not surprisingly refer to *alcohol poisoning*. In fact, your body tries to protect you against alcohol poisoning by inducing you to vomit if you have consumed too much alcohol.

The scientific term for the adaptation of cells and neural functioning following the continued exposure to drugs is *neuro-adaptation*.

The signs of withdrawing a drug from your body are typically the opposite of how the drug affects your body. For example, heroin use not only results in euphoria and reduced pain sensitivity, it also causes constipation. Heroin withdrawal, on the other hand, results in depression, increased pain sensitivity, and diarrhea. Alcohol causes sedation whereas acute alcohol withdrawal results in hyperarousal and possibly, seizures. Because these withdrawal effects can be life threatening, you need to be medically monitored during the detoxification period. Thus, detoxification typically takes place within the context of a specific detoxification program, a hospital, or residential treatment facility.

The time period between abruptly stopping the substance and experiencing withdrawal symptoms varies depending on the substance of use. For example, withdrawal symptoms from alcohol may be noticeable within hours of stopping drinking. Withdrawal symptoms from diazepam may take several days to occur and can peak five to ten days after withdrawal.

Detoxification: What Is It, and How Does It Work?

Detoxification (commonly known as *detox*) is the process you undergo if you're physically dependent on alcohol and/or other drugs and you want to rid your body of these substances. Some people are addicted to a combination of alcohol and/or other drugs (known as *polydrug abuse*). For them, the detoxification process typically involves more than one substance. This chapter is limited to the medically accepted guidelines for the detoxification from alcohol and other drugs of abuse, including prescription and nonmedical drugs.

 Detoxification isn't a treatment for addiction but rather a method to manage the symptoms of drug withdrawal. You should be wary of "treatment plans" (perhaps dictated by third parties) that only involve detoxification.

 Overcoming a drug or alcohol addiction takes more than simply clearing your body of the toxins that underlie the physical addiction. For a case study that backs this up, read the sidebar "Detoxification isn't enough." Addiction has many aspects, and some of the most powerful are also some of the more subtle aspects. Detox doesn't treat these other aspects of addiction. For example, you must figure out how to deal with the cues that trigger you to engage in the addictive behavior. You need to try one or more of the treatments discussed in the other chapters of Part III to get help. Thus, although detoxification is a fundamental component of treatment for a serious drug or alcohol addiction, it doesn't address the powerful psychological aspects of the addiction.

Coming to the realization that you have a substance addiction is a process. You can read more in Chapter 6 about the process of deciding on when you need to seek treatment. Your experience isn't unique if you find yourself going through detox treatment a few times before coming to understand that treating addiction takes more than detoxification. Still, detoxification is usually a fundamental component in a comprehensive treatment strategy.

Detoxification isn't enough

Mary was addicted to cocaine and prescription and nonprescription drugs. She used prescription medication like benzodiazepines to help her sleep and to calm her agitated nerves. She consumed large quantities of Tylenol daily to combat headaches.

She got started using cocaine through her boyfriend and friends. At first, she only used cocaine when she was at parties with her friends, but slowly she began using it in the evenings after work. At these times, she and her boyfriend would snort cocaine to get high. Gradually, she came to use cocaine after work even if alone. Because she started to have trouble sleeping, she went to her doctor to see whether she could get something to help her sleep. She didn't tell her doctor that she was using cocaine. Instead she blamed her sleeping problems on feeling anxious and irritable at work. Her doctor prescribed diazepam (otherwise known as Valium). She began using diazepam every night to help her sleep. At first it seemed to help, but in time she noticed that her sleep problems returned. A glass of wine at night seemed to help, so eventually she had a drink or two of wine every night to help her sleep. She also took the diazepam.

What Mary didn't know was that she had built up a physical tolerance to the diazepam and needed more to achieve the same result. Her poor sleep patterns and her chronic cocaine use were the primary causes of her headaches. Her overuse of Tylenol to treat her headaches followed the same course as the diazepam. Over time, she had to keep increasing how many Tylenol tablets she took daily to help her headaches.

A number of events lead Mary to realize that she was physically addicted to cocaine. She believed that all she had to do to overcome her cocaine addiction was to go through detox. She was confident that if she could rid her body of the physical addiction, she would not be tempted to use cocaine again. She went through a detox program for both her cocaine and diazepam addiction. Upon discharge from the detox program, she was sure she had licked the problem. However, within a few months, she was back using cocaine on a recreational basis. Soon it escalated to a daily use pattern. For a second time, Mary went into a detox program to withdraw from cocaine. She still believed that she could resist taking cocaine if she could just overcome the physical dependence. She now thought she was especially vulnerable to the physically addictive properties of cocaine, and as long as she got help with withdrawing from cocaine use and she never used cocaine again on a recreational basis, she would be okay. However, it wasn't long before Mary found herself addicted to cocaine for a third time.

The goals of detox

In the short term, detox has three immediate goals:

- ✔ **To provide a safe withdrawal from the drug(s) of dependence, allowing you to be drug-free.** Detox from a serious drug or alcohol addiction usually takes place under close medical supervision, often within a residential treatment facility. Detoxification from milder levels of addiction may be treated successfully on an outpatient basis, but you should seek medical supervision.

Not only can acute withdrawal symptoms be life threatening, but if you do try to go through detox on your own, you may resort to street drugs to help ease the pain of withdrawal. Some of these street drugs can interact with your addictive substance to cause serious physical problems and even death.

- ✔ **To provide a humane withdrawal that protects your dignity and confidentiality.** Detox programs are run by staff that are very familiar with and experienced in helping folks deal with withdrawal symptoms. Bouts of distress, irritability, and sickness are treated compassionately and competently.

- ✔ **To prepare you for the next phase of treatment.** Just as the staff will talk to you about treatment options after detox, some of the patients going through detox at the same time as you may be able to provide you with first-hand knowledge of follow-up treatment options.

Overcoming addictions is a process. You may relapse following your first few attempts at quitting, but every relapse episode provides you with important information about what you need to do differently the next time you go through detox. You can approach each subsequent detox program more realistically and more knowledgeably.

Each detoxification you undergo will encourage you to get a more complete and effective form of drug dependence treatment. In other words, knowing that you can get free of the substance will motivate you to get treatment for the other aspects of addiction that keep you psychologically "hooked."

The process: In the body

The detoxification process takes time, but the exact amount of time needed is often difficult to predict. Individuals react differently to chemical dependence, and some people have *polydrug* (multiple-drug) addictions. The medications used to treat withdrawal mask or suppress the withdrawal symptoms. Because these treatment medications can be prescribed for long periods of time (sometimes for years in order to reduce vulnerability to relapse), spotting exactly when the side effects of withdrawal have ceased can be difficult.

The process: In the mind

During detoxification, you may experience significant anxiety. And previous withdrawal attempts may dominate your thinking. Reassurance from an experienced clinician who can medically manage your withdrawal symptoms is strongly recommended.

One surprise in store for you following the detox procedures comes if you ever decide to return to using the drug. The brain adapts more quickly to drug use the second (or third or fourth) time, and this quicker adaptation means increased *tolerance* (need more drug for the same effect) and increased *dependence* (brain cells object if no drug is in the system). When you became physically dependent on a drug, your brain changed, and some of those changes remain in place even after detox. These leftover changes in your brain cells render you more vulnerable to becoming addicted faster upon a relapse to drug or alcohol use.

Each addictive substance has a typical set of symptoms experienced for specific periods of time. Table 10-1 provides good guidelines about what to expect.

Table 10-1   Lengths of Time for Withdrawal Symptoms to Cease Following Cessation of Substance Use

Substance	Time of Onset of Withdrawal Symptoms after Stopping Substance	Typical Length of Time for Withdrawal Symptoms to Cease
Alcohol	6–24 hours, peaking on the 2nd day	3–5 days
Short-acting benzodiazepines (such as lorazepam and alprazolam)	Within 24 hours, peaking within 1 day	Gradually subside over 2–4 weeks
Long-acting benzodiazepines (such as diazepam and clonazepam)	Can take 5 days to start, peaks around day 9	Gradually subside over 2–4 weeks

Substance	Time of Onset of Withdrawal Symptoms after Stopping Substance	Typical Length of Time for Withdrawal Symptoms to Cease
Following a 2–3 day binge on stimulants (cocaine, cocaine crack, amphetamines, methamphetamine, and crystal methamphetamine)	24–48 hours	24–48 hours
Following regular use of stimulants (cocaine, crack cocaine, amphetamines, and methamphetamine)	2–4 days	2–4 days
Opiates (such as heroin and morphine)	8–12 hours	5–7 days

Many different types of benzodiazepine medications are available. Some get absorbed into your system faster (fast-acting drugs) and some take longer to be absorbed (long-acting). You experience the drug effects sooner with fast-acting than with long-acting benzodiazepines. You also experience withdrawal symptoms faster with short-acting benzodiazepines than with the long-acting ones.

Different drugs affect different neurotransmitters in the brain producing the high or the calm. These chemicals in the brain cells are responsible for both the drug effect and the drug withdrawal effects.

Knowing What to Expect with Detoxification Treatments

In the following sections, we go over what you can expect when you go through a detox treatment for a specific substance like alcohol withdrawal or opiate withdrawal. In the following list, we cover some of the common principles or pointers that most detox treatment programs try to follow:

✔ Detoxification alone is rarely enough to treat a substance dependency. The goal of detox is to get you safely withdrawn from the substance; detox isn't meant to be a full addiction treatment. We strongly encourage an effective course of follow-up treatment to deal with the other aspects of your addiction.

✔ Get help with detoxification from a medically approved treatment facility.

   • Considerable research has been done on finding the best and most effective treatments for detoxification. A good facility always has the best and most innovative treatments according to the most recent research. The detox treatments used in these medically approved treatment programs are those that have been proven to be safe and effective.

   • You can receive promising, newly discovered treatments in medically approved detox treatment programs. Many of the medically approved treatment facilities will alert you to treatment options that although promising, have yet to be fully tested for safety and success. Depending on the facility, you may have the option to try one or more of these new treatments. See Chapter 13 to learn more about alternative treatments.

✔ Detox is usually very hard. Your body cries out for the drug you've been using, and you may be tempted to find relief from the withdrawal symptoms in unhealthy ways. For this reason, many detox programs try to ensure that you don't have access to any unauthorized medications or street drugs.

✔ Everyone is treated like an individual when it comes to withdrawal. The time frame and severity of withdrawal symptoms vary from one person to another.

✔ Detox programs use every means possible to decrease your withdrawal symptoms safely. Many programs provide both medications and supportive counseling to help you get through the acute withdrawal period as quickly and as comfortably as possible.

 Most importantly, remember that detox aims to get you off drugs and alcohol safely. Detox doesn't treat any of the other aspects of addictions. After detox, you need to get additional treatments for your addiction.

 Hallucinogens such as LSD, DMT (dimethyltryptamine), mescaline, and Ecstasy don't produce physical dependence and aren't associated with physical withdrawal symptoms.

Detox from alcohol and other sedatives/hypnotics

As we discuss in Chapter 2, sedatives are drugs that produce calming and sleep-inducing effects on the body. Alcohol and benzodiazepines, a type of prescription drug, are the two major drugs in this group. In this section, we go over the details of withdrawal from these two drugs.

Alcohol

In most cases, alcohol withdrawal can be performed on an outpatient basis. The exceptions are when you have a severe dependence on alcohol or a polydrug addiction.

You need the most support on the second day after your last drink of alcohol — when the withdrawal symptoms are usually at their worst. The amount of time it will take for your withdrawal symptoms to subside depends partly on your overall health and partly on the severity and duration of your addiction. If your health is poor, you will need to undergo a slower and longer detox treatment process.

The range of symptoms you can experience when you stop drinking varies, depending upon how severely dependent you are on alcohol. These symptoms can include: restlessness, irritability, anxiety, agitation, loss of appetite, nausea, and vomiting. You will experience increased arousal as evidenced by tremors, elevated heart rate, and increased blood pressure. This *hyperarousal* affects your sleep, so you'll have difficulty sleeping, and when you do sleep, you may experience intense dreaming and nightmares. Other symptoms include: difficulty concentrating, poor memory, impaired judgment, increased sensitivity to sounds, and changes in your skin sensations (the creepy-crawly feeling).

All of these symptoms can be very bothersome, but they're not life threatening. The more dangerous withdrawal symptoms that can occur following termination of a serious alcohol dependence problem are delirium, hallucinations, elevated body temperature, and seizures. The latter need to be monitored carefully by a physician. For this reason, detoxification from a serious alcohol dependence problem is often performed on an inpatient basis.

Benzodiazepines

Not surprisingly, the severity of withdrawal symptoms from stopping benzodiazepine medications (such as diazepam) depends on the dose of medication you've been taking, the length of time you've been taking the drug, and whether the drug is fast-acting or long-acting. Most medical prescriptions of these sedatives are at a low-dose level and are prescribed for the treatment of anxiety problems. Withdrawal symptoms are milder from low-dose prescription levels.

What is considered a low-dose level varies depending on which benzodiazepine is being prescribed. For example, 6 milligrams of alprazolam (Xanax) is equivalent to a 60-milligram dose of diazepam (Valium). The dosage also depends on your age and the purpose for the prescription (for example, treatment for anxiety disorder or a sleep problem).

Withdrawal symptoms from the benzodiazepines can be confused with a return of anxiety symptoms. You may have a difficult time telling the difference between true withdrawal symptoms and the symptoms of an anxiety disorder. So work to achieve a complete withdrawal before assessing whether further treatment is needed for your anxiety problems.

The range of withdrawal symptoms reported includes nausea, vomiting, irritability, tremor, coordination problems, insomnia, restlessness, blurred vision, sweating, loss of appetite, and anxiety. Withdrawal from benzodiazepines must be medically managed. You will be gradually withdrawn from (tapered off) your benzodiazepine. You may be prescribed another type of benzodiazepine to lessen the discomfort of the withdrawal symptoms and to prevent serious medical consequences. (For more on this, see the section "Medications for treating benzodiazepine withdrawal.") Any abrupt discontinuation of high-doses of benzodiazepine may produce severe withdrawal symptoms. These may include seizures, disorientation, psychosis, and depression.

Symptoms of withdrawal from short-acting benzodiazepine (lorazepam) are more severe than symptoms from long-acting benzodiazepine (diazepam).

Detox from stimulants such as cocaine and amphetamines

The most common symptoms following a two- to three-day cocaine or amphetamine binge are sadness *(dysphoria)* and irritability. The most common withdrawal symptoms following regular use of stimulants, like cocaine or methamphetamine, consist of dysphoria, irritability, difficulty sleeping, and intense dreaming.

If you also abuse alcohol, marijuana, or benzodiazepines, you're not alone. Typically, you turned to these others substances to reduce the irritability caused by chronic stimulant abuse. Detox in these cases is complicated, because you must be withdrawn from multiple substances.

Detox from opiates

All *opiates*, which include heroin, morphine, hydromorphone (Dilaudid), codeine, and methadone, produce similar withdrawal symptoms. However, they differ as to how quickly withdrawal begins after use has stopped and how long it lasts. In addition to the type of opiate used, the severity of the withdrawal symptoms depends on the total daily dose, the interval between doses, the duration of use, and your overall health.

The symptoms of withdrawal from opiates can be grouped according to what parts of the body they affect the most. There are four groups:

- ✔ Gastrointestinal distress, including diarrhea and, less frequently, nausea or vomiting

- ✔ Pain, typically either joint pain, muscle tenderness, or abdominal cramping

- ✔ Anxiety

- ✔ Sleep disturbance

Detox from marijuana

There are only minor withdrawal symptoms from marijuana use. You may experience some feelings of irritability and have difficulty sleeping for a few days when you discontinue chronic use of marijuana.

Detox from inhalants/solvents

Detoxification from chronic use of inhalants/solvents is very similar to alcohol detox. The withdrawal symptoms are similar as well. Please refer to the section on detox from alcohol if you want to find out more about what to expect with inhalants/solvents withdrawal.

Medications That May Help

Specific medications may help you detoxify from almost all of the serious drug dependence problems. And because this is an area of intense study, new treatments are approved frequently. In the remainder of this chapter, we go over the most effective medications used for drug and alcohol detox.

A great Web site for the latest information on drug abuse treatments is www.drugabuse.gov.

The goal of detox is to get you off the addictive substance in as safe and comfortable a manner as possible. All of these detox medications aim to do that. They're only prescribed for a brief time to get you over the withdrawal period.

Medications for alcohol problems

Depending upon the severity of your alcohol dependence, you may be able to be withdrawn from alcohol on an outpatient basis. The detox treatment team can advise you on your best treatment options.

If you have a choice, a residential detox treatment program is safer than an outpatient program. Although guidelines help the clinical team determine whether your dependence problem can be treated on an outpatient basis, we do know that when it comes right down to it, the severity of withdrawal symptoms in any particular person is hard to predict.

The most common medications prescribed for withdrawing from alcohol dependence are sedatives such as the benzodiazepines. Because these medications have a sedating effect on the body similar to alcohol, they're helpful in lessening some of the hyper-arousal withdrawal symptoms, such as seizures and tremors. The real advantage of benzodiazepines is that they're a different substance from alcohol, and they can be managed in a more controlled way because the dosages can be titrated.

Some of the commonly prescribed benzodiazepines are chlordiazepoxide (Librium), clonazepam (Klonopin), chlorazepate (Tranxene), and diazepam (Valium).

In some instances, you may be prescribed a medication that specifically controls seizures. One medication is Carbamazepine (Tegretol). Beta-blocker medications are also frequently prescribed. These medications help reduce or prevent a rapid heart rate, elevated blood pressure, sweating, and tremors. With severe alcohol dependence, you may experience hallucinations upon withdrawal. An antipsychotic medication called haloperidol (the trade name is Haldol) has been found to effectively treat hallucinations.

Medications for treating benzodiazepine withdrawal

Withdrawing from benzodiazepines typically involves a slow and gradual weaning off process. Even if you've been taking the benzodiazepine medication for only a month, you should taper off gradually. *Tapering off* means that you will be prescribed a progressively milder dose that helps your body adjust to having less and less drug. In many cases, you will be able to withdraw from these medications on an outpatient basis. The exception is with the last two administrations of the medication. Depending upon the severity of your withdrawal symptoms, your treatment team may advise that you be admitted to a hospital for the period of time you're withdrawing from the last two administrations of the drug. Even though the last administrations of the medication are usually quite low dosages, your body may have a bigger reaction than in previous reductions. As an inpatient, the severity of your withdrawal symptoms can be monitored more closely.

As mentioned earlier, the withdrawal symptoms from the short-acting benzodiazepines are more intense than those with the long-acting medications. Thus, although tapering off works well for the long-acting drugs, it may not work so well for the short-acting drugs. Often, your medical team will suggest switching you from a short-acting drug to a long-acting one and then gradually taper you off the long-acting one over a one- to two-week period.

Medications for treating opiate addiction

The approach to detoxification from an opiate addiction involves prescribing medications to help relieve the withdrawal symptoms, switching you from heroin to another type of opiate drug that is associated with fewer side effects, and then gradually tapering you off this alternative opiate. The medication most commonly prescribed to help lessen the intensity of most withdrawal symptoms is clonidine (Catapres). Unfortunately, this medication doesn't help relieve the symptoms of muscle aches or sleep disturbance. Nor does it lessen drug cravings. The latter symptoms of aches, sleep disruption, and cravings are helped by switching you to another opiate drug that is associated with fewer withdrawal symptoms.

The three alternative opiates that you may be switched to are methadone, LAAM, and buprenorphine. Because all three of these drugs are used to help relieve drug cravings and prevent relapse, we discuss them further in the section "Maintenance medications and craving reducers." In most cases, you will be gradually withdrawn from these alternative opiate medications. If you're at very high risk of relapse to a heroin addiction, you may be maintained on methadone for a long period or even for the rest of your life.

Medications for stimulant abuse

Withdrawal symptoms associated with stimulant withdrawal typically subside in two to four days (refer to Table 10-1). No specific medications for stimulant withdrawal exist. However, you may be prescribed a mild medication to help relieve sleep disturbance and distress.

Maintenance medications and craving reducers

Some medications help reduce the cravings for opiates and alcohol. They also help reduce the pleasurable effects so that if you slip and reuse these substances, they produce fewer of the desired effects. These medications are referred to as *maintenance drugs* because they can be used on a longer-term basis to reduce the harm of drug addiction by reducing cravings for or by blocking the high associated with the drug you previously abused. Because the effects of maintenance drugs are fairly benign or at least less risky than the illicit drug, they can be tolerated for extended periods of time. We go into further details on some of these drugs in the following sections.

Naltrexone

Naltrexone is a craving-reducer for both alcohol and opiates. It acts on the opiate system in your brain, blocking the sensations of pleasure that can be associated with alcohol and opiate intake. Research indicates that you're two times less likely to relapse and resume drinking alcohol when you're taking naltrexone. If you do slip and have a drink, Naltrexone also increases the likelihood that you'll recover from the relapse and resume abstinence. The drug is typically prescribed for a three-month period.

If naltrexone doubles one's chances of abstinence, why doesn't everyone use it? One reason is that it is associated with some negative side-effects. These include nausea and stomach cramps.

Plus, because naltrexone blocks the effects of opiates in the brain, it worsens opiate withdrawal symptoms. You should wait at least five to ten days after being drug-free from heroin before taking naltrexone, and even longer if you have just come off methadone, LAAM, or buprenorphine.

Although naltrexone does reduce cravings for alcohol, it fortunately doesn't interfere with the experience of other kinds of pleasure. Nor does it interfere with nonopioid pain medications such as acetaminophen, aspirin, and ibuprofen.

Like detox treatment, naltrexone isn't effective as a sole treatment for alcohol addiction. You need additional treatments for help with the other aspects of addiction.

Antabuse (disulfiram)

Antabuse produces a highly unpleasant sensitivity to alcohol. The unpleasant symptoms persist until the alcohol is completely excreted from your body. The unpleasant sensations are numerous and include flushing, headache, breathing difficulty, nausea, vomiting, sweating, thirst, chest pain, rapid heart rate, dizziness, blurred vision, and confusion. The symptoms can sometimes be life threatening. They can last up to an hour in the case of mild reactions and several hours for severe reactions.

Campral

Campral (or acamprosate calcium) is a new drug that was just approved by the Federal Drug Administration in August 2004 to help prevent relapse following alcohol withdrawal. This medication is so new at the time of writing this book that we don't yet know how much it will cost. Nor is very much known about how it works except that it is thought to modify the effects of one of the brain's chemicals, GABA. The result is that it reduces the pleasurable effects of drinking alcohol. Research indicates that people taking Campral as a maintenance medication for the treatment of alcoholism are about twice as likely to remain abstinent as people who aren't taking this medication following alcohol withdrawal.

One big advantage of Campral is that it doesn't have much of an effect on the liver, so it can be used in most people who have liver disease. The exception is with people who have very severe liver disease. Other contraindications for its use are pregnancy, kidney disease, or ongoing drug abuse.

LAAM (ORLAAM)

LAAM is an opiate, like methadone, that is used to help taper you off heroin. (For more information on methadone, see the section "Methadone Treatment.") LAAM is still under investigation as a maintenance drug, so take-home doses aren't allowed in North America at this time. Also, LAAM can't be given to pregnant women. LAAM is a longer-acting drug than methadone, so withdrawal from LAAM takes longer. But the advantage is that the withdrawal symptoms are less severe than those associated with methadone withdrawal.

Buprenorphine

Buprenorphine is another new drug that is being used as a maintenance drug to help users stay off heroin. Withdrawal from buprenorphine takes longer than from methadone, but the symptoms are less severe and more easily controlled. In 2002, the FDA approved it for use in the United States in two forms. It can be prescribed both alone (Subutex) and with naloxone (Suboxone). The combination drug with naloxone is intended to discourage abuse of buprenorphine. If you do attempt to abuse the combination pill by dissolving it and injecting it like heroin, naloxone will block the opiate effects and result in opiate withdrawal symptoms. When combined with buprenorphine in a pill form, on the other hand, naloxone doesn't affect the absorption of buprenorphine. See how tricky the scientists and clinicians are getting? They have to be, because of the tremendous compulsion users feel to use a drug, a compulsion that may be overwhelming if there isn't some type of deterrent.

Methadone Treatment

Methadone is a drug commonly used to help users withdraw from heroin. During the initial detox phase, you will be treated with methadone on an inpatient basis. Furthermore, after you're through the detox phase, you may be kept on a maintenance dose of methadone as an outpatient. In either mode of treatment, you may have to undergo mandatory drug testing to verify that you haven't relapsed to heroin use.

You may also have to qualify for methadone treatment by having your physician verify that your physical dependence warrants it. Only the most severely drug dependent patients are maintained on methadone indefinitely. Others are eventually weaned off when it can be done successfully.

What is methadone?

Methadone is a long-acting narcotic (that is, an opiate) that because of its actions on the opioid receptors in your brain, acts as a stabilizing agent. When taking methadone, your physical dependence is managed, allowing you to deal with your drug-seeking behaviors (which typically include illegal acts to get the drug or the money to pay for it). Methadone does produce a high, but because the effects are less intense than with heroin, users are less likely to abuse it. Nevertheless, because methadone *is* physically addictive, its use is highly regulated. Patients are only given a limited number of days of prescription, and they must undergo random blood testing to verify that they haven't relapsed to heroin use. (The effects of narcotics on the brain are discussed more in Chapter 5.)

Methadone myths

We'd like to dispel a few misconceptions about methadone that you may have heard. We've included a list of various false notions about methadone:

✔ It is easier to overcome the psychological effects of a heroin addiction when taking methadone.

FALSE. Although methadone does reduce the physical cravings for heroin, it does *not* help reduce the mental cravings. You still need to work at countering the mental desire to take heroin.

✔ Methadone is worse for your body than heroin.

FALSE. Methadone is safer than street drugs, because it is medically regulated and manufactured. Like street drugs, methadone can cause serious health consequences if taken in overdose. However, because methadone is medically regulated, you're less likely to overdose on it. Furthermore, because it isn't associated with the euphoric rush of heroin, you're unlikely to desire more than the prescribed dose.

✔ Methadone harms your liver.

FALSE. Although methadone is cleared from your body by the liver, it doesn't harm the liver. Even if you have liver damage, you can take methadone.

✔ Methadone is harmful to the immune system.

FALSE. It is not harmful to the immune system.

✔ Methadone causes people to use cocaine.

FALSE. You may well have progressed from cocaine use to heroin use, but no evidence indicates that methadone increases your chances of taking cocaine.

✔ The lower the dose of methadone, the better.

FALSE. The best dose of methadone for you is the one that controls your drug craving. You will likely need 60 to 120 milligrams of methadone to control your craving for heroin.

Who should choose methadone treatment?

If your detox efforts in withdrawing from heroin or morphine have been unsuccessful, then you should try methadone treatment.

Except in rare cases, methadone treatment in the United States has not been approved for treating heroin addictions in adolescents.

Does it work?

Methadone is the only opiate treatment that has been proven safe and effective for opiate withdrawal and dependence. It is taken once daily and it successfully suppresses opiate cravings for 24 to 36 hours. It not only reduces the cravings associated with heroin use, it also blocks the euphoric high from heroin. Because methadone isn't associated with the extreme highs and lows of heroin or morphine use, you won't experience the uncontrolled cravings for methadone that you do for these other powerful narcotics.

Chapter 11

Twelve-Step Programs

As our modern society truly becomes more modern, we increasingly accept human fallibility. It is quite clear, wherever we look, that humans are far from perfect. As a result, we have to deal with failure — and need support and understanding when we do.

Twelve-step programs are superb examples of caring and understanding in the face of failure and stigma. These programs respond to the ultimate plea for understanding, "If only you knew what it's like. If only you could understand what I'm going through." Twelve-step programs help because participants can genuinely say, "We've been there, we understand." One of the responses to the plea for understanding is for members in the program to share their stories — including the good, the bad, and the ugly parts.

Types of Twelve-Step Programs

The purpose of twelve-step fellowship is to teach and support skills related to recovery. In the beginning of your recovery program, the structure and availability of twelve-step meetings can be critical. These meetings provide a refuge and help you overcome your resistance to asking for help. They can also assist you as you learn to manage the triggers of your addictive behavior and the other compulsive reactions that may plague your lifestyle.

Compulsive behavior refers to wasteful or self-destructive actions that are repeated because they temporarily reduce anxiety. Addictive behaviors fit this definition. The empty promises to quit made by addicted people are empty because addicts are in the grip of emotions they can't control or resolve. Often, these emotions are closely related to anxieties. To escape the grip of unrelenting distress, they flip to the other side of the spectrum, adopting a risky, what-the-hell attitude. Finding better and better understandings of what triggers your own compulsive-addictive behaviors can be very important in recovery.

Bill Wilson (Bill) began Alcoholics Anonymous in 1935 and established the AA tradition. Wilson and others codified their approach in the *Big Book,* the book that guides addicts through the process of recovery. The main criterion when attending a meeting is that members admit they have a problem. ("Hi, I'm Jane and I'm an alcoholic.")

Although AA was created for alcoholics, the treatment approach has been so successful that many other types of twelve-step programs have been developed — programs that address nearly every type of addiction. The focus may differ because the guidance provided depends on the types of issues the addicted person faces. In many cases, the person has a *polydrug problem* (using several different types of drugs, including alcohol). In addition, people may have other addictive behaviors (sex, gambling, money, overeating, work).

Over 2 million people worldwide participate in AA.

You can find more than 50,000 twelve-step groups in the United States and over 100,000 worldwide. The following is a partial listing of twelve-step programs that are available in most cities:

- ✔ Al-Anon (support for families with an addicted member)
- ✔ Alateen (support for teens with addicted family members)
- ✔ Alcoholics Anonymous (AA)
- ✔ Debtors Anonymous (DA)
- ✔ Gamblers Anonymous (GA)
- ✔ Marijuana Anonymous (MA)
- ✔ Narcotics Anonymous (NA)
- ✔ Overeaters Anonymous (OA)
- ✔ Sex and Love Addicts Anonymous (SLAA)

In some communities, you may have to crossover and attend a meeting that doesn't quite address your specific addiction. Nevertheless, the principles are consistent: regular meetings, participation if you're comfortable, and fellowship.

The Actual Twelve Steps

The hardest part of joining AA is walking through the door at your first meeting. So you should know that you will be welcomed. Most people agree that the experience is a good one, and for some, AA is exactly what they're looking for. After you've been attending meetings on a regular basis, you may want to ask another experienced member to sponsor you. Find someone at the meetings whom you respect, and ask that person how he has achieved his recovery. See whether you feel comfortable with and can trust this person. If the person passes your personal tests, ask her to sponsor you. Your sponsor will get you started with respect and caring and guide you through the process known as *the steps*. Working through the steps in AA is the cornerstone of recovery. The preamble that follows is how AA describes its membership.

AA Preamble

Alcoholics Anonymous is a fellowship of men and women who share their experience, strength, and hope with each other that they may solve their common problem and help others to recover from alcoholism.

The only requirement for membership is a desire to stop drinking. There are no dues or fees for AA membership; we are self-supporting through our own contributions. AA is not allied with any sect, denomination, politics, organization, or institution; does not wish to engage in any controversy, neither endorses nor opposes any causes. Our primary purpose is to stay sober and help other alcoholics to achieve sobriety.

What follows are the Twelve Steps of Alcoholics Anonymous. The steps are taken in order, but folks often a need to revisit a step and reinstate some of the commitments and understandings.

1. We admitted we were powerless over alcohol — that our lives had become unmanageable.

2. Came to believe that a Power greater than ourselves could restore us to sanity.

3. Made a decision to turn our will and our lives over to the care of God as we understood Him.

4. Made a searching and fearless moral inventory of ourselves.

5. Admitted to God, to ourselves, and to another human being the exact nature of our wrongs.

6. Were entirely ready to have God remove all these defects of character.

7. Humbly asked Him to remove our shortcomings.

8. Made a list of persons we had harmed, and became willing to make amends to them all.

9. Made direct amends to such people wherever possible, except when to do so would injure them or others.

10. Continued to take personal inventory and when we were wrong promptly admitted it.

11. Sought through prayer and meditation to improve our conscious contact with God as we understood Him, praying only for knowledge of His will for us and the power to carry that out.

12. Having had a spiritual awakening as the result of these steps, we tried to carry this message to alcoholics and to practice these principles in all our affairs.

The Twelve Steps are reprinted with permission of Alcoholics Anonymous World Services, Inc. (A.A.W.S.). Permission to reprint the Twelve Steps does not mean that A.A.W.S. has reviewed or approved the contents of this publication, or that A.A.W.S. necessarily agrees with the views expressed herein. AA is a program of recovery from alcoholism only. Use of the Twelve Steps in connection with programs and activities which are patterned after AA, but which address other problems, or in any other AA context, does not imply otherwise.

Working Your Program

In twelve-step programs, you hear the phrase "working your program" a great deal. Working your program means:

✔ Accepting guidance and practicing the steps of recovery.

✔ Replacing the behaviors and thinking of addiction with the behaviors and thinking of recovery.

✔ Actively participating in the fellowship.

What do we mean by recovery? *Recovery* is a process of transformation. Your whole life has been yanked out of balance by chemicals and actions that have undermined positive balances, values, and achievements. *Recovery* refers to recovering the simple but healthy balances that made you feel good when you ate, exercised, made love, and engaged in good, honest, wholesome friendships. Somewhere along the line, either by relying on the quick fix of a chemically induced buzz or by being overwhelmed by a sudden set of very painful experiences, you began the habit of seeking artificial solutions to life's challenges. Recovery means rediscovering your own natural resources to meet those challenges. In doing so, you feel natural satisfactions and develop a natural sense of confidence in yourself.

Hitting bottom and working toward recovery — one day at a time

You aren't alone if you remember your first drink, hit, or bet with excitement and nostalgia. You may recall the temporarily positive impact of the behavior, whether you felt anxiety reduction, the thrill of the chase, or an escape into pleasure and euphoria. This memory trace can be so powerful that it can counteract the real life experience of spiraling downward. You can get used to the downward slide, even numb to it, until you hit bottom. Then you realize that you have no more room to slide. Things can't get any worse. But hitting bottom can also be the beginning of the big turn-around. The bottom can be the start of recovery — where it hurts most is where your healing can begin.

Whether you've hit bottom or not, taking one day at a time is extremely important. Psychologically, this mindset exerts considerable power. You don't want to look back and relive past mistakes, and you don't have to look into the future either. The focus is on living *today* in an addiction-free state.

Keep track of your days in recovery. People who are recovering tend to keep track of their days of sobriety or behavioral control. They celebrate "birthdays" that symbolize their achievements in recovery. They don't take even one day for granted. Live *one day at a time*.

A friend was coming up to a three-year birthday and when asked how long he had been sober he said it had been 1,092 days — not three years. That's what we mean by one day at a time. Don't get ahead of yourself. The process of recovery is too hard.

Discovering spirituality

Spirituality can be important in recovery because addiction can become so powerful, it competes with the spiritual power people feel during religious and meditative ritual. In other words, after you're addicted, more and more of life is consumed with looking forward to each addictive fix. Your substance or behavioral addiction takes the same place that religious or spiritual commitment may have once occupied in your life. Rediscovering spirituality can help you reorder your life and reconnect with your own spiritual power, helping you to put your addiction in perspective. A spiritual view reminds you that you are *more* than your addiction.

What if you don't feel so spiritually oriented? It's a good question because you can't fake spirit. If you don't feel spiritually oriented or motivated, don't pretend that you do.

But sometimes the difference is one of form rather than degree. Spirituality is a highly personal matter. The form of spirituality right for you may be very different from what's right for someone else. Many people have some idea of a transcendent core that continues after the body dies. Many people also believe in some order to life that can be comprehended and used to guide one's actions. Such beliefs, however, don't necessarily coalesce into a particular religious or spiritual view.

If you feel spiritual in this way, you don't need to force your feelings into a given structure. Instead, follow your own feelings about how your spirit is strengthened. If some of your feelings are confirmed by your participation in twelve-step programs, great. If some aren't addressed in twelve-step programs, that's fine too. Take what works for you and leave the rest alone.

Using affirmations

The value of slogans or affirmations to the recovering process depends very much on you as an individual. Depending upon what is meaningful to you, keeping a special thought in mind can be motivating. *Affirmations* are basically reminders of the positive sides of the processes of growth and transformation. As much as you may believe that you don't need such reminders, they can actually make a difference as to what thoughts, emotions, and actions are emphasized in your life.

Turning Leaf Press provides a slogan per day on the Web at http://turningleafpress.com. The slogan we found when we looked was "You are the answer to someone's prayers."

Deciding Whether a Twelve-Step Program Is Right for You

Only you can decide whether the traditions and steps will really be helpful for you. The basic approach of AA and other twelve-step programs is to identify a problem and then assess your willingness to make a call, go to a meeting, and stay with the program.

Twelve-step programs work best if you're willing to admit to your addiction and you honestly want to stop. If you have reservations about wanting to stop ("I hope that one day I'll be able to drink again"), then quitting is harder, and the approach is less of a match. The core of the twelve-step approach is the admission that the addicted behavior must stop with no compromises: a *complete* stop.

Most people with addiction disorders want to experiment with a return to addictive behavior. Your desire to return to a normal state is typical of other chronic illnesses. The diabetic may experiment with sugar levels and the asthmatic with exposure to allergens. The usual response to experimenting with addictions, however, is that the addictive behavior gets re-established. Simply put, experimentation leads to relapse.

The following questions were developed by AA and are used to help you decide whether AA is for you. These questions are similar to our assessments in Chapter 5.

Answer yes or no to the following questions:

- Have you ever decided to stop drinking for a week or so, but only lasted for a couple of days?

- Do you wish people would mind their own business about your drinking — stop telling you what to do?

- Have you ever switched from one kind of drink to another in the hope that this would keep you from getting drunk?

- Have you had to have an eye-opener upon awakening during the past year?

- Do you envy people who can drink without getting into trouble?

- Have you had problems connected with drinking during the past year?

- Has your drinking caused trouble at home?

✔ Do you ever try to get "extra" drinks at a party because you do not get enough?

✔ Do you tell yourself you can stop drinking any time you want to, even though you keep getting drunk when you don't mean to?

✔ Have you missed days of work or school because of drinking?

✔ Do you have "blackouts"?

✔ Have you ever felt that your life would be better if you did not drink?

The preceding twelve questions have been excerpted from material appearing in the pamphlet, Is A.A. For You?, and have been reprinted with permission of Alcoholics Anonymous World Services, Inc. ("A.A.W.S"). Permission to reprint this material does not mean that A.A.W.S. has reviewed and/or endorses this publication. AA is a program of recovery from alcoholism only. Use of AA material in any non-AA context does not imply otherwise.

Problems with Twelve-Step Programs

As the twelve-step programs have become more and more common, a number of participants have voiced their dissatisfactions with twelve-step programming. Some of these participants, both men and women, have found it constricting to "accept that one is powerless" against the addiction and therefore submit to the guidance of a "higher power." To some people, the twelve-step program principles conflict with an acceptance of an individual's personal inner strength and resources and power to affect change. In this section, we go over some of the criticisms that have been leveled at twelve-step approaches. In Chapter 12, we describe a number of groups that provide approaches that are effective alternatives to the twelve-step program.

What the critics say

Critics point out that twelve-step programs don't help everyone, although they're sometimes presented as if they can. The percentage of successful recoveries, when compared to the total number of program participants, is relatively modest — this is the reality that often leads to modifications of programs. AA's own surveys show that of the people who attend a meeting, nine out of ten drop out within the first year. Similar research hasn't yet been done on

Narcotics Anonymous (NA) and other twelve-step programs, but we suspect that dropout rates are similar.

With a 90 percent dropout rate, it's clear that twelve-step programs are far from perfect. However, the prevailing attitude is that people who fail the program are the problem, not the program itself. Members who resist or criticize twelve-step programs are told, "Utilize, don't analyze." Thus, the very process by which people everywhere evolve and mature — by thinking critically, exploring new ideas, and implementing change — can be treated as a heretical process if directed toward twelve-step programming. This resistance to innovative thinking about the model can lead to blind adherence and an absence of scientific inquiry about it.

Any comments on the program are labeled as "the addiction talking" rather than being viewed as honest attempts to understand and perhaps modify existing programming. If you're the kind of person who tends to creatively dissent and challenge, twelve-step programs are probably not going to work for you because they offer little tolerance for incisive, creative questioning.

Is a twelve-step program enough?

The other relevant question is whether twelve-step programs are sufficiently powerful to help you reach a full recovery. The best answer to this question relates to how powerful the approach seems to you. If you don't experience yourself as being especially enthusiastic about or confident in twelve-step programming, then the approach isn't likely to have the power for you that it has for someone who is more committed and enthusiastic.

Keep in mind that the approach is supposed to have the power to help you make positive transformations of your own thoughts, emotions, and behaviors. The strength of your belief in this transformational power is an important factor in actually helping you to make these transformations.

If you don't feel the power of twelve step, it may just not be there for you. If that's your experience, don't waste time feeling rejected or angry. Go where you find the power of healing.

Chapter 12

Joining Self-Help and Support Groups

*O*ne of the most common self-help approaches is the twelve-step program. Because of its widespread popularity, we have devoted a whole chapter (see Chapter 11) to it. But some people don't find this approach helpful. Some are opposed to the spiritual part of the twelve-step approach or to the view that you're powerless at fighting an addiction on your own. Others don't like the expectation of a lifelong commitment to AA.

A number of other self-help approaches have emerged as alternatives to the twelve-step program. In this chapter, we review some of them. Although some of these alternatives may not be directly available in your community, a surprising number offer support via the Internet or telephone.

Self-help approaches typically involve *moderators* who have personally recovered from addictions. They also actively involve you in peer support and counseling. Your peers in the group can be powerful role models for you. You may find it reassuring and encouraging to speak with a counselor who has experienced the highs and lows of the recovery process and has developed the means to successfully overcome his own addiction.

You too serve as a role model for others. This kind of group responsibility and support may be your first step out of the self-absorption of an addiction into a more giving, caring relationship with others.

In the early stages of quitting an addiction problem, you will probably need more than self-help approaches. Research has shown that your chances of quitting and staying clean are greater when you use a combination of treatment approaches. Self-help approaches can be one helpful tool in this combination. You can read more about combining treatment approaches in Part III of this book.

Secular Organizations for Sobriety and Save Our Selves (SOS)

SOS was founded in 1978 by Jim Christropher as an alternative to the AA approach. Although SOS was initially an approach for overcoming alcohol addiction, it now aims to help people overcome all types of addictions, including both substance and behavioral. Like AA, SOS advocates lifelong abstinence from your addictive substance. However, SOS maintains that you can find that power to resist using and abusing within yourself.

The SOS approach

SOS is an independent, worldwide organization. According to SOS, each person must find his or her own recipe for recovery. SOS doesn't provide a standard approach that participants must fit into. Rather, they encourage you to try several methods so you can find the approaches that work best for you. In keeping with their openness to different methods for different people, SOS has no problem with you simultaneously utilizing other treatment approaches such as AA. And SOS also provides guidance for family and friends.

Although the SOS approach isn't structured, it offers a toolkit of strategies on its Web site to help you achieve abstinence. SOS lists over 40 tools on its Web site at www.secularsobriety.org.

Here are some examples of the SOS tools:

✔ **Abstinence:** No matter what, there is no valid reason to drink again.

✔ **Determination:** Never turn back, especially if things get rough. You've gotten another chance at life. How many really have that chance? Sobriety doesn't fix everything, but it makes everything possible.

✔ **Honesty:** Get things into the open. Get rid of the shadows and darkness of the past. Shine some light on the dark things, and they lose their power. Even problems can be dealt with reasonably when they're truthfully reviewed.

✔ **People:** Human contact is powerful. If you meet people who are in recovery, your interactions with them can fight the old patterns of isolation.

SOS is most likely to appeal to you if:

✔ You feel that you have the power within yourself to overcome your addiction.

✔ You wish to maximize flexibility in your treatment approach.

✔ Abstinence is your priority.

✔ You feel you could benefit from group support.

Joining an SOS group

You can visit the SOS Web site (www.secularsobriety.org) to find out about meetings in your community. You can also register if you're interested in helping establish a meeting group in your community. The Clearing House helps link people from the same communities so they can establish their own local meeting group. It also provides a 24-hour online meeting, allowing you to access the support of SOS wherever you can make an Internet connection.

Rational Recovery

Rational Recovery (RR) is another self-help approach that emerged as an alternative to the twelve-step programming. It was founded by Jack Trimpey. In his book, *Rational Recovery: The New Cure for Substance Addiction,* Trimpey explains that he founded this alternative to AA because he didn't accept its insistence on submitting to a Higher Power for the strength to abstain from alcohol. Jack Trimpey went to AA for help with his alcohol addiction but found it undermined his ability to abstain. After many years of struggling with his addiction, he came to a point where he decided that he'd had enough. After he made a personal decision to quit drinking for good, he found that quitting was much easier than he thought.

The Rational Recovery approach

The RR approach emphasizes abstinence through self-reliance and common sense. To underscore how RR differs from twelve-step programs, Jack Trimpey published *The Small Book* in 1992. The book summarizes the self-help strategies advocated by RR. Its active core technique is called Active Voice Recovery Technique (AVRT), which is a thinking skill that empowers you to follow through on your decision to quit being addicted. It optimistically describes how human beings *naturally* recover from substance abuse. Trimpey makes the point that AVRT is what people have been doing for eons to end addictions. The fundamental belief of RR is that after you've made the decision to *really* quit, you *will* quit.

RR may appeal to you if you want an approach that relies heavily on your own capacity and motivation. Like SOS, RR embraces the notion that many different pathways lead to change. You're encouraged to find pathways that work best for you. Although RR advocates abstinence, total abstinence isn't mandated as the ideal goal for everyone.

Joining Rational Recovery

In the book, *Rational Recovery,* Jack Trimpey describes tools and strategies for self-directed change. For example, a number of strategies based on current theories of cognitive-behavioral change are described to help you resist your cravings to use. RR proponents believe that support groups can foster an unhealthy dependency that may undermine your sense of self-mastery. Thus, they no longer hold meetings for support. Rather, they encourage you to learn AVRT by reading *Rational Recovery* or by taking a course on its Web site (www.rational.org).

Self-Management and Recovery Training: SMART

The welcoming slogan on the SMART Web site is "Get free for free with evidence-based SMART recovery." SMART developed out of a split between some members of RR and its founder, Jack Trimpey. The SMART approach is based more directly on the theories of cognitive-behavioral change that are best supported by scientific evidence. Like SOS and RR, SMART advocates self-management strategies that rely on your inner abilities and motivations. Thus, you need not believe a Higher Power is necessary to help you overcome an addiction.

The SMART approach

SMART offers free face-to-face and online self-help groups. The group believes in the power of social support and the importance of relapse prevention. Thus, it encourages members to attend group meetings. But the group doesn't insist on a particular set of tools or strategies. Rather, SMART changes its approach over time, based on the outcomes of research studies. They adopt the strategies that have the best track record in research. Their tools and strategies target four key areas of cognitive-behavioral change:

- ✔ Enhancing and maintaining the motivation to abstain

- ✔ Coping with urges to use

- ✔ Problem solving (managing thoughts, feelings, and behaviors and finding practical solutions)

- ✔ Lifestyle balance (balancing momentary and enduring satisfactions)

 SMART's recovery tools and strategies are based on psychological principles that can be readily combined with other approaches, including pharmacologic approaches that feature the use of various anti-addictive drugs (see Chapter 10).

 SMART provides members with the support, tools, and strategies to come to decisions about change. It also helps pinpoint the best strategies for effectively changing. SMART recognizes the many needs that underlie addiction problems, and helps you develop strategies for eliminating or managing these needs in healthier ways.

Joining SMART

You can directly access information on SMART from the Web site (www.smartrecovery.org), which states that the group sponsors more than 300 face-to-face meeting groups around the world. SMART also runs 13 online meetings a week, which you can join if you have access to the Internet.

If you're interested in approaches like SMART that focus on the underlying factors in addictions, you can learn more about the psychological approaches to treating addictions in Chapter 8.

 Typically, addictions evolve because the addictive substance or behavior is helping you feel more relaxed, less lonely, and more content — temporarily. Giving up the addiction means finding new ways to enhance your well-being, improve self-confidence, and overcome feelings of isolation or loneliness. Psychotherapy approaches address these underlying issues.

Women for Sobriety (WFS)

Women for Sobriety (WFS) was founded in 1975 by Jean Kirkpatrick, a recovering alcoholic. She founded WFS as a female alternative to AA because she felt that female alcoholics already spent too much time hating themselves. She felt that what women needed was a supportive group that would help them feel better about themselves and take their special needs into account.

The WFS approach

The WFS program is described in Kirkpatrick's book, *Turning About: New Help for the Woman Alcoholic.* The group advocates abstinence. Women with all types of addictions are welcome. The focus is on building self-esteem and empowering women to make life choices that sustain their sobriety. Its motto is: "We are capable and competent, caring and compassionate, always willing to help another, bonded together in overcoming our addictions."

Anita's experience with AA

Anita is a mother of three children. Her husband has a successful law practice in a medium-sized town. Anita is an energetic person herself. She's very sociable, involved in all of her children's recreational activities. Her friends would describe her as the life of the party. However, inside she feels worthless. Her mother was an alcoholic, and as a child, Anita adopted the role of caretaking her younger siblings and father. As an adult, she wanted desperately to have what she believed was a normal family. She had always imagined herself cooking wonderful meals for her family, being an ideal mother, keeping an immaculate house, having a loving and intimate relationship with her husband, having no problems of her own, and always being there to support her husband and children. She expected her husband would be home most nights for dinner. She also expected that he, too, would participate in their children's recreational activities, and would appreciate and love her deeply.

She felt it was her fault when her family life didn't turn out the way she'd imagined. Instead of having a normal family life, she started experiencing her husband as being distant, working long hours, and having no time for their children's recreational and social activities. He seemed to take her caretaking activities for granted.

Her drinking started as a way to numb her feelings of disappointment and worthlessness. It wasn't long before her drinking got in the way of her mothering activities. She was frequently late to pick her children up from school, and sometimes didn't even get there. She would frequently lose sight of appointment times. Meal preparations deteriorated so badly that their oldest son, who was just 10 years old, started to caretake his younger brother and sister. Her old childhood and family pattern was repeating itself. When the school principal confronted her husband about his wife's neglect of their children, and when her husband threatened to leave her and take full custody of their children, Anita finally went to her first AA meeting.

Although AA helped her get sober, it did little to help her sense of worthlessness. In fact, AA's focus on humility and recognizing one's flaws only reinforced Anita's feelings of worthlessness. After each AA meeting, she felt squashed down rather than encouraged and bucked up. She learned about Women for Sobriety through another woman in her AA group.

Discovering WFS was a transformational experience for Anita. Here were women like herself who were also struggling with empowering themselves to assert individual rights and regain self-esteem. Women at WFS were learning to no longer subjugate their needs to their family demands. Through WFS, Anita learned to balance her need to take care of herself with taking care of her family. She also learned that both men and women are affected by sex role stereotyping and that her husband's lack of involvement in their family life was not because he didn't love his family. Rather, he believed that the most loving thing he could do for his family was to be a good provider. As Anita learned to validate her own needs she was better able to communicate with her husband. As a result she and her husband have been able to work together in finding ways for Anita to take time to look after herself. Her husband has found more time to share in family activities.

If you're female and looking for a support group that specifically addresses the common needs of women with addictions, WFS may be for you. It encourages the use of meditation, diet, exercise, and positive-thinking strategies. It will probably be especially attractive and helpful to women interested in a holistic approach to addiction treatment.

Joining WFS

You can obtain information on WFS groups in your community and on other services of WFS by visiting its Web site (www.womenfor sobriety.org). It offers online chat rooms, newsletters, literature, tapes, videos, conferences, and information on community and group meetings.

Religious Organizations

A number of religious organizations within the community offer support groups for individuals and families. If you're religious, you may want to ask at your own place of worship about an affiliated support group for addiction problems. Also, Christian Recovery

International (www.christianrecovery.com), the National Association for Christian Recovery (www.nacronline.com), and the Jewish Alcoholics, Chemically Dependent People, and Significant Others (www.jacsweb.org) offer information on numerous religious support groups for addiction problems.

Chapter 13

Alternative Treatments

· ·

· ·

*I*n the last decade, increasing numbers of people have been seeking out alternative treatments in North America and in Europe. Currently, more people consult alternative treatment professionals than consult licensed physicians, a statistic reflecting this shift in direction and attitude.

Despite the trend, there has been reluctance to invest the funds needed to precisely assess alternative treatments. As a result, we're in a transition. Some suggestive evidence, case studies, and anecdotes about alternative treatments are available. But the scientific method hasn't yet been applied with sufficient precision. In most cases, we know less about the evaluation of alternative treatments than we know about the evaluation of standard medical treatments.

The important consideration in any experimentation with alternative therapies is to ensure your safety by concurrently maintaining conventional treatments and frequent contacts with trusted licensed physicians. You don't want to ignore the wisdom of several centuries of medical science. Go for the best combination of treatments you can find — but be sure some of that combination includes the best that Western medical science has to offer.

Although we don't cover all the alternative treatments that are used in addiction treatment, our goal is to describe some of the more important ones and to provide a framework for deciding what to try and how to try it out. The thorough scientific evaluation of these treatments is still in evolution, despite the fact that people have voted with their feet and beat a path to alternative health professionals. So although you need to evaluate the scientific data that exists, you should evaluate it critically and be willing to trust your own experience of what works for you.

Acupuncture in the Treatment of Drug Abuse and Addiction

What is acupuncture? And why would anyone believe it might help with addiction? The practice of medical acupuncture involves inserting needles in the body in various combinations and patterns. According to the theory of acupuncture, the choice of needle patterns stimulates the flow of qi (pronounced chee), a subtle type of invigorating energy. Different disorders are caused by obstructions in the flows of energy through the meridians or channels by which they circulate throughout the body. Treatment involves inserting needles into the channels affecting the disordered organs to stimulate the energy circulation that restores energetic balance and proper organ function.

Many people are convinced of the benefits of acupuncture due to its long history of use in Oriental medicine. How could so many people believe they have been helped, over a history that spans several thousands of years, if there were no beneficial effects?

The point about the long history of traditional acupuncture is an important one because it brings up another question. Could a treatment work well in one environment and not in another? Perhaps it could. First, because of the *placebo effect* where a person's positive expectations affect the outcome of the treatment. Second, whenever you take a treatment out of its natural cultural environment, you're changing that treatment. When we put acupuncture to the Western scientific test, in a Western medical clinic, we're inevitably changing it. You may argue we're changing it in a minor way. However, we really don't know just how major or minor the changes are. What we do know is that the acupuncture being tested, in the end, is different from the acupuncture that was practiced throughout the ages in China and other parts of the Orient.

In Western science, evidence about acupuncture varies. In terms of treating drug abuse and addiction, the correlational evidence is much stronger than the clinical trial evidence.

 A clinical trial is where individuals agree to undergo an experiment in which they will be randomly assigned to receive a particular treatment. The new treatment that is being investigated is called the *experimental* treatment. (It's called experimental because the scientists don't yet know if it works as well or better than the standard treatment.) Sometimes, the comparison treatment condition is a placebo because the scientists want to test whether the experimental treatment works better than the effects people can bring on themselves through having positive expectations about treatment.

Which results do you trust, the correlational results or the clinical trial results? We can't say for sure, but there are two perspectives to consider. The first is that the difficulties involved in conducting a high-quality clinical trial in acupuncture are so extensive that such a trial hasn't been done satisfactorily. From this viewpoint, you can trust the correlational evidence more, because this evidence is derived from easier forms of experiments that, because they're easier, have been undertaken more effectively. The second view is that the clinical trials provide the most exacting evidence of effectiveness, and acupuncture just doesn't measure up under these stringent conditions of testing.

We will go over examples of both types of evidence, so you can see for yourself what makes sense.

Acupuncture research

Much animal research in acupuncture is devoted to testing whether the treatment reduces addictive behavior. First, addictive responses are induced (for example, in laboratory rats), then the strength of the addictive responses is tested following acupuncture treatment. For example, rats induced into a nicotine addiction (the addictive ingredient in tobacco) are given acupuncture and then observed. The treated rats show decreases in addictive behaviors consistent with lesser addiction levels. An important aspect of these studies is that the same anti-addictive effects observed externally, in terms of behavior, are also observed internally, in terms of biological responses.

The human research is more variable, although similar. One important question has been whether acupuncture assists patients in withdrawing from addictive states. If it does, its anti-addictive action may be effective in rebalancing the biological processes that become disordered during drug abuse and addiction. If true, the anti-addictive effects of acupuncture may also be effective in preventing relapses.

In several randomized clinical trials with humans, acupuncture has effectively reduced the addictive withdrawal responses of patients detoxing from nicotine, alcohol, cocaine, and opiates. However, the picture isn't all clear because other clinical trials, specifically done with nicotine and cocaine addiction, have yielded opposite results — little or no differences between acupuncture effects and the effects of a sham needle treatment. The sham treatment is meant to look like acupuncture, but the needles inserted aren't placed in any real acupuncture points. Thus the sham treatment is purposely ineffective. If it turns out to be as effective as acupuncture, then either a new, effective needle treatment has been discovered (highly improbable) or there's some placebo response involved that suggests the action of acupuncture isn't crucial to the benefits derived.

How do you interpret these positive and negative study results? You may conclude that some studies were done more precisely and that the more precise studies showed either the positive or the negligible results. Or you may conclude that some patients are highly responsive to acupuncture, and others are unresponsive. Whenever results are compared across patient groups, the data of each group is analyzed as a whole. Therefore, there is an overriding of differences in the responses of individual people.

Plainly put, if the most acupuncture-reactive patients were compared with the control groups of these studies, different results may be obtained from the ones reported. In practical terms, it may be that certain sectors of the patient population, or the general population, have a strong response to acupuncture. Other sectors are less responsive. In most of the studies, thus far, both responsive and unresponsive sectors are mixed together in the evaluation of responses. Practically speaking, if you, individually, are a strong responder to acupuncture, you may have a more positive response than those reported in the studies.

This kind of responder research could be done systematically, but the science in this area hasn't progressed to this point yet. Therefore, you could be justified, on the basis of current findings, to try out acupuncture as part of a treatment regimen. Then you can evaluate how strong your response is — and see whether you feel you're a responder and, if so, whether you want to continue with treatment to derive the benefits.

Ibogaine Treatment

Ibogaine is a fascinating, plant-based remedy believed to have anti-addictive properties. As a biochemical, it's referred to as an alkaloid that alleviates opiate dependency and withdrawal. It has been categorized elsewhere as a hallucinogen (like peyote) and was perhaps originally used for its anti-addictive action by the tribes in West Africa that discovered it.

Historical beginnings of ibogaine treatment

Despite the observation that the visions associated with ibogaine can be stressful, it has a history of underground use starting in the early 1960s. At that time, it was transported to North America in sufficient quantities to become known as an anti-addictive substance. One of its discoverers, Howard Lotsof, gave it to seven heroin and cocaine addicts and reported that five of the addicts stopped their use for 18 months, experiencing few or no withdrawal problems. Lotsof pursued efforts to patent the drug, finally succeeding in 1985 with a patent for its use in opioid withdrawal. Addiction treatment with ibogaine began in informal clinics in the Netherlands as early as 1989, and has progressively expanded so that clinics now use it in the U.K., Canada, Slovenia, and Mexico. Although ibogaine is legally used in most countries, it is, unfortunately, outlawed in Belgium and the United States. Although scientists in the United States continue to try to evaluate its effects, at this time there is insufficient research data to warrant FDA approval.

How ibogaine may work

The research on ibogaine is simple to interpret, because most of the reliable studies have been done on animals. Most indicate ibogaine reduces opiate withdrawal symptoms and alcohol dependency. For example, in morphine-dependent mice, ibogaine reduced physical withdrawal reactions. In rats that have been preconditioned to be alcohol-preferring, ibogaine reduced the subjects' desire for alcohol intake, with minimal side-effects on food intake.

Ibogaine research

With humans, ibogaine research has been controversial, partly because of its hallucinogenic properties. In low doses, ibogaine is a mild stimulant. At high doses, users report emotionally provocative visions, some pleasant and some harrowing. One formerly addicted patient who credits ibogaine with 3 years of sobriety after 15 years of addiction, stated, "It was like dying and going to hell 1,000 times." Because this described his experience after ingesting ibogaine, you can see why ibogaine wouldn't be addictive in itself. Ibogaine may induce an emotional catharsis that motivates users to never again ingest anything that is addictive.

At this point in time, don't use ibogaine without being under the careful supervision of a physician experienced with its use. Although not yet legal in the United States (at the time of printing), some clinics in Mexico, the Caribbean, and Europe administer it. One of ibogaine's investigators, K. Alper of the New York University

School of Medicine states that ibogaine seems to work on "every neurotransmitter system we know about." Certainly, one of its important actions is as an antidepressant agent that acts on the serotonin levels in the brain. The available data suggests that ibogaine is safe, but careful supervision of patients is also indicated.

Nutritional Therapy

If you believe nutrition is important for health, it follows that you'd believe good nutrition is especially important for recovering from an addiction. Furthermore, scientific evidence suggests that nutrition can play a major role.

Addictions and poor nutrition

Recently the first comprehensive examination of the link between substance abuse and eating disorders revealed that over one third of the people who abuse drugs or alcohol have an eating disorder. This statistic contrasts with the 3 percent of the general population with an eating disorder. Furthermore, about one half of people classified as having eating disorders also engage in the abuse of alcohol or drugs. What does this mean?

Simply put, if you have an alcohol or drug abuse problem, you're more likely to additionally have an eating disorder. And if you do have an eating disorder or an eating problem, the result for you is probably poor nutrition, which combines with the chemical imbalances in your body that exist because of your use and abuse. And the reverse is also true — if you have an eating disorder, you're also more likely to have an alcohol or drug abuse problem. Both problems combine in creating chemical imbalances.

 Because an unfortunate side-effect of most addictions is a poor diet, your recovery process will benefit by following a healthy diet. What constitutes a healthy diet? Start with what is recommended by authoritative bodies such as the U.S. and Canadian governments (www.health.gov and www.hc-sc.gc.ca/).

 Pay attention to your diet. A good nutritional approach is important in counteracting your substance abuse and behavioral addiction tendencies.

But what is good nutrition?

Even in this era of the Atkins Diet and controversies over how much protein you should eat, everyone agrees you should eat fresh fruits and vegetables. Increasing your consumption of fruits and vegetables is associated with a reduced incidence of cancer and heart disease, as well as other chronic illnesses. You just can't go wrong with these basic staples of good nutrition.

Another valuable dietary change is reducing daily intake of sugars and refined carbohydrates. These foods are broken down easily and raise the levels of your blood sugar precipitously. Then they burn out quickly. You naturally produce higher levels of insulin to match your blood sugar levels, so when the burnout happens, you're left with too much insulin in your blood, and the result is fatigue and often, a lower mood. If you're going to consume carbohydrates, consume complex carbohydrates — whole grains and cereals. These types of carbohydrates are like the logs that burn longer in your fireplace. They get broken down slowly and thus raise your blood sugar levels more gradually and evenly — and your blood sugar levels are maintained at higher levels for longer periods. This results in more energy and evener moods.

This point about carbohydrates and nutrition, generally, can be very important and difficult for those who abuse alcohol. Because alcohol intake impairs absorption of nutrients by interfering with two major body organs, namely the liver and the pancreas, following withdrawal, it's important to be on the lookout for imbalances of fluids, calories, and electrolytes as well as vitamin deficiencies involving pyridoxine, thiamine, and vitamin C. Furthermore, because you get accustomed to a good deal of carbohydrate intake in the form of alcohol, you can find yourself experiencing an acute, refined carb deficit after withdrawal. The result is a residual sweet tooth. You find yourself prone to eating lots of sugars — pastries, ice creams, chocolates, and hard candies. You will probably have to adjust gradually to a lower carb intake or, alternatively, to an intake of the healthier complex carbs. This transition usually requires a good deal of attention and discipline.

Macrobiotic diets

Among the special diets that can help people overcome health problems, this Oriental-style vegetarian diet has been promoted as one of the most effective. It emphasizes low fat intake and eating whole grains, vegetables, and nonprocessed foods. It may prove helpful in dealing with food allergies, chemical sensitivities, and addictive tendencies.

The macrobiotic diet is an oriental diet that is based on ancient Chinese philosophy. It is a nutritional attempt to balance the *complementary opposites* known as yin and yang — the forces that the Chinese believe must be kept in harmony to achieve good health.

These forces are woven into every aspect of life. Their characteristics are as follows:

- ✔ Yin is said to be expansive, cold, wet, slow, passive, sweet, loose, and dark.

- ✔ Yang is contractile, hot, dry, fast, aggressive, salty, tight, and light.

Alcohol and drugs are extremely yin in character.

The macrobiotic dietary regimen strives to bring daily dietary intake into balance, based on balancing the yin qualities (for example, cold, wet, sweet) and yang qualities (for example, hot, dry, salty) of food. According to this Chinese philosophy, some food substances are neither yin nor yang but rather in-between. The most balanced foods in the yin/yang continuum (though not necessarily in nutritional science) are brown rice and whole grains. Hence, these foods constitute the foundation of the macrobiotic diet.

To this foundation, the macrobiotic regimen adds foods reflecting different degrees of yin and yang, selected in accordance with the individual's dietary needs and temperament. In practice, this usually works out to a diet consisting of:

- ✔ **About 50 to 60 percent whole grains, including brown rice, barley, millet, oats, corn, rye, wheat, and buckwheat.** Keep in mind that whole grains are considered the best types of carbs to consume in current Western nutritional circles.

- ✔ **About 25 to 30 percent fresh vegetables.** Especially recommended are *cruciferous* vegetables (members of the cabbage family) and other dark green and deep yellow vegetables. They should be grown organically and locally, if possible. Macrobiotic advocates recommend lightly steaming or boiling them, or sautéing them with a small amount of vegetable oil. For purposes of the macrobiotic diet, vegetables fall into three categories:

  - **Eat frequently:** Cruciferous vegetables, including arugula, bok choy, broccoli, cabbage, cauliflower, collards, kale, kohlrabi, mustard greens, radishes, rutabaga, turnip greens, turnips, and watercress; also included are Chinese cabbage, dandelion, onion, daikon, orange squashes, and pumpkin

  - **Eat occasionally:** Celery, iceberg lettuce, mushrooms, snow peas, and string beans

  - **Avoid:** Potatoes, tomatoes, eggplant, peppers, asparagus, spinach, beets, zucchini, and avocado

✔ **About 5 to 10 percent of your food in the form of beans, soy-based products, and sea vegetables.** In this category, tofu (soy bean curd) is a favorite. Sea vegetables to consider include wakame, hiziki, dombu, noris, arame, agar-agar, and Irish moss.

✔ **About 5 to 10 percent of your food as soups.** Miso soup, a broth made with soybean paste, is a popular choice. Also permissible are soups made with vegetables, grains, seaweed, or beans.

Macrobiotic diets and substance addiction

From the macrobiotic perspective, an overabundance of substances like drugs and alcohol creates an imbalance of too much yin in your diet. Accordingly, you need to counteract the dominance of yin in your diet with more yang substances. From this perspective, if you establish a balance between yin food items and yang food items, you will reduce your craving for alcohol and drugs.

The research on macrobiotic diets as an aid to substance abuse treatment

At this time, no scientific evidence supports the idea that a macrobiotic diet will reduce your urges for alcohol or drugs. Nevertheless, evidence shows that when addictions dominate your life, a healthy diet is neglected. Moreover, some of these addictions (alcohol abuse/addiction) impair your body's ability to properly process the nutrients in foods. Macrobiotic diets do help ensure a more nutritionally balanced diet than what you are likely achieving when consumed by an addiction.

Meditation

Meditation techniques were once difficult to scientifically evaluate. This is changing radically as we enter a new era of exciting findings indicating that meditating offers important benefits.

Underlying this revolution-in-the-making are innovative ways of detecting subtle brain signals within different parts of the brain. By using sophisticated forms of MRI and electroencephalograph tests, subtle changes in neural signals can now be detected at a rate of 1,000 times per second. With these tests, we've discovered that high levels of neural activity in the left prefrontal cortex are associated with states of happiness, vitality, and alertness. High levels of activity in the right prefrontal cortex, in contrast, are associated with emotional distress, depression, and anxiety. The consistency of these findings raised questions as to whether people could be taught mental disciplines to shift to the patterns associated with happiness and vitality.

Could people, for example, be taught to activate the brain sectors associated with happiness while deactivating the brain sectors associated with depression? If so, would these disciplines help one to cultivate happiness and alertness, and increase vitality?

Preliminary answers have been derived from studies of Buddhist meditation masters and regular citizens. During a form of compassion meditation, the advanced meditators demonstrated a remarkable leftward shift in prefrontal brain activity — a shift that stimulated those same brain areas associated with positive emotion, vitality, and alertness. Although this was an important finding, it was possible that it required many years of meditation discipline to train this leftward shift. Could these meditation techniques be useful for regular people who are unable to devote years to meditating?

To demonstrate that these same shifts were possible for ordinary citizens, a randomized study was conducted on healthy employees from a large company. Half the group was randomly allocated to an eight-week training in mindfulness forms of meditation, and the other half was placed on a waiting list group and assessed but not trained. The results indicated significant increases in left-sided activation for the meditators when compared with the nonmeditators.

A brief introduction to mindfulness

Mindfulness meditation involves the non-avoidant awareness of the thoughts, emotions, and sensations that arise in one's immediate experience. No particular thoughts are emphasized. All are related to in the same way.

Attention is first directed to breathing sensations until a thought, image, emotion, or sensation is perceived. Then *that* thought, image, emotion, or sensation is noted, and attention is redirected back to breathing sensations. This simple process continues for 10 or 15 or 30 minutes, or for as long as a person wishes. One can be in a seated position (recommended) or lying down. The technique can be summarized in the following way:

- Attention is directed to breathing sensations

- Awareness arises of a thought, image, emotion, or sensation

- Practice detachment from this awareness

- Attention is redirected to breathing sensations

- Awareness arises of the next thought, image, emotion, or sensation

- Practice detachment from this awareness

- Attention is redirected to breathing sensations

These findings demonstrate that a brief training in mindfulness meditation generated positive effects on brain function similar to those achieved by advanced meditators. Briefly put, ordinary citizens were able to learn meditation techniques that assisted them in cultivating positive emotional states, vitality, and alertness.

How does this relate to addictions? Addictive states are associated with people becoming dependent on substances or engaging in behaviors that, temporarily, generate excitement and satisfaction. The hardest part of detox and recovery is that after withdrawal, you have to find *new* ways to sustain positive states of mind — without the substances or behaviors that once did the trick.

As we have seen in the experimental results, meditation techniques, particularly mindfulness approaches, can be useful in cultivating positive states of mind. Rather than subjective reports of positive changes, we now can observe actual brain signals — the actual biology associated with positive emotional states. With meditation techniques and new methods of observation, we may be ushering in a new era of *seeing* what is healthy and what isn't healthy for the mind — and then being able to engage in activities, like meditation, that help us make the critical transitions from unhappiness to well-being.

Harm Reduction Approaches

Harm reduction programs entail reducing the worst dangers of drug and alcohol use by programs that don't aim for or require complete abstinence but instead reduce use-associated risks. For example, if a teen with drinking problems can't abstain, she can still relinquish a driving license and, in doing so, reduce the risks associated with driving under the influence.

Perhaps the most recognizable harm reduction programs are those relating to opiate addictions that include needle exchange programs (which ensure reduced use of dirty needles that transmit infectious diseases like HIV/AIDS and Hepatitis C) and methadone maintenance programs. These methadone programs provide controlled, midway steps between total abstinence from opiates and the dangers of street use. Methadone programs provide a regular dose of opiates that don't produce a high or a deficiency leading to craving and re-engagement with street use. (See Chapter 10 for more information on methadone treatment.) Although these are concrete examples, the principles of harm reduction are widely applicable.

The other noticeable example of harm-reduction programs in North America and parts of Europe are the introduction of decriminalized marijuana programs. Such programs don't encourage use but do reduce the legal penalties that are sometimes much more damaging than actual use.

The following principles are important to understanding what harm reduction is:

- ✔ Accept for better and worse that licit and illicit drug use is part of our world and work to minimize harmful effects rather than simply ignoring or condemning them.

- ✔ Understand that drug and alcohol use is a complex phenomenon that encompasses a continuum of behaviors from severe abuse to total abstinence, and acknowledge that some ways of using drugs and alcohol are clearly safer than others.

- ✔ Establish quality of individual and community life and well-being — not necessarily cessation of all drug use — as the criteria for successful interventions and policies.

- ✔ Call for provision of services and resources to people who use drugs and to the communities in which they live in order to assist them in reducing attendant harm.

- ✔ Ensure that drug users and those with a history of drug use routinely have a voice in the creation of programs and policies designed to serve them.

- ✔ Affirm that drug users themselves are the primary agents of reducing the harms of their use, and seek to empower them to share information and support each other in strategies that meet their actual conditions of use.

- ✔ Recognize that the realities of poverty, class, racism, social isolation, past trauma, sex-based discrimination, and other inequalities affect people's vulnerability to and capacity for effectively dealing with drug-related harm.

What is difficult about harm reduction is deciding where to draw the line between reducing the harm of abuse and making it easier for abusers to keep abusing. This boundary is best understood in terms of each individual's situation and how he or she responds to harm reduction efforts. If you feel that someone's exploiting a harm reduction program, the situation must be dealt with as effectively and as immediately as possible. Exploitation threatens the harm reduction program and enables the addicted individual to avoid confronting the necessity of limiting or stopping use.

Chapter 14

Teen Treatment

Y ou may be a teen or a concerned adult. Either way, you're worried about someone who seems headed toward addiction or is already addicted. In some cases, that someone is you.

Experimentation with drugs, alcohol, and tobacco is common with teens. You're young. You want to explore. You've seen and heard warnings but you're curious. One way or another, advertising suggests alcohol, tobacco, and drugs are *worth* exploring.

Socially speaking, smoking, drinking, and drugs are icebreakers. They help get things going and make you feel "in" with a group. You can find a mental or emotional groove that makes worry and loneliness seem distant and irrelevant.

But, if you're still reading this, you know it isn't all good. You're aware of a signal inside, a warning signal that's bugging you to look at the other side — the *destructive* side of drugs and alcohol. It's time for a straight, honest look.

Why Alcohol and Drugs Are More Destructive When You're Young

Statistics show the younger you are when using drugs and alcohol, the greater your chances of becoming addicted. If you start using alcohol regularly at age 13, there's a 43 percent chance that you'll become an alcoholic. By comparison, if you start at age 21, there's a 10 percent chance. In other words, by starting young, your chances of getting addicted are four times higher.

If you've already started using, what do you do? All available statistics indicate you should stop or, at the least, slow down. The longer you use and the more you use, the harder it is to stop. If you can't stop or reduce (on your own), get help as soon as you can.

The younger the brain and the earlier the use, the more the brain becomes dependent on use (of drugs and alcohol).

It's easier to damage a growing brain

While you grow and develop, your brain decides which biochemicals it needs to be healthy. The most important brain chemicals, called *neurotransmitters,* influence your mood, sleep, and appetite, among other things. If you take drugs and alcohol during your teens, your brain confuses these substances with natural neurotransmitters and incorrectly reads your level of development or maturity. Your brain unfortunately programs itself for wrong settings. You crave drugs or alcohol to correct these imbalances.

Teens have a tough time these days

Another reason why substance use is more destructive for teens is its association with emotional problems. You're more likely to use when unhappy. If you use, you're likely to get more unhappy and to make problems worse — even though, for brief periods, it may seem that your problems go away.

Let's face it, being a teen right now is no picnic. According to statistics, you may be experiencing major emotional challenges. If you're feeling frustrated, anxious, depressed, or confused, you're not alone.

The one fact that captures current teen problems is the rate of teen suicide. Teen suicide has *tripled* in the last 60 years. A recent survey showed nearly 10 percent of college students seriously considered suicide, and 1.5 percent made actual attempts.

If you're a parent or adult reading this, please take this finding as a warning. Take all talk of suicide seriously. Don't pass it off as "just talk."

If you can't stop feeling sad, anxious, and overwhelmed, get support and help. These feelings can't always be managed on your own. Asking for help is okay.

If we work back from the alarming suicide statistics, we see the stress of being a teen increases the likelihood of you having mood and anxiety problems. So wanting to believe that a cigarette, drink, or drug can help you relax is understandable. After all, a lot of advertising suggests that drinking, smoking, and taking prescription drugs bring on quick switches in mood.

But alcohol and drug use makes things worse, not better. The more you avoid problems, the worse your problems become. Then you have even more problems to avoid.

Confront fears and anxieties. One important result of current research shows that avoidance only fuels anxiety. The more you avoid fears or anxieties, the bigger they grow in your imagination, and the more troublesome they become.

Another key point is that after the high, drugs and alcohol leave you in bad shape, mentally, to solve problems. Although alcohol may lower anxieties and inhibitions in the short-term, it has depressing effects over the long-term. So you're more depressed after drinking than before drinking. And Ecstasy (also known as E or MDMA), a drug that first became popular at raves, gets you up because several neurotransmitters (serotonin, dopamine, norepinephrine) are artificially released from storage sites. But it leaves you down after six hours of high because, by then, you have *depleted* (used up) these same biochemicals.

Evidence suggests Ecstasy has neurotoxic effects, actually damaging the terminals that release the neurotransmitters and creating longer-acting or permanent imbalances. All of these effects are more powerful and long lasting, the younger your brain is.

What to Do When You Suspect Substance Abuse in a Loved One

In the preceding section, we tell you that young people are more susceptible *to* abuse and more damaged *by* it. Furthermore, young people are less able to find a way out of the downward, slippery slope of use, abuse, and addiction. If you're a friend or parent and you suspect someone is slipping down the slope of abuse, contact a trusted professional or friend to discuss how you can help. That may seem like a scary step, but it's the single most efficient and effective action to take. A modest amount of personal consultation can make a big difference in how persuasive you are in encouraging your troubled friend or offspring to get help.

Depending on where you live and your preferences, the professional you speak with may be a family physician, pediatrician, or counselor (preferably within a substance abuse program).

Professional advice will help to clarify the situation and your feelings. You will be more effective in approaching your friend and getting help. Professionals can advise you on how to use the influence of your relationship to dispel denial and support solutions.

Advice for parents

If you're a parent, consider what treatment options are immediately available in your community and how you can support treatment by financing it directly, through third-party insurance, or via a government-funded program. After you raise the issues of use, abuse, or behavioral addiction with your child, you want to act quickly to guide her to appropriate treatment. Any hold-up weakens your influence to guide her in the right direction.

Take care of as many details as possible — before you intervene with your child about use, abuse, or behavioral addiction.

Advice for good friends

If you're a friend or concerned peer, you need to discuss the situation with a trusted adult before proceeding. It's not that you don't know what you're doing. You probably know the situation better than anyone else. But you need help navigating the adult system. It's preferable that the adult be a parent, guidance counselor, or school administrator. Even if you don't get the response you want from the first adult you talk to, persist, because you're doing the right thing. Sooner or later, you'll find a responsible and sensitive adult who will help.

Even though some of the actions necessary in starting treatment must be undertaken by an adult, you, as a friend and peer, have an extremely important role. In fact, you may have the *key* role if you've observed your friend get into trouble with excessive use on several occasions. Your recall of those situations can be very important in helping your friend come out of denial about his or her problem.

Case one: Part athlete, part addict

John was from a large family in a rural area in the Midwest and had the good looks, athletic skills, and charisma to be a sought-after date for the prom. However, other elements about John's life weren't so apparent. He had been adopted as an infant and had gnawing questions about the circumstances that caused his birth parents to give him up for adoption. He felt an underlying uneasiness and insecurity that didn't seem to go away, no matter how well he played on the sports field — and no matter how much respect he earned with his skills. He fell in with a group of team-mates who got together for beers after games and on weekends, and he found something new in this experience of drinking. The background buzz of insecurity that plagued him seemed to go away for a while.

It wasn't long before John wanted the tranquilizing effects of alcohol more of the time — not just after games and on weekends. He began to save beers and have older teammates buy extras so he could have some beers around on weekdays. He began drinking alone — in private. Soon, he found that it was difficult to function as smoothly if he didn't have at least a few beers each day and then that few grew in number. Meanwhile, he had to adopt more and more special measures to keep look-ing normal to his peers and his parents, and to hide his drinking.

Oddly enough, his athletic performance didn't drop off at first. Gradually, however, he began to find that he had less endurance, even though he continued working out at the same levels. Also, his reflexes and coordination were no longer as reliable, and he began to flub key plays. But by then, he felt trapped into regular drinking, fearing things would get worse, and his athletic performance would suffer most if he stopped drinking suddenly. He felt stuck and trapped in this seemingly private problem — except for the buzz amidst his friends and fans, that something wasn't right. For more on what happens to John, see the sidebar "Case one treatment suc-cess: Athlete finds inner peace" later in the chapter.

The individual you're concerned about and want to help may be afraid to admit to a problem. Part of this anxiety is related to believ-ing that someone will find out the secret that is destroying him. He may also fear that acknowledging the problem will cause a mass rejection by peers, or disappointment or anger in parents. You can be immediate proof that someone will be concerned and supportive, and that people do care for your friend's whole person, not just the easy, good-times sides. The importance of your role in this respect just can't be overstated. You are very important to this person.

A word about denial

Denial is a huge part of the addictive process. Drugs and alcohol are used when people are trying to have a good time or when people are having a hard time. Use also happens in situations where people are having a hard time but are trying to have a good time. In the latter situation, you can see denial in action. Although you shouldn't try to shame the person you're concerned about, expect denial and be prepared to counteract this denial right from the start.

Don't say a word to someone you see as being on the slippery slope to abuse unless you're willing to be firm and direct, without being critical. Be especially firm in encouraging your friend to seek and accept help. Also, save your energy and refrain from any confrontation unless you're willing to be *empathic* — to make a sustained effort to understand what it's like to feel so far out-of-control that alcohol and drug use are the only reliable ways to feel good.

Be prepared for a long haul to a healthy recovery

Addiction can't be cured like a sore throat. The problems of abuse take a while (several months to several years) to resolve. Nonetheless, the first step you take covers the most ground. Then, be prepared to persevere for several reasons:

- ✔ The person you're concerned about may resist taking action. You may enter a period of impasse where the cat is partially out of the bag — you and the person you're worried about know the issue won't go away. On the other hand, the time is not yet right to get to the bottom of it all. Tolerating this uncertainty and strain and continuing to love the person are parts of the work needed to bring the abuser out of denial.

- ✔ Getting to the right treatment match may take a while. A variety of outpatient and residential programs are available for teens — one size doesn't fit all. The first effort at treatment may not be exactly right, and if that's the case, adjustments will be needed. The remaining sections of this chapter help you fine-tune the process so you're making the best possible choices, guided by the best information available. Try to review the case examples in the sidebars of this chapter, because they illustrate a few of the many forms the slippery slope to addictive behavior can take. As you read, try to think about the specific form your friend or child's situation is taking. There is much that you can understand, as long as you think about the details of what you have observed.

Case two: Golden girl with a diet pill addiction

Joan was a straight-A student who scored off the chart on every achievement test she took. There was no doubt she'd be one of the smartest kids in whatever school she'd attend. But she didn't see her intelligence as such a great advantage. She felt emotionally at loose-ends, unable to comfortably connect with people. She often fell into a pattern of being very entertaining and funny, rather than relaxed and authentic.

She was also attractive but had a tendency to gain weight — nothing too noticeable, but she wanted to be slimmer and to have the body every man wanted.

When her mother offered her diet pills one evening to help her study for final exams, she was interested in whether the pills, taken regularly, would do the trick for weight control. Well, they certainly did the trick for studying. She pulled an all-nighter and had energy to spare during the next day to do well on two separate exams. She couldn't seem to find a downside to these little diet pills.

Soon she found out where her mother kept the pills and started taking them regularly. It worked — she lost the pounds she had worried about. Living in an affluent suburb, she found she could buy a regular supply of diet pills. However, there *was* a downside. She began to find it hard to go to sleep — and even when she fell asleep, she'd awaken in the middle of the night. She had to start wearing more makeup to hide the circles under her eyes and she found she was quite jumpy during the day. She always felt edgy. She was worried because her heart often raced and she felt that sometimes it skipped beats.

She was becoming, step-by-step, an amphetamine addict. She couldn't miss a day for fear of crashing and entering into that awful depression she had just tasted just once — when her supply was temporarily interrupted. She still was the golden girl of academics in her school — except now she had a secret. Even her boyfriend and her parents didn't know. She was in addictive trouble. For more on what happens to Joan, see the sidebar "Case two treatment success: Golden Girl becomes successful artist" later in this chapter.

Making the investment in teen treatment

On a purely practical level, you need to communicate with an insurance expert to see what degree of outpatient or residential treatment is covered by your regular health insurance plan. An addicted person rarely resolves his or her addiction without help.

Also the situation of addicted individuals can become very dangerous, very quickly. Thus, there is a continuum of services that may
be critically helpful at different times: outpatient treatment, family-
based treatment, drug (urine) testing, residential treatment. Often,
such programs must be accredited by specific organizations for
you to be reimbursed (in part or full), and you need to know what
accreditations are necessary before considering and discussing different alternatives. In some cases, the only insurance expert you
need will be your insurance agent, but in other cases, you'll have
to find another skilled individual familiar with your program who
can read the fine print of policies and interpret precedents.

Getting Treatment as a Teen

Treatment may be a frightening word at first, but focus on the
bright side from the start. In your determination to get the very
best help, you'll find that the help you get will address all the
important questions you have about life and about living in a
healthy, meaningful way.

You may feel confused and low in confidence because you have
now acknowledged unsolved problems. But regardless of how you
feel, you are now taking a very important step. You now have the
humility to know you need to ask the tough questions about life.
Some of the toughest seem very simple: What *is* healthy? When it
comes right down to it, how do you know what's good for you?

That question is an important part of your renewed effort to
search. The search starts with choosing to change and to find the
treatment that helps you do that. In the end, be assured, you must
choose to change, and treatment will help you through the part you
haven't been able to do on your own. No one can effectively treat
you against your will. Your parents may choose a treatment setting, and you may go along with their choice, but you won't really
be helped until something clicks — until some inner *yes* happens,
some inner light turns on, and you feel something is learned and
understood right there, right in the immediate situation. Until you
feel you're absorbing some wisdom, whatever is happening will be
going in one ear and out the other.

You need to do the treatment in a setting where you feel you'll really
learn something valuable. This starts with you trying to be honest
with yourself about what really seems right and what doesn't.

Asking for help: Any time is a good time

You tried to stop on your own, and it hasn't worked. The feelings and urges return. Your mood swings, and your frustrations and anxieties return.

If you feel you're slipping, the first step is to feel some pride about your willingness to deal with the problem. Many famous, highly skilled people have had the same problem, so it's not a problem that strikes only the weak. In reading this, you're showing the strength and courage needed to get to the root issues and putting yourself on the path to recovery. Now, keep going. Just keep taking one step after another; little steps, like reading this section, can be very important.

The sooner you're in contact with a trusted, competent counseling professional, the more likely you are to use your concern and energy to best advantage. Some of the most important help this person gives you is when you acknowledge you have a problem but you're unclear about how serious it is or what to do about it. A skilled counselor can help you with your feelings and help you to find solutions.

If you're concerned about yourself, you have to take the step of talking with a trusted adult. We're not saying that trustworthy adults are all around and easy to find. For example, you may not feel comfortable talking to either of your parents, or to any of the school counselors you know. If so, don't give up. In Chapter 21, we list some teen help centers in the United States. Or you can go directly to a clinic or a doctor. There *is* a trustworthy adult out there, somewhere, who will listen, be nonjudgmental, and guide you. You're doing the right thing even though it may seem the right thing should be easier to do. Keep going.

Finding a counselor

Certainly, one very important part of the program you choose is your counselor. No worthwhile counselor will try to intimidate you into going along with a program. No worthwhile counselor will get you to stop asking honest questions or to stop calling attention to stuff that doesn't make sense. No, the counselor knows what you're going through, knows how you got there, and knows how to get you back into good shape. The good counselors realize that you're going to have to find a match between what you're confused about, what you want, and what they're offering. The good counselors may be tough, but you don't doubt their kindness and their essential interest in you as a separate, living, breathing, thinking, and feeling human being.

You must take the first step and dial the phone. The good counselors are out there — they can be found. But because you're a unique person, you may have to do some searching to find the right counselor for you. And this person may not come in the packaging you'd expect. She may be shorter or taller, or more or less attractive, than the people you imagine. She may seem smarter and brainier, or less intellectual and more practical, than you imagine. The important thing is that something this person says — something that happens in your mind and your emotions when you're with her, sticks and doesn't go away. You feel that great relief, that sense of trust that this person is showing you something about life that is reliable and useful — and makes you appreciate life more than you did before. The good news is that you can find this person — the good news is that this person, once found, will help you a lot.

In selecting a counselor, make sure you ask about his training and experience in counseling youth. Many counselors specialize in treating either youth or adults. Obviously, you want to connect with a counselor trained in counseling youth.

Relating to your counselor

In most cases, your counselor will have an independent practice or will be associated with an established residential or outpatient program.

If your counselor has an independent practice, you will probably go to his office for scheduled sessions that usually last between 45 minutes and 2 hours. The focus will be on talking. Initially, you'll talk about how you began using and why, and how you have continued. Be aware that your therapist will be doing a lot of listening, and while listening, he may be taking notes that permit a later review of what you've said. This initial stage can make you feel very uncomfortable because the things you're talking about are painful — you will likely be describing periods of insecurity and anxiety, situations where you made a bad choice or did something you knew was wrong. It may feel strange talking to a virtual stranger about stuff you haven't told your friends or your parents. Keep in mind that you're engaged in a process that has been tested and found effective for quite some time. Keep in mind that it is a confidential process that allows you to speak freely, without worrying about the consequences of what you say. The only consequences you carry away from a session are those that have to do with changes in the way you feel and think and the choices you make.

Your counselor should have no other relationship with you aside from being your counselor. This kind of single-focus relationship coordinates with the principle of confidentiality (that your communications with her will be kept secret). In combination, these conditions help you to talk freely without being worried that what you're saying will be communicated to anyone else in your life. In other words, you're able to talk without worrying that what you're saying could cause problems for someone or influence any other situation. In order for someone to be that separate from the rest of your life, she must be a virtual stranger in the beginning.

At the start, there must be distance between you and your counselor, but this distance need not be a difficult barrier for very long. You should begin noticing that the quality of your counselor's listening is different from that which you usually expect from other adults — your teachers, parents, and relatives, for example. In fact, the quality of listening should be different from that which happens with your friends as well. You should feel that someone is listening to you *very, very carefully* — that your counselor is somehow picking up on what you're saying with surprising accuracy and understanding. And that because he's listening to you so well, you begin trusting that something good can come from your conversations.

We call the experience of feeling heard, *empathy.* It is the experience that someone is right there, understanding what you're saying and feeling (while you're talking).

The other experience that is important is what we call *alliance* or the experience of feeling that this person you're talking to is somehow in your corner, and a valuable ally. Your counselor is valuable not because he agrees with everything you say, but because he shows you the utmost respect in how he listens. Furthermore, he's completely honest in his responses to you. You may be motivated to show your best side to your counselor and minimize your difficulties — that's natural. But you'll notice that he isn't fooled when you skate around a difficult point and is, instead, patiently waiting for you to get down to more honest, earnest communication. Because the honesty involves you acknowledging more emotional negativity, your counselor is the very opposite to what has been described as a fair weather friend — he wants you to feel free and not judged so you can reveal the worst sides of your story and yourself, as well as the best. Just disclosing those issues that you have previously kept hidden has been shown to be helpful.

Does your counselor have to be a recovered addict in order to help you?

The short answer to this question is no. Just like a cardiologist doesn't have to have heart disease to be a good heart doctor, a counselor doesn't have to have come through the process of recovery from addiction to be a good counselor. Your counselor may be someone who has simply found the counseling process interesting and fulfilling, and hasn't had to confront addictive kinds of problems. Although it can be an advantage for a counselor to have been through recovery, it can also be a disadvantage. Sometimes, the method of recovery has left such an imprint on the counselor that she winds up taking an inflexible approach in counseling. On the other hand, having been there with an addiction can be helpful, because your counselor can refer to her own experience and feelings and recall direct events that parallel those you're dealing with. On this point, you have to judge for yourself how helpful or unhelpful it is that your counselor has had a recovery experience. Personal experience with an addiction is certainly not required to be a successful and effective counselor.

Also consider what counseling *isn't* going to be like. For instance, the good counselor doesn't give you answers and tell you what to do. He or she will listen and help, but you will have to make decisions about what things in your life you want changed.

Counseling in group programs

You may choose to work in a *group format,* where a group of people like yourself gathers to talk under the direction of the counselor. Sometimes, this format seems to be the least desirable, particularly if you feel automatic negativities about other people who have addiction problems. One typical thought is "It's bad enough dealing with my own problem, why choose to be in a situation where I have to deal with other people's problems as well?"

Although this may be a deciding point for you, do look at the other side of the picture before rejecting group treatment. The other people with addiction issues may be valuable to get to know simply because they *are* like you. They understand. They're going through the same thing. Being in a group may even help you reach some important realizations more quickly than you would in individual treatment. No one is a loser just because he somehow got involved with the slippery slope of use and abuse. The common ground in group treatment isn't the past of abuse but finding a new path for living that deals with today and makes past problems a distant memory.

Case one treatment success: Athlete finds inner peace

Although it took trying a number of programs, John eventually found a residential program that took him away from the environments he found so difficult to manage. He has had to stay completely sober and refrain from even the occasional beer to progress with his career and eventually, to begin and sustain his own happy family life. He made contact with his birth-mother and has maintained regular contact with her for several years, including face-to-face visits on Mother's Day during which she gets to play with John's son — who also shows the promise of being a superlative athlete.

One advantage of group treatment is that you're able to give help to others in the group while you receive help — and sometimes that feels more natural. Also, you learn, from direct example, about the different stages people go through as they experience progress and the inevitable bumps on the road to recovery.

And group and individualized treatment aren't mutually exclusive — you can do both at the same time or you can do them in an alternating pattern: first individual, then group, and so on. The point is the two are *complementary* (they can complete each other), and you don't have to make any decisions in favor of one as opposed to the other.

Furthermore, family-based treatments (that include other family members) can be an important component of group-based treatments. The more your family truly understands you, the more truly supportive they can be.

Residential treatment: Group and individual treatments

If your circumstances and your old friends make it impossible to stop using, get away from it all for a while, and take up a new residence within a program designed to provide intensive and personal therapy in an environment that nurtures positive change.

This approach is particularly important if you feel the temptations of continuing to use are so high that you can't trust yourself to stay clean. Getting into residential treatment ensures that your temptations are reduced to a minimum and opportunities and rewards for healthy activity are maximized. Residential treatment is all about replacing old habits with new, positive, healthy habits.

How is this done? First, residential programs place you in an environment that restricts you from situations that are tempting and exposes you to situations where you experiment with (and can establish) a whole new set of healthy habits. Some residential treatment programs for youth, for example, are set on working ranches where a good deal of activity is directed toward tending and riding horses. Other programs focus on adventure learning, involving expeditions to wilderness areas where you experience the beauty and freshness of the great outdoors while learning survival techniques, camping, and navigation skills. You also engage in specific challenges like climbing or rappelling down cliffs or kayaking through different levels of rapids. The idea behind these programs is to experience nature in a full and raw way and, in doing so, to find your own healthy, inner nature. Being in a place of natural beauty is an emotional up that is drug-free, and points the way to other natural highs that can form the basics of a healthier lifestyle.

Other residential programs have therapeutic specialties that directly address the particular addictive problem you've been plagued with. For example, if your problem is an addictive behavior like an eating disorder, some residential programs focus solely on that problem, guaranteeing expert help. If you do have an eating problem, these types of programs can be very helpful because they address the problem on all levels, from the meals you're served to the group and individual counselors you meet with.

Case two treatment success: Golden Girl becomes successful artist

Joan eventually found her way to intensive outpatient psychiatric therapy and, after three years of intensive, psychodynamically oriented treatment, left the big city in which she had lived, to attend a university in a rural town in California. It took a good deal of outpatient therapy for her to free herself of the recurrent temptations to use amphetamines, but out of her therapy emerged a new commitment to visual arts. She had always enjoyed being an amateur artist, but had not allowed herself the freedom to consider it a serious vocational choice. However, after she granted herself that freedom, she discovered she had considerable talents, enough to propel her to a very successful career as a freelance artist. Now, as she says, she is positively addicted to working away in her artist's studio, making art in a way that produces a healthy high.

And some programs are specialized for the type of drug addiction you have (cocaine, opiates), once again ensuring that the people you work with will talk with you in detail about your experience and the changes you've been going through. They will also help you see what you need to do to free yourself.

The time that you spend in a residential treatment setting can vary widely although the typical span of time begins with five to seven days and can extend to several weeks or even several months. Some programs add academics so that you can simultaneously keep pace with your grade level courses or get additional tutoring that helps you catch up if you've fallen behind while troubled by addictions.

For those of you who are religiously oriented, some residential treatments have spiritually based programs that encourage use of scriptures or multicultural spiritual approaches to augment and complete your recovery program. Some of these carry with them the advantage of being supported by church foundations and charities, limiting the costs that will have to be paid while you're in residential treatment.

Harm reduction programs for youth

At any stage of treatment, harm reduction programming is very important. Basically *harm reduction* focuses on reducing the risk of harm associated with any engagement in addictive behaviors and/or any use of substances. Examples include needle exchange programs, substituting methadone for heroin, educating about HIV risk and the importance of safe sex (condom use), implementing driving laws that limit how many passengers a teenage driver can transport, and so on. Harm reduction programs follow several principles. Read Chapter 13 to learn more about harm reduction programs.

Remembering That Slips Aren't Freefalls

Slips, or interruptions in your program (which can include temporary lapses back to using), are learning experiences. You see that a high from using feels bad afterwards. You experience real remorse about the slip and can link your remorse to plans to avoid the triggers that got you slipping.

Your teens are just one period of seven or so years, and your lifespan will extend much, much longer. On the news are many stories of youth who were once heavy users, abusers, and addicts who then went on to completely reverse these problems and become societal leaders.

Whatever the immediate situation, the wheel is still spinning; you are constantly growing, physically and psychologically. Remember to never give up on yourself: Find what the good life is for you! And remember this if you're a friend concerned about someone who may be heading for addiction. Hanging in for the longer-term is an important idea because things can change in a major way. Don't give up hope or condemn anyone who has recently slipped. Youth is a time of resilience when there is the capacity for a great deal of change and redirection.

Ultimately, the best way to counteract the slippery slope of abuse and addiction is to take the approach of starting over, knowing you have plenty of time to build the right life for you.

Part IV
Life in Recovery

The 5th Wave   By Rich Tennant

"Remember, it's not proper etiquette to immediately talk business on a golf outing. Wait until at least the 6th hole to bring up the pool toy account."

In this part . . .

Recovery focuses on building a healthier, more natu-rally satisfying life. It includes practical learning about how to avoid slips and relapses. In this part, we describe barriers to recovery and guide you in overcom-ing them. Everyone experiences temptations to slip, and many people do slip and relapse. We show you how to get back on track after a slip and how to pull yourself out of a relapse. We review how to re-establish sound social, family, and work relationships and how to rebuild a sound financial footing. Invariably, family and friends are also learning how to recover their own balance, especially in how they relate to you. We provide guidance to family members and friends in how to help you in your recovery.

Chapter 15

Overcoming Barriers to Recovery

A big gap lies between thinking about quitting an addictive behavior and deciding to quit. There's also a big gap between deciding to quit and quitting decisively. How do you bridge these gaps? How do you overcome the barriers between you and recovery?

If you're reading this book, you're thinking about making a change. But you may find yourself still in conflict. You may hate what your use and abuse are doing to you, but still look forward to the next hit. You may want to change, but dread starting treatment and getting down to it. You may feel you should work harder at recovery, but find momentum difficult to gather.

In this chapter, we focus on overcoming the barriers to successful recovery. We go over the essential pointers — with emphasis on pacing, self-acceptance, forgiveness, and serenity.

Be Prepared: The First Step That's Too Often Forgotten

Statistics prove that most people who undergo treatment for addiction experience relapse. (For more information on relapses, see

Chapter 16.) No one likes relapsing. No one likes preparing for it, because relapse is often viewed as failure rather than as part of recovery. Even when you understand that relapse is part of recovery, the experience is painful. Remember, you're human, and we humans are slipping and sliding and making errors all the time — in every area of endeavor and effort.

Accept that recovery is a moving target. It's a *process* of invigorating and positive change. Although you may hit points where you find satisfaction and can relax, you're never completely cured. But you can recover, and recover so well that you're better off than ever before.

In simpler terms — you can do it. You have the resources: the energy, the intelligence, the motivation. Everything you need is right there, inside. You can face your obstacles and barriers and clear them away, just like clearing away debris after a storm.

Yes, recovery will always be a challenge — but a challenge you can meet. Just accept the hard work and take very little for granted.

Building Your Skills for Recovery

You won't get anywhere on the road to recovery unless you're honest with yourself. Accept your fallibility, but take responsibility for your actions.

You have to realize that you're not your addiction. Your addiction is just a set of behaviors — a series of things you once did — not part of your basic core. You *are* more than your addiction. As you recover, you discover this, because you discover more of your real self — your natural self.

So what are the critical skills you need to get started? We list some to start with below:

✓ **Refusal:** Although refusal may seem the simplest part of recovery, it's not really so simple after all. You need to develop the skill of saying, hearing, and accepting no. Refusal is more than just saying no to others. You have to say no to yourself and mean it. You must accept that the addictive behavior is *no longer part of you!* Why this emphasis? Because life has twists and turns. Saying no and accepting it (no matter what the situation, no matter what the emotion) is the basic skill you need. Your refusal can be courageous, creative, and life giving. Refusal is a foundational skill in recovery.

Can you help Harriet?

After reading this chapter, put yourself in the shoes of an expert and review Harriet's situation:

Harriet was ready for recovery. She had a 20-year history of alcohol and drug abuse and had been involved in more sexual relationships than she could count or even remember. She had a job and a child who she loved. But she hated her life, and she hated herself.

Harriet went to treatment through her company's Employee Assistance Program. She went to AA, she worked with her sponsor, and she stopped her addictive behavior. She wanted to change, and she wanted a man to love her.

But Harriet hated her life. She was disgusted with the way she had behaved in the past. Harriet had to work on forgiving herself. She had to refuse to give in to her desires to get involved with a man. She had to heal. She had to learn.

It's time for you to be Harriet's support person. Help Harriet help herself. Give Harriet your best advice.

Hint — focus on Harriet's psychology. Review the section "Building Your Skills for Recovery" in this chapter and advise Harriet on three things that will help her.

1. _____

2. _____

3. _____

✔ **Surrender:** Maybe surrender sounds weak, but it isn't. The best generals throughout history knew when to fight and when to avoid fighting. If you admit that you're addicted, your addiction is the superior force. Surrendering the belief that you can reduce addiction to a convenient level is a key skill. Accept that your brain and body are vulnerable to addiction and that addiction is a powerful force to contend with. Our practice is full of people who are powerful in their chosen activities — from elite sports to corporate leadership — but who readily admit their powerlessness over addiction. Twelve-step and other abstinence programs center on this very point. Accepting that you need treatment and expert help in beating addiction is what we mean by surrender — the summoning of humility in the face of addiction is the skill of surrender.

✔ **Commitment:** You have to maintain your commitment and your resolve to change. You must have a plan that you're confident in. Recovery isn't a New Year's resolution. It may be a matter of life or death and is certainly a long-term process.

✔ **Action:** Deciding what actions are necessary and acting decisively are good all-around skills — and essential skills for recovery.

Deciding what's necessary and what isn't and then trusting your decision so you vigorously and thoroughly carry it out — those are skills you can and must cultivate in recovery.

✔ **Healing time:** You need to devote some definitive time to healing. With all the change you're undergoing, you need time to just "be in the moment" with no demands to be any particular way. Relaxing for a while — giving up all notions of progress — accelerates healing.

Pacing: Taking Things One Step at a Time

Your recovery is a journey, and every journey has a pace. You decide the pace. Go too fast, and you get exhausted or injured. Go too slow, and you stagnate and lose momentum.

Rather than trying to prescribe the precisely right pace for you, we give you pointers about how to tell when you're going too fast or too slow.

You're going too fast, so slow down

Surprisingly, the most common problem is going too fast. You know you're going too fast when your ideas and emotions are far ahead of your behavior. For example, you may have virtually completed recovery (in your head) and yet in reality, you've barely progressed through detox. You can get ahead of yourself, mentally, and then become disappointed or demoralized because you can't match your mental momentum with real changes and real actions.

If this description fits you, slow down. Take things one step at a time — both in how you think and what you do. Remember, you don't want to stumble on your path of recovery. Your balance and traction are best when you focus in on what's happening in the immediate present.

You're bogged down and slowing down, so pick up the pace

You know you're going too slowly when it feels like nothing is decisive and nothing is really moving. You can become bogged down to the point where you start rolling backwards. But the only real direction, the only lifegiving, lifesaving direction is forward. If you feel bogged down, you probably *are* bogged down, and you must get moving forward again.

If you feel stuck, straighten up, put your foot on the accelerator, and move forward. You may need to imagine and envision your goals more clearly.

Pacing with time

A routine with structure can be very helpful. The predictability can be comforting and can strengthen your motivation to go forward.

In recovery, a good routine involves some time spent reflecting on addictive behavior. You may achieve this reflection in different ways: a meeting, a meditation, or a counseling session.

In recovery, start with your sleep-wake cycle to build up your routine. When you keep regular hours, you form a basis for routine that is comforting. If you go into rehabilitation, you'll see a predictable daily schedule that will remind you of school or boot camp in the military.

Remain flexible but consistent in routines. You don't want to get too rigid and, therefore, stressed about change. On the other hand, you don't want to be wishy-washy with yourself. You're building strength. Keeping with your life-routine is like keeping with a daily workout. You're going to have to put work in, to get success out.

Pacing with activities

Another key to pacing is to focus on structured activities. You will be very tempted to build Rome in a day. After you decide to change, you feel an inner pressure to get on with it. Carefully pick activities that help you in your recovery process. Remember that with every minute, hour, or day you spend in recovery, you're building strength and a personal history of success.

Pacing with activities means that you pick activities purposefully. Some are picked for pleasure, some because they boost you up with an experience of success, and some because they're difficult and strenuous but must get done anyway. Eliminating the nonessentials and focusing on the must-do's are important in pacing yourself past obstacles.

Building Resilience

Although anticipating every obstacle to recovery is impossible, we do know that you must build up strength and resilience for the challenges ahead. In this section, we give you some pointers on how to do that.

Maintain personal hygiene

It may or may not surprise you to discover that people with addictions neglect themselves. You may neglect your needs and your personal care. We have often started people on the road to recovery simply by focusing them on acts of hygiene. Washing, brushing your teeth, combing your hair — each activity is simple but each boosts your morale.

Explore your senses

You have five senses (sight, hearing, touch, taste, and smell). Each is connected to a part of your nervous system that is connected to pleasure and pain centers of the brain. Focus on activities that retrain your senses to bring you fuller experiences of the natural pleasures of life.

In the grip of addiction, you probably lost your ability to experience your senses. Many of your natural senses became dulled. Exercises in which you focus on specific senses and specific sensual events serve to "rehabilitate" your sense awareness. Many drugs target the pleasure centers of the brain, giving you a shortcut to powerful but artificial gratifications. The sensing exercises re-establish the natural pathways to pleasure. These are the natural ways to feel good — the healthy ways. You can't get yourself into trouble by stopping to smell the roses.

What is your favorite smell? How about your favorite touch? What is your favorite taste? What works of visual art are appealing to you? What music do you find most compelling?

Take some time to appreciate each sense and then write a few phrases that describe what was special about each sensate experience:

Sight: _____

Hearing: _____

Touch: _____

Taste: _____

Smell: _____

 Take time to deeply explore the unique aspects of your experience. Explore each sense separately and in different combinations. Using your senses in this way reinvigorates the neural pathways and enables you to sense more completely.

Exercise

Whether you love to or hate to, you need exercise to build resilience. Why? Because exercise helps you discharge stress, generate energy, reduce fatigue, and increase endorphin levels (those natural opiates that ease pain and enhance well-being).

Aerobic exercise involves muscle movements that raise the heart rate by about 80 percent for periods of 15 minutes or longer. When done consistently, aerobic exercise speeds body metabolism, so your body converts food and oxygen to energy more quickly. Aerobically exercised muscles develop more *mitochondria* — those important cellular structures that, like tiny power plants, produce energy. The more mitochondria in your muscles, the more energy you produce, and the more energy and strength at your disposal.

Another important resilience-building aspect of aerobic exercise is that people who do work out regularly sleep more deeply and more consistently. Aerobic exercise helps your muscles relax while sleeping, encouraging better restoration of your body and mind.

Still another benefit is that aerobic exercise triggers a release of your body's own pain-reducing chemicals. You feel less pain and discomfort when exercising regularly. Aerobics and even milder forms of exercise have even been shown to have effective antide-pressant effects for people with mild-to-moderate depression.

Although everyone can do some form of aerobic exercise, slow walking is a good place to start. Combine the walk with an increase in observational skills. Check out architecture, birds, trees, and flowers. Pace yourself. You don't have to go all out at first. Your body will send you signals about when to get more intense. It is more important to first get consistent with every day or nearly every day exercise. Breathe. Focus on taking in more air and oxygen and feeling more alive.

Exercise boosts your self-esteem and mood — two items that need boosting when you're in recovery. Exercise helps you fight those low, painful moments when you're tempted to give in to your addictive urges.

Handling Your Everyday Fears

Worrying about yourself and your life (including the future) is a threat to your recovery. But worrying may also have a purpose in making you act more prudently. You must act to control your worry, however, because worrying about things you can't control is paralyzing.

The work of worry

Thinking of the future is smart. For example, saving money for retirement or for a rainy day is sensible. Doing so gives you flexibility and a certain control of your destiny.

Worry is part of thinking that allows humans to anticipate future negatives (associated with anxiety and low-level fear). Worry, if tied to a plan of future action, is healthy. But first you have to decide what you can and can't control.

The work of worry is best done in front of a piece of paper (or in today's world, a computer). Write down your biggest worries. Then go further; write down your smaller worries as well. Opposite each worry, make a note as to what you can do about it. (If you're honest with yourself, you'll recognize that you can't do anything about certain worries.) Keep a record. Then put the record away until the next day.

Worry for a maximum of 30 minutes a day. Don't do the worry work within three hours of going to sleep. Don't be afraid to ask for help. And remember that other people have had similar worries.

How Millie handles a very real worry

Millie was worried about getting a job. She had lost three years of her life in addiction. She thought that she would be judged as weak and fragile. She knew, though, that as part of her recovery, she needed to be honest and accept responsibility for her past actions.

Millie couldn't control how others judged her. However, she could control how she presented herself and her story. For example, at a job interview, if asked to explain a gap in her resume (due to her addiction), she could respond with a positive statement highlighting what skills she can bring to the job. She didn't need to drag herself through the mud. The job interview concerned how well she could do the job.

For instance, the interviewer asked her what happened after she worked in New York (the period she lost to addiction). Millie replied, "I hit a rough spot in my life and had to take time away from work. It's funny, though, during that tough time, I learned how strong I was. In this job, it sounds like I'm going to have to be very persistent. I'm willing to stay focused. I'm motivated and self-reliant."

Death and dying

You may or may not be surprised to discover that many people with addictions aren't particularly concerned about dying. These folks are often more concerned with the problems of living. Rather than a fear of death, they have a hatred of the pain and emptiness that living seems to bring. Their main need is to learn to live again.

Nevertheless, the fear of death and dying does play a major role in the lives of some who face addictions. The usual expression of this fear is a panic anxiety, a feeling of terror where almost everything feels out of control. At these times, the system producing adrenaline goes into overdrive, producing shakiness, shallow breathing, chest tightening, sweating, dizziness, and dry mouth. This experience may feel like a heart attack and can lead to a visit to the emergency room.

Fear of death may result in many different reactions — ranging from avoidance of risky activities to frequent, unnecessary visits to the doctor. If you do suffer from these kinds of fears, you may find it helpful to learn more about how these fears affect your thinking and behavior. You may also want to learn about the various ways of treating these fears. In Chapter 21, we provide resources that may help with a number of problems — including anxiety. You may also want to speak with your doctor about getting a referral to a mental health professional who can determine whether you have a panic disorder.

Abandonment

The fear of abandonment is fundamental to some people. Unlike monks living in cloistered monasteries, most people don't want to be left alone: No one likes to be rejected, and no one wants to be found wanting by another person.

The best ways to handle the fear of being abandoned are to:

- ✔ **Learn to appreciate your own company.** Learn to enjoy time to yourself where you can get to know yourself and can look after your own needs.

- ✔ **Take an active interest in others.** In particular, learn to listen actively.

- ✔ **Venture out.** Join groups, participate in activities, or find clubs or events that put you out in the world.

Handling Your Fears about Recovery

Giving up a habit is difficult, and addictions are especially well-engrained habits. You can usually come up with many reasons to stay the same and give in to your habits. But that giving in is probably your fear talking. You may need to bring your fears — both short-term and long-term — out into the open where you can clearly confront them.

Accepting your human qualities — your fallibilities and vulnerabilities — is key to an attitude of recovery.

Short-term fears: Withdrawal problems

As we detail in Chapter 10, some drugs are relatively easy to quit, but others are more difficult. If you've gone through a withdrawal process, you may have acquired a learned fear of the pain and discomfort related to withdrawal. Thus, if you've relapsed and are contemplating getting back on track with recovery, one fear that may stand in your way is the fear of going through withdrawal again.

The opiates are usually a withdrawal challenge. Some say withdrawal feels like a bad flu; others say it's like an agonizing sickness. Whatever the experience, the fear of these symptoms, much like fear of dental procedures, has to be confronted and managed. Good medical care helps. But the fear must be brought out into the open and confronted with an experienced counselor or guide.

Long-term fears

Recovery is a marathon, a protracted effort in changing your way of living. In the long run, you must change your basic attitude toward addictive behavior and build up your coping skills. You have to confront your emotions or even a curious *lack* of feeling, which is often the cover of an emotion that is suppressed.

Boredom

Boredom, which can be described as the emptiness that's sometimes experienced when you've been stressed for a long time and are close to exhaustion, is a risk factor for relapse. Boredom can occur when you've experienced either insufficient stimulation or too much. You may feel bored when life feels humdrum, especially after a period of hard partying that is now completely over. In any case, the fear of boredom can take many forms including a feeling of disgust about boredom — hating the feeling that life is empty.

Discomfort

Some addictions start with physical pain (as a result of injury or congenital defects). The discomfort that you have to endure, particularly with chronic pain, may result in the dependence on painkillers (opiates, analgesics). If you overcome this dependence, you may be left with having to tolerate the pain all over again, and you may fear this possibility. Fear is usually a powerful motivator, particularly when combined with pain. But fear of pain can be brought out into the open and confronted.

Helplessness

Helplessness is a psychological condition in which you believe that *no matter what you do,* desired outcomes (good job, loving spouse, nice kids, nice possessions) will never happen. A state of helplessness follows when you consistently try to avoid negative outcomes, like pain, and yet every effort you make at avoidance fails. Eventually, you just want to give up. Any state of helplessness or futility, particularly if prolonged, is a risk to your recovery.

Sometimes, the antidote to helplessness is vigorous activity. Sometimes the antidote is *to give in* to simply experiencing the feelings of futility until you discover some alternative feelings rising to the surface. Then follow these alternatives — they usually point you in the right direction.

Avoiding Self-Hate: A Slippery Slope to Relapse

You may have heard people talk about the slippery slope to relapse. This phenomenon refers to the tendency to slide back into old behavior patterns. Those patterns, in turn, start a bigger, faster slide back into addictive behavior. Self-hate is one kind of slippery slope where a threat to your recovery begins with negative thinking. If you continue to dislike and despise yourself for past behavior, you become more vulnerable to relapse.

To challenge negative thinking, start with an inventory of your strengths and weaknesses. Focus on your skills and behavior, not on your personality. Watch for labels (stupid, ugly, unlovable, loser) and get rid of these descriptors from your language.

Next, engage in activities that boost your self-esteem. Exercise, play your favorite musical instrument, write a letter — do something just for *you* that also makes you feel like you've accomplished something, no matter how small. Focus on the fact that you've been successful at something! Success is an important antidote to feelings of unworthiness.

Or perform some service that benefits others. Humans are social beings who benefit from community. When you give, you get feedback from those who have received, and you feel good. When you feel good, particularly if you let it sink in deeply, you have more confidence and determination to overcome the barriers to your recovery.

The classic question is "What does a person have to do to feel worthwhile?" We reply: Feeling worthy is natural. All newborns have value — you never lose it, you simply cover it over. Find the sources of your self-hate and clear them away.

You may think that you have to be loved by someone else in order to feel good. The fact is that others don't have to love you for you to love yourself. You must start with an acceptance of yourself. Accept your fallibility; accept that you aren't perfect and will make mistakes. Accept that you must forgive yourself for past mistakes, while at the same time accepting responsibility for them. Seek the advice and opinion of others who give you honest feedback. Forgiveness evolves with honest, open communication among people who care — whether they're professional counselors, friends and loved ones, or caregivers.

Some people consider payment for treatment or therapy as a kind of paid friendship. But therapy *isn't* friendship. It's an honest communication where people examine their core beliefs and feelings in the ongoing situations of their lives. Therapy can help you uncover and release the layers of self-hate to find true self-acceptance. Seeing the lovable bits within yourself can feel at first like a tiny flame, a flickering light that is elusive, fleeting, and tenuous. In time, this light will strengthen. It will become something you can turn to for solace and inspiration.

Putting judgments on hold

One established technique to challenge self-hate is to put all judgments about yourself and others on hold. Stop the shoulds (I should have done this; he shouldn't have done that). Playing "the should game" is a genuine waste of your time. Instead, look for the root cause of the behavior — the thinking and the feeling behind it. Listen to yourself and try to understand, rather than judge and label. So if you're thinking, "Look at her, she's such a loser; she cries at weddings," you may want to consider rephrasing your thoughts to "She cries at weddings; I wonder what feelings she may be experiencing and why?"

Recognizing negative moods

Negative moods and feelings are a normal part of life. No one is perfect, and if people act like they are, watch out. If you learn to recognize your feelings, you can use them to understand what's important to you. When you feel happy, you know what you're like. When you feel sad, you can understand what is hurting you by tracing that sadness to its origins. At any one time, you can describe your feelings (in other words, your moods or emotions). Feelings include happiness, sadness, anger, tension, anxiety, guilt, and many others. Recognizing your negative moods is an important skill to learn because these moods may trigger relapse.

So assume that you have normal human emotions. And remember, if you want to understand your feelings, you also need to pay attention to your thinking — that is, to the statements and images that occupy your mind.

Assessing your sadness

Sadness isn't clinical depression but rather a mood state. You may feel low, down, tearful, and unhappy. The cognitive theme associated with sadness is loss; something important is missing. You know when you're feeling sad because you have an empty feeling in the pit of your stomach and an "ache" in your heart and chest.

Assessing your anxiety

Anxiety is a complex mood state associated with feelings of threat. Something is threatening your world — you perceive a danger. The feelings are tension, worry, and agitation. You may be sweating or trembling, and you may feel your heart beating rapidly.

Assessing your anger

Anger is a protective mood. It can protect you from a perceived or a real assault. This assault may not be physical. It may be an attack on your pride or character. If you feel angry, you may be on the attack, yourself, or you may be defensive (hurt and pouting; what we call *passive-aggressive*). Two primary themes are associated with anger states. The first is frustration, when you're blocked from achieving a goal or deprived of an important need. (Animals get very frustrated when blocked from their food dishes.) The second is resentment, the sense that you're being treated unfairly, when something is unjust or not right. Anger feelings may include hostility, outrage, and the old favorite, just being mad. Usually you "don't want to talk about it" — but talking about it is good.

Assessing your guilt and shame

Guilt and shame mood states are complex. Shame is defined by your morals and social group and is associated with letting yourself and your social group down. Guilt typically occurs when you have violated a standard or an expectation. These expectations may be based on your family's beliefs or the code of a social institution (church, school). With shame, you feel humiliated; with guilt, you feel embarrassed. A court of law can find you guilty. Your family and your neighbors may judge your actions as shameful.

Recognizing stressful situations

Stress undermines your commitment to recovery. Your resources to counteract stress aren't unlimited, so having to deal with a lot of stress in your life takes energy away from dealing with overcoming your addiction. Thus, dealing with stress as quickly and thoroughly as possible is very important.

Check out the resources in Chapter 21 to assess your stress level.

Stress is a term used to describe times when events, either internal (expectations and disappointments) or external (job loss or separations), tax or exceed the person's ability to cope with them. No one can avoid stress, and some stressors actually provide you with a challenge that you may enjoy (the good stress or *eustress*). For example, crowding can be stressful, especially if you hate being in that situation, but on a crowded dance floor, it may be fun.

Felix and Felicia

Felix knew that no one cared for him. Since he was a young boy, he had been neglected and spent most of his time alone. He wanted to be close to his mom, but she was never there for him. Later in his life, Felix was thrilled to meet Felicia. She was incredible. But Felix just couldn't commit to a relationship with Felicia because he couldn't see what his girlfriend saw in him. He wanted to be married but if he married, he knew it wouldn't last.

Felix hated being alone but when Felicia comforted him, he felt "too needy" and asked her to leave. In fact, he kicked her out, often precipitating an argument based on his jealousy. Felix was in conflict. He wanted to commit to Felicia but instead rejected her. A comedian once quipped that he would never want to join a club that would have him as a member. Felix didn't get the joke; he lived it.

Felicia decided that she was ending it with Felix. They had been dating for four years, and he backed off whenever she mentioned the future. She spoke with her therapist. She had to move on. She ended it.

Felix said "Fine, I knew you'd leave me eventually. I never loved you." He was in agony. The only thing that seemed to help was getting loaded. He had to numb the pain. He cried. He was depressed. He developed a serious drug dependency.

The couple attended couples counseling. Felix learned about his pattern of rejecting Felicia because he felt angry (really self-hating) when he was dependent. He learned that at these times he was going against a silent rule that he had given himself when he was a child ("I'll never depend on anyone but myself"). Felicia learned to give Felix some space and let him work out his conflict rather than getting angry and hurt, which just reinforced his resolve not to commit. On the addiction side, Felix realized that he was using alcohol to cope but also to anger Felicia so that she would reject him (a self-fulfilling prophecy). Felix had to deal with his drinking first and then expose himself to some painful therapy experiences. He did it, and we're proud of him (so is Felicia).

If you're under chronic stress, then you're at risk in your recovery, and you have to deal with that risk as soon as possible. Many ways and many teachers can help you deal with stress. In Chapter 21, we provide some links to stress management resources.

Taking Action: Storming the Barricades

There comes a time when you let your actions speak. No more talking, no more excuses, no more delay. The time to take action has arrived.

Taking action to commit to change

Commitment is an interesting concept to talk about, but what does it really mean? To *commit* means to take a stand, to be counted, to say what you believe and what you want. If you want to change, the producers of Nike sporting equipment tell us to "Just Do It." But it isn't that easy. It's better to say: "Stay the course." Don't waver in your willingness to change your life. Know that you'll encounter many, many challenges but only one final pathway. The pathway to change your addictive behavior, to change the course of your life, is right in front of you. If you waver (and you almost certainly will), recommit to the change, learn from the mistakes — and get back on course.

Taking action against triggers that increase cravings

What are the triggers that increase your craving? Say that your worst trigger is that uncomfortable feeling when you're trying to impress a new group, trying to fit in. They want to party, and you know that you would love to join them. But you also know that being with that group will expose you, will tempt you, to take coke. (For more on triggers, turn to Chapter 7.)

So you need to take action! Can you afford to go to the party as a clean-and-sober person, and increase your risk of addictive behavior? The answer to this question is highly personal. One thing is clear — you must counter the *cravings,* those stimuli that set off the urge to engage in addictive behavior.

Ultimately, you need to discover the ways to counter cravings that work best for you. Here are some tips to get you started:

- ✔ Drink water when feeling the acute urge to get a hit or a drink. Cravings are time limited.

- ✔ Remind yourself of all the personally meaningful reasons why you started your course of recovery.

- ✔ Remind yourself of all the effort you've made and the success you've had in your recovery.

- ✔ Find healthy ways to counteract negative mood states (see information later in this chapter).

- ✔ Be prepared to leave the risky situation promptly.

When in doubt, stay away. If you go, be prepared to leave immediately. If you leave, be prepared to call your support system.

Taking action to build self-confidence

How do you improve self-confidence? Where does it come from? *Self-confidence* refers to your self-perceived ability to handle situations, to achieve your goals, and to manage the tough situations in life.

Confidence in life starts with a sense of pleasure, looking after basic needs such as nurturance, achievement, and affection.

When you were a baby or a small child, how could you look after these needs yourself? You couldn't control those things. Many factors influence the nurturance and security you felt as a child, including your parents' skills and abilities in caring for you. Psychological research shows that beyond basic needs for food, a baby's attachment to his mother is a critical aspect of development. During these early years, you learn many things, including how to comfort and soothe yourself. No one can pick or control his or her caregivers during these early years. Your parents were what they were, you can't change that now, so consider forgiving them for their errors and forgiving yourself. Forgiveness helps release you to move ahead in your recovery.

For more information on the influence of the early years on later development, go to http://imaginewhatif.com/Pages/Mustard.html and read about the impact of early development on later illness.

Self-confidence as a youth and adult depends on competencies (as well as appearance, but we won't go there right now). You want to build skills and competencies so that you can handle different situations you will encounter in life, perhaps even caring for others. (Now that's a scary thought; being responsible for another human being — or a pet.)

This learning and skill building can be lifelong, so it's conceivable that the older you get, the more self-confident you are. Maybe that's why seniors seem to know it all — maybe they do!

To build self-confidence, quiet your internal critic, because self-criticism and perfectionism are destructive. Then begin building your skills and knowledge in most any area and you start to feel better about who you are.

Taking action against negative moods

Experiencing negative moods isn't bad. In some ways, negative moods make us feel real, but nevertheless they're unpleasant. As a result, we don't want you to stay in a negative mood state for too long (more than a day or two).

Use your moods to help understand yourself. Find those cognitive themes (the thinking associated with your negative moods) and determine how true they really are in this situation. If you feel sad, think about a sense of loss or disappointment that you may have experienced. If you're anxious, think of what is threatening you and figure out where the danger is, including the danger to your self-esteem. Try to take advantage of the negative mood (what a concept!) and view it as if it were a shadow — that is, a momentary darkness to a positive mood when the sun isn't shining. What could that positive mood be? Think deeply and be honest with yourself. Don't accept the idea that you're thinking about nothing.

When feeling a negative mood, ask yourself: What does this say about me, my future, the world? Next, consider how true your responses are. Here are some questions to help you judge the validity of your thoughts:

✔ What would I think of (insert the name of your best friend) if he had this experience?

✔ Are there alternative ways of thinking about the situation?

✔ If (insert name of your best friend) said this to me, what would I say to help her get perspective?

✔ Am I jumping to a conclusion without much evidence to base it on?

✔ Am I magnifying the consequences of the event?

✔ Am I trying to predict the future?

One in five people who suffer from an addiction also have a mood or anxiety disorder. Don't hesitate to seek professional advice.

Chapter 16

Handling Slips and Relapse

· ·

In This Chapter

▶ Seeing the difference between a slip and a relapse

▶ Understanding relapses

▶ Examining and understanding your relapse tendencies

▶ Preventing relapse by restoring balance in your life

· ·

*T*he fundamental feature of relapse is that you cycle backward toward addictive behavior despite your best intentions. Relapse isn't rational. It happens when emotions dominate. You're driven by *conditioned responses* (learned responses triggered by certain events) that dominate your rationality. These conditioned responses dominate because you don't take the preparations and precautions that can bring them under control.

In this chapter, we tell you how to differentiate between relapses and slips. We tell you what you can learn from these pauses on your journey and we give you some tips on getting your balance back after a relapse.

Slips Versus Relapse: What's the Difference?

When you're in recovery but decide to resume an addictive behavior, you slip or relapse. For example, we receive many calls right after clients have taken a first drink (or joint or hit). A *slip* is when you fall back into the addictive behavior for a short period and then get back on track, working on your recovery. A *relapse* is when you return to the addictive behavior, and immediately slide back to the same level where you left off. (For example, if you're addicted to alcohol, your drinking levels may go right back to the destructive levels you were experiencing before treatment or before you quit.)

Alan Marlatt, an expert in relapse prevention, describes the key to the transition from slip to relapse as hinging on the perception of your first use. If you see the use as the start of a binge or a run, you may be willing to make the call for support. If you don't see the slip as the start of a potential relapse, you tend not to make the call for backup. Without support, the second and third use can lead to the one-hundredth use.

Aftercare plays a critical role in long-term recovery. In a recent four-year follow-up study from the Caron Foundation, more than 60 percent of clients who regularly attended some form of aftercare following treatment remained abstinent from drug or alcohol use, compared with 40 percent of clients who attended sporadically, and 30 percent of those who didn't attend aftercare at all.

Why Relapse Happens

Why does relapse occur? Typically, your thinking starts to drift away from recovery, and the urge to behave in an addictive way takes hold. You may lose sight of your recovery goal. You may not be getting much pleasure or satisfaction from your life, or stressors may begin to build up. You know that every day you have to do some work on recovery, but working isn't easy.

You can almost count on it

Relapse is alarmingly common, although not inevitable. We know of several people who hit a stage in their lives where they stopped and didn't go back. (At least, so far — 20 to 30 years later.) These people emphasized their *choice* in recovery. They *decided* not to engage in the pattern of addictive behavior. Nevertheless, the unfortunate fact is that most people in recovery do relapse at least once.

Relapse rates for alcohol and drug addiction range from 50 percent for resumption of heavy use to 90 percent for brief slips. These rates for addictive diseases don't differ significantly from rates for other chronic diseases.

Without being too fatalistic, relapse is best viewed as a probable learning event during recovery. When you relapse, you're at great risk for regression or even dying via overdose, so manage the event very carefully. How can you quickly limit relapse and minimize its impact? Ask yourself, "How quickly will I get back on the path to recovery?"

Triggers for relapse and what to do about them

Early in the process of recovery, many triggers are tied to old associations with friends, addictive situations (bars, parties, casinos), and paraphernalia (a pipe, a racing form, music). The media is a powerful trigger because addictive behaviors are often portrayed as desirable. For example, the party scene in some commercials combines sex, being cool, being free, and being wild . . . all in 30 seconds.

Be aware that a particular smell, sound, or image can set off your urges. Be aware that urges can be set off suddenly (in a "flash") and powerfully. As fast as information can be processed in your brain, an urge can be triggered.

Urges and cravings are linked, for the most part, to *subcortical brain processes* that involve little thinking on your part, but still exert powerful influences on you. Because you don't think *about* these processes, they're difficult to counteract and tend to dominate your mind. This very domination of your thinking can drive you to a relapse.

To counteract urges, you may have to do something that radically alters your experience at both cortical (thinking level) and subcortical levels (nonthinking level). For example, intense physical exercise can counteract the power of the subcortical messages that comprise urges. Other methods to counteract urges include taking a very cold shower or treating yourself to a pleasurable, nonaddictive experience, like a deep massage or an excellent meal. The more able you are to direct your experience away from the addictive urges, the more you gradually weaken the conditioning underlying the urges.

How do you avoid these relapse triggers? For a start, learn how to deal with the trigger after it is set off. Resolve that when the trigger hits you (for example, the smell of alcohol, seeing a casino ad, being at a party), you will talk about it to a trusted person. Get away from the trigger if you can (yes, leaving the party is better than relapsing). Focus on your recovery goal and think about the changes in your life since you've started your recovery. Call another trusted person to talk about your experience. (The sponsors you connect with by joining twelve-step and other support groups for recovery can be very helpful.)

Some of the most difficult triggers are the ones that are most internalized, often associated with emotional blind spots and automatic thinking (sometimes known, in AA circles, as *stinking thinking*). In other words, the thinking that you haven't really challenged (for one reason or another) can often be the most troublesome. Stinking thinking can set off a slip or relapse by creating a certain momentum in your thoughts.

High-risk situations and their remedies

Most relapses are associated with four high-risk situations. The situations include times when you feel the following:

- **Frustration and anger:** Anger and the sense of deprivation that's often associated with it can be the drivers for rebellion and relapse. You may think, "I don't care anymore," or "I deserve it after what I've been through." Resentment and self-pity fall into this category. Thoughts like "Why me? Why can't I control it?" may rear their ugly heads.

  You can't afford to dwell on this type of thinking, because you can't control it. Call someone and discuss your feelings. Remember that you can feel lousy without having to go back to your addiction. Feelings will pass. Sometimes you can deal with them directly.

- **Social pressures and demands:** Social pressure and demands can be subtler: We're all social beings and respond to the pack. Sometimes, returning to the demands of life (and specifically your roles in life — mother, worker, executive, rock star) creates a chronically stressful situation.

  You may need some advice on how to cope with your roles. Find out how other people who've been in the same boat coped. Look for ways to change unmanageable stressors, and if you're overwhelmed in your role, find an alternative. Recovery is the primary concern now.

- **Interpersonal temptation:** The interpersonal temptations are very risky. New relationships may bring challenges, like when someone says, "Ahhh, come on, just have one." For someone on a recovery path of abstinence, "just one" may set off a run.

You may want to be a normal drinker, user, and so on, but it just doesn't work that way. A good friend of ours once described his response to the interpersonal pressures we're talking about. He said, "Yeah, I'd love to have a drink with you. But you know, I wouldn't stop with one, and even if I did stop, the next day I'd want another one. Pretty soon, I'd be lying around my house with a needle in my arm." In these situations, you may just have to be blunt and honest. But start with "No, I don't drink, use, gamble, or do that."

✔ **Feeling great:** How, you ask, can feeling good lead to relapse? Many people with an addiction admit that feeling great lulls them into a false sense of security. When you're feeling particularly good, you can deceive yourself that you're strong enough to taste your addictive behavior just once again — for fun.

Be aware that you're playing with fire. Few experiences of well-being can withstand the pressure of addictive urges, after they're restimulated with use. Your confidence level when things are going well may be high, but the risk for relapse doesn't go away.

The good news: Relapse is preventable

A relapse-prevention approach helps you develop a profile of past use behaviors and current expectations about high-risk situations. The first task is to study these risky situations and to understand how certain thoughts and feelings may precede the actions of getting into the risky situation. Controlling these thoughts and feelings is very important. Always have a plan to call for support. And preferably, have two or three people to call.

 It may be useful to think of a craving for addictive behavior as similar to hunger. The only difference is that hunger is natural, and your entire biology centers on getting adequate nutrition. An addictive craving isn't natural; therefore, it will fade into the background if managed correctly.

Learning from Relapse

To begin to avoid relapse, you must develop understanding of why you relapse, a willingness to avoid triggers, and an acceptance of both the positive and the negative consequences of your actions.

Examining your relapse

To learn anything meaningful from a relapse, you have to dig deep into your psyche and get brutally honest with yourself. Put on your detective hat and ask these questions of yourself:

- ✔ **Who?** The who is easy, just look in the mirror. But be aware that "you" change under different conditions.

- ✔ **What?** What did you actually do? Be specific. Only describe your behavior.

- ✔ **When?** When did you do it? Describe the timeline and plot it out just as you would if writing a script.

- ✔ **Where?** Where did these behaviors occur? Describe the situation in as much detail as needed.

- ✔ **Why?** Now, this is a tough one. Be honest and dig deep.

Write your responses down. Writing has the effect of slowing your mind, allowing you to think more clearly and with more emotional connection.

When answering these questions, describe your inner thoughts, your feelings, and, most importantly, your motivations. Great directors of film, sales people, psychologists, and detectives know how to find the person's motivation. *You* have to find your own.

Doing things differently next time

How can you prevent future relapses? Focus on the skills you need to develop or refine to gain a greater sense of self-confidence and self-control in future situations. These skills include figuring out how to limit or abstain from your addictive behavior, how to combat urges and cravings, how to relax, and learning to effectively deal with the underlying emotional issues that make you vulnerable to relapse. (We discuss these skills more in Chapter 15.)

Gary's relapse story

Gary relapsed after six years of being clean and sober. He went on a self-destructive binge that lasted weeks. We had to let him go and work on protecting his family, his friends, and, if possible, his assets.

Gary finally made contact. He was sheepish but quick to react with resentment. Gary hated being controlled. He hated being dependent. He refused to knuckle under. He wasn't going to make an excuse.

Gary said, "I relapsed. I don't know why." That was it. No excuses. What was surprising was the anger that his lack of explanation generated. Everyone who loved him wanted an explanation. "He owes us an explanation! He's so self-centered. He doesn't even care enough to make an excuse."

Gary agreed to examine his relapse. He answered the same questions we present in the "Examining your relapse" section. His responses follow:

✔ **Who?** Me — I accept responsibility. No one else was to blame. I'm tired of blaming everybody and everything for my binges.

✔ **What?** Started out at my old local bar. I don't know why. [Therapist note: Gary leaves the whys for later. They get in the way. Just give us the facts.] Left after two drinks. Went to the strip club. Drank heavily. Talked with girls. Met X — very nice, kind. Used cocaine — can't remember any more what happened after that. Came to in a seedy motel near the airport. No money.

✔ **When?** At 3 p.m. started out at my old local bar. Left at 3:30 p.m. after two drinks. At 4 p.m. went to the strip club. Drank heavily. Talked with girls. At 8 p.m. used cocaine. At 10 a.m. came to in a seedy motel near the airport.

✔ **Where?** My old local bar — I knew not to go there — so stupid [Therapist note: No labels necessary — they block the discovery process]

✔ **Why?** Why did I go? I was bored, pissed, happy — you pick one! [Therapist note: We get the sarcasm but listen to the feelings. Start with pissed.]

Gary had ten or so people who he could have called when he had the urge to drink. But he didn't make the call. ("I didn't want to bother anyone.") The reality was that Gary refused to call. He was angry (the number one reason for relapse is anger), and he didn't want any interference.

Digging into the anger, we were surprised: Gary had been flirting with a young server at a local restaurant for months. On the eventful day, he was feeling great. He had made some money and he went to the restaurant. He finally got up the courage to ask her out, and she turned him down flat. Ouch. Gary went to the bar and started his binge.

To block his tendency to go back to his local bar, Gary went by and spoke to the owner when he was sober (compulsive gamblers also take this step with casinos). He took responsibility for his actions by asking them to refuse to serve him the next time. The owner told Gary that he would help. He asked if he could call the police if Gary wouldn't leave, and Gary said yes.

Getting Your Balance Back

We say it again: Relapse is part of recovery. And relapse prevention is hard work but achievable. Slips are easier to manage than relapses — so catch the slips when they're still slips. Get help as soon as you need it. Assume you need help rather than trying to go it alone.

The severity of your addictive behavior is an important factor here. If your past severity of addictive behavior was high, you have a greater need for multiple, powerful approaches to relapse prevention.

Medications may help

A few medications may help reduce your cravings. The SSRI drugs are the most commonly used. Disulfiram (antabuse) for alcohol abuse, methadone for heroin dependence, and naltrexone for alcohol abuse (but not for opiate dependence) will be considered by your physician if you ask. (See Chapter 10 for more on helpful medications.)

Getting back on track

Okay, you've relapsed. Now, what? What are the next steps? What should you do?

- ✔ Go to a meeting. Call your support system. Be honest, open to feedback, willing to change. Just do it.
- ✔ If you get hopeless (for whatever reason), get help immediately!

What's going to keep you on the straight and narrow?

- ✔ Go to a meeting. Call your support system. Be honest, open to feedback, and willing to change. Just do it.
- ✔ If you get hopeless (for whatever reason), get help immediately!

(The repetition here is intended. This advice is critically important, and we want to emphasize it.)

Deciding whether you need some extra help

How do you know if you need extra help? If you agree with any of the following statements, get help:

- ✔ Your program just isn't working.

- ✔ You are starting to white-knuckle your sobriety. In other words, you've recently survived several near misses of relapses or slips.

- ✔ You tried to control the behavior but before long, you were right back at it.

- ✔ You feel like giving up and packing it in.

- ✔ You've just heard some shocking news. You can't believe it.

Chapter 17

Handling Work and Family During Recovery

. . . .

In This Chapter

▶ Dealing with relationship problems

▶ Solving family problems

▶ Making sense of work problems

▶ Dealing with financial difficulties

▶ Looking at relapses

. . . .

During your recovery, life doesn't stand still. You may have to address problems at work, struggle to maintain personal relationships, and, of course, confront family issues. In this chapter, we offer advice in these areas. We also discuss how families are affected by addiction. Addiction is a family disease, and no one escapes the effects.

Our basic point, throughout this chapter, is that when you start treatment, new relationships begin with your family and friends. You're finding out how to deal with problems in a different and better way. The key issue in relating to your family's problems is that the best help you can give them starts with you staying in treatment.

You have taken the lead in admitting your problem and getting into treatment. In the course of treatment, you will progress by admitting and solving more problems.

 Treatment fundamentally reverses the addictive process for you and your family. You learn to trade the unnatural highs of addiction for the natural highs of good relationships. It's a worthwhile trade; the best trade you can make.

Dealing with Relationships During Recovery

When you finally commit yourself to treatment, everyone you know seems relieved. They're behind you and give you all the support you need. But it doesn't remain so simple for long. The changes you make, as you progress in treatment, cause further changes in your family and friends.

For more than 50 years, psychologists and psychiatrists have tried to understand how families and close relationships work. During this time, one thing has become increasingly clear. Every member of a family reacts to every other member. Some of your family's changes may be surprising. In this chapter, we help you prepare.

Dealing with positive changes

Although some positive changes may be welcome, some may be hard to accept. In order to accept them more readily, you must trace back how you have affected your family in the past.

While you were in the grip of addiction, your family was under tremendous pressure. When you're in treatment, however, this pressure on your family reduces. As a result, everyone may seem more lively and happy. If you're away from home (in residential treatment somewhere), you may feel that your family is better off without you — a lonely feeling.

The bottom line is that others may seem relieved after you enter treatment. Be aware that your loved ones' positive, relieved responses — reactions to not having to worry about you so much — may kick off resentments in you. Rather than act on the resentment, watch yourself. Watch for any behavior on your part that could bring your family down. Also beware of adopting the attitude of "I'm suffering, so they should suffer." Instead, accept the effects of your formerly addictive behavior on your family — it was bringing them down.

Rarely are your family members and friends better off without you, if you stay clean. What you're seeing is that when you're under better control, they're happier. When you get healthier by accepting treatment and staying clean, they get healthier as well. After you see this calmly and clearly, you realize that these are very positive chain reactions.

Dealing with negative changes

You may be surprised to hear that after you start treatment you may have to deal with negative changes as well. Why? Remember that each family member (or each person in a close relationship) is causing reactions in the other(s). Sometimes, your addiction causes the people around you to curb their wilder behaviors. When you get into treatment, there's a reduction in pressure that can cause them to lose it and get wilder. Instead of doing healthier stuff, they act out and do riskier stuff.

For instance, say your addictive actions caused your son to curb his wilder actions. Now he may feel it's his turn to walk on the wild side. Rather than learning from your positive actions, he may try out his version of your former wildness. Remember that this wild behavior is your son's attempt to find balance. He's not trying to mess things up — he's trying to make sense of what feels messed up to him.

You can't expect those close to you to become saints just because you've made positive changes. You must be ready to tolerate their bad behavior just like they tolerated your bad behavior. This tolerance doesn't mean you should encourage bad behavior, just don't expect your family to be perfect.

Case study: The Macademus family

No one could figure out what was going on with the five Macademus children: Joe (16), Angela (14), Christina (13), Lucy (11), and Josephine (7) were all unusual kids. They kept to themselves, never had guests over, and seemed to be seething with resentment much of the time. Even little Josephine got in trouble in first grade. What was up with these kids?

The parents, Chris and Jackie, seemed quite normal. They were frequently at work and weren't home much, but that wasn't that unusual. Finally, Angela called her teacher a name (XX###&&@@OO!!) and stomped out of class. The teacher went to the principal, and they arranged a meeting with Chris and Jackie.

The parents maintained that nothing was wrong. Everything was fine. But just two weeks later the same meeting was reenacted because each one of the Macademus kids was now acting out — all in the span of one week.

At the second meeting, under the increased demand for straight answers, the true story came out. Mrs. Macademus had an addiction problem — and she had just completed her first ten-day inpatient program. The kids were having trouble coping with her absence. This important turn in her battle against addiction was difficult for them to tolerate.

Dealing with Family Problems

In dealing with family problems while in treatment, remember the one thing that helps your family most: staying in treatment.

As you progress with recovery, you get stronger and better able to help members of your family make changes that are healthy for them. During earlier treatment phases, however, you may have to pace yourself. You can help only up to a certain limit. That limit is defined by being able to continue the thing that helps most: namely, staying in treatment. Any situation that threatens treatment must be dealt with in a way that deepens commitment to, and involvement in, treatment.

Your counseling relationship should help with many of your family problems. Given your past use and abuse, your family will inevitably have problems. Even if you've taken pride in keeping your addicted life separate from the family, at some level they've felt the effect of your problems. Kids and spouses have intimate radars that pick up what's happening, even without understanding any details. They often sense that something isn't right — although they may not know that what they're sensing is your addiction problem.

Furthermore, all families inevitably have problems. Whether you feel your family's problems are related to addiction or not, you sometimes get emotionally upset by them. You will probably be more sensitive than before to these problems, and you will need to figure out how to deal with them in a more effective way.

 In your counseling, you must disclose family problems. Disclosure is the first step toward solutions and to understanding how your progress contributes to the progress of each and every family member. If you don't feel you can share family problems with your counselor, think about finding a different counselor. Family problems are very, very important to your treatment progress.

Do the right thing: Be a good role model

The most important part of your treatment, in family terms, is your role modeling. By doing the right thing, you exert pressure on your family members to do the right thing. Of course, your treatment and recovery help you better understand what happened when you were failing to do the right thing — when you were addicted.

You were negatively role modeling. Now that you've reversed directions, you'll see the difference. And what a difference you can continue to make on each and every day by moving further in the right direction.

How families are affected by addiction

Families affected by addiction have similar problems in dealing with the truth. In summary, families of addicts have the following two problems:

- ✔ Often, a lot of energy is spent denying troubling realities.

- ✔ Frequently, related attempts are made to present an ideal family image to the outside world. Or, at least, an image that is much better than how things really are.

Both characteristics need not be present: Some families are more dominated by denial, others by efforts to present ideal images.

Regardless of which characteristic dominates more, solutions involve openly disclosing problems while letting go of ideal images. You've taken the lead in admitting your problem and getting treatment. In the course of treatment, your progress will depend on admitting to even more of your problems. The simple truth is you admit to having problems before you can solve them. Admitting problems takes courage.

The process of admitting problems is easier to agree to than to follow through on. Your self-esteem and self-respect feel compromised when disclosing shortcomings. You feel humbled. But remember that feeling ashamed is part of the process. These initial feelings fade, and you eventually have a stronger sense of self-esteem because you rebuild your self-respect on a solid foundation.

Being in treatment gets you ready to view yourself and your family with your eyes fully open. Admitting to problems is tough, but try to focus on the good feeling of building a foundation of truth beneath you. The added good feeling is that you're helping to build that same firm foundation under your family members as well.

An old recovery phrase that may help you keep perspective is "Progress not perfection." When applied to living within a family, it means dropping ideas about being the perfect parent, brother, or husband and humbly acting in support of the better way. This humility also places more emphasis on how you behave and less emphasis on what you demand from your family. Whatever you do demand from them, be sure that you have demanded it from yourself first.

Making positive changes in family relationships

Family members always react to each other. The degree varies, but reactions and counter-reactions go on continually. They go on so much, in fact, that we take them for granted. We develop hard and fast expectations that a particular family member *always* reacts in a certain way. What we don't realize is that our hard and fast expectations influence family members to keep reacting in the same old way.

The important point is that positive changes happen in families when we drop expectations and observe real reactions. Change happens when people do things differently — even small things. If we observe closely, we can rearrange situations to induce the small changes that add up to major, significant changes.

The trickiest part, however, is choosing where to direct efforts — selecting which behavior you should persuade someone to change. Naturally, the more the behavior you want changed matches a behavior the person feels should change, the more your efforts meet his motivations. Clearly identifying where this match will occur makes a key difference.

Families with addicted members tend to deny certain realities while upholding the ideal family image. Engaging in positive change involves reversing this: dropping the denial and acknowledging problems — dropping the ideals and embracing realities.

Originally, the family denial patterns probably related to your addictive behavior. Efforts were made within the family to deny your addiction — just as you tried to keep it secret. But these patterns eventually go beyond the abuse and include other situations. Now you need to change your family's norms by addressing the problems previously avoided.

Solving family problems by changing norms

All people and all families keep track of certain *norms* (the ways things usually happen). Norms exist in every family — some norms are healthier, some are less so. To create positive changes, you need to induce small changes and have them happen consistently so that new, positive norms get established.

By being in treatment, for example, you establish a new norm that says it's okay to seek and find counseling assistance. The new norm begins with you finding your way to good counseling. Then, your example and your positive experiences give you leverage to suggest help to others.

The same is true for the norm of talking through problems honestly and thoroughly without pretending that something doesn't bother you (when it does) or that an issue is unimportant (when it's important to you). Your counseling relationship helps you prioritize the issues that are most important for you to address with family members and choose what strategies to use when bringing up issues. These strategies help you communicate in the ways that are the most likely to be positively received. Try to maximize positive responses while minimizing defensiveness.

Bring up issues at a pace so that they can be dealt with effectively and with enough accompanying positive regard that each person is reassured of love and respect. Only so many issues can be raised at any given time. If too many issues are raised, people get flooded with anxiety or react depressively rather than positively. Remember, you're asking for someone to change, so when you bring up too much all at once, your loved one may experience your comments as a critical rejection.

Making long-term plans for positive change

If the best approach to change involves some pacing (and we think it does), then a long-range plan for change is helpful. This plan ensures that you don't try going too far, too fast. It also acts as a reminder so that you don't let opportunities for change slip by.

Expect meaningful change within intimate relationships to take about one year. A long-term plan often involves determining what changes you want to make during a six-month or one-year time span. Eventually, the long-term plan takes the place of the ideal family image that members once aspired to protecting. Rather than trying to protect a fantasized image, there is systematic movement toward a positive goal.

In your long-term plan, give consideration to the balanced use of family resources. In some families, each spouse may feel he or she is carrying the greater load of family responsibilities. But a true equalization of responsibilities can take time to arrange, because outside factors may be involved — like jobs, work hours, training programs, or a move of the entire family.

In any case, after family members commit themselves to a dynamic model of change rather than a denial-based stagnation, you need to work together on plans for change that unfold over reasonable time periods and progress toward goals supported and understood by all family members.

All of these changes involve movement from an imbalanced power structure, where decisions are made by and favor just a few members, to a more representative structure where each member is given an equal opportunity for personal development.

Dealing with Work Problems

If you're one of the providers for your family, any work problems for you (while in treatment) immediately affect your family. This brings work issues into the recovery picture.

Scenario one: You were hardworking to begin with

Many extremely hard-working and productive people become addicted. If this is true of you, then your addiction problems perhaps began with, or were linked to, a type of work addiction. In other words, some version of chronic overwork may have contributed to your developing another life; the life of a drug, alcohol, or behavioral addict. For more information on work addiction, turn to Chapter 3.

If this profile fits, you may have proved yourself so valuable to employers and colleagues that a job is waiting for you after completion of treatment. Or if you're in outpatient treatment, your colleagues and employers may remain supportive while you take the time needed to do treatment and recovery thoroughly. The simple fact is that your work performance, productivity, and earning power will improve considerably after good treatment.

On the other hand, if this profile fits, your life requires much transformation, especially your work life. As valuable as you are to others, your view of yourself is most important. You may have become accustomed to a precarious balance of overwork, use, and abuse. With that balance shifted, you may lose a surprising amount of confidence in your ability to produce. Either you previously pulled off enormous spurts of productivity, followed by addictive behavior, or you maintained yourself in highly disciplined states provided you could let it hang out in the end by using and abusing. Whether these patterns fit or not, the basic patterns we're talking about involve extremes: extremes of work and then extremes of addictive behavior. Both are unhealthy and threatening to your career.

If you're in the unfortunate situation where your employer truly expects extreme work habits from you, then you probably need to look for another job. You may be undervaluing yourself as a worker and, as a result, being exploited by someone who's unfairly reaping benefits from your overwork. Look around to see whether people with your equivalent skills are working more reasonable hours and still earning a reasonable income. Try to do these comparisons as systematically as possible. This may not be easy, because salary information is typically private. However, you can get a pretty good idea of the work hours of peers and their compensation levels if you put your mind to it. Underselling yourself as a worker is most definitely a risk factor for slipping back into the addiction.

While in treatment, your confidence may roller coaster through ups and downs, both at work and with your family. Many successful, productive people have superstitious ideas about success. And with a shift in behavior, like getting clean, these ideas about success get jumbled. You may develop serious questions about whether you still have what it takes. You may wonder whether your career will nosedive into humiliating failure. The important point to remember is that getting treatment and ridding yourself of addictive behaviors will increase your productivity.

Although you may have to seek and find *new* modes of being productive, you have increased your potential by getting into treatment and getting free of addiction. It's simple biological and psychological reality. You're increasing your capacity to perform.

Scenario two: You lost your job due to your addiction

Your addiction problems may have deteriorated your career to the point where you don't have a secure job waiting on the other side of treatment. If this is true, you're going to have to adjust to painting on a whole new canvas. You're restarting a career or initiating a new one — and your family may face periods where your financial support is reduced or nonexistent.

This can be embarrassing and demoralizing. Your self-image, as provider, may be threatened. You may no longer feel the strength that comes from filling this important role. It may be painful to hit this bottom. But the fact remains that being in treatment is the most important thing you can do, right now, to ensure and increase future earnings.

Whatever your career was like before, working with an addiction (in the background) was like pursuing it with one arm tied behind your back. Now, when you resume career building, you'll be working with two good arms. Whatever you once achieved, you may increase or double it when addictive behaviors no longer impede your progress.

Meanwhile, your family may be struggling. Your kids may have to drop out of college or high school and get jobs. Your spouse may have to work longer hours or get a second job to make ends meet. You may need to sell property or cash in bonds or stocks. The costs may be considerable, but hard work rarely injures anyone unless it's addictive. Your treatment is worth everyone's hard work because you're so much better able to give when further along in your recovery. Healing is an investment. The best investment you or your family members ever made.

Addiction is, to a major degree, the result of valuing external substances over the inner you. In recovery, *you* become the focus: your inner resources, inner truths, inner capacities, and inner needs for harmony — they're all emphasized over externals. And this reversal in experience is appropriate. The basic message is that the inner you is the most important you, and after the inner you recovers, everything gets better, including the work you do to support your family and yourself.

Dealing with Financial Problems

While in treatment and when coming out of it, you can find your financial resources substantially reduced. You may be in considerable debt. All your previous denial and excess now add up to dollar signs tinged in red and proceeded by minuses. What do you do?

Although downsizing expenditures, expectations, and financial obligations are the basics of solving these problems, try also to understand the behavioral side. You have to come to terms with depleted finances. The psychological side of debt reduction involves revaluing good, old-fashioned work while reducing reliance on materialism. You need to get over your feelings of being unable to do without something, other than the basic necessities, of course. You may think you need cars, planes, boats, pieces of art, houses, clothes, memberships in clubs, or trips to different places around the globe. You may think you also need gourmet dinners, jewelry, vintage alcohol, or the status that comes with entertaining lavishly. Whatever material objects you think you need, they don't add up to happiness or well-being.

At some level, you already know this. But like many of us, you're susceptible to the advertising that runs like a broken record via TV, radio, billboards, the Internet, and by simple word of mouth. Marketing induces you to want something so bad, you buy it whether you can afford it or not. Marketers have no interest in your well-being. They're pursuing figures (market-share, profit-margin) that help their careers. If you multiply one marketer by several hundred thousand or million, you have the steady influence in our culture that suggests you buy, buy, buy — and feel guilty or shamed if you don't.

You must step away from this merry-go-round to get back on your feet financially. Bluntly stated, you have to refrain from buying stuff you don't absolutely need. You won't be able to do this if you see it as simple impoverishment. Instead, find a way to focus inward and discover inner harmony so that a real change of view can occur. You have to feel good about doing the right thing in the way you're living. In many ways, you're reversing the addicted lifestyle. When addicted, you put up with disharmony to get and use a substance that, supposedly, made everything better. Before you knew it, you were putting up with a great deal of conflict for highs that were brief escapes from a world of trouble.

Now you're transforming your world of trouble into a world that works. The major commitment needed is hard work. You have to face the hard work of generating income (however you wind up doing it) and the hard work of saving the income you generate. Both add up to the hard work of doing the right thing.

You know the right thing because it feels right. With the new skills of inner exploration learned in treatment, you become clearer about what feels right. You find that it isn't substances that make your life good, but people. With each relationship that improves — and each relationship that involves real compassion — you realize different highs (better highs) than ones you experienced before.

The inner wealth that comes from good relationships and personal harmony is what helps you refrain from buying what you don't need.

Ralph's addiction, recovery, and financial recovery

Ralph had been addicted to gambling for 15 years. His record was spotty, but he did work as a skilled laborer when he could. In the years before he quit, he spent more and more time at the racetrack. Ralph no longer had any credit. He was broke. Ralph hadn't paid taxes for ten years. He was nearly certain that he'd be dead soon — why pay the government? He gave at the track!

Ralph's good friend Johnny (they'd known each other since grade school) talked Ralph into going to treatment. He knew Ralph's family and wanted to help Ralph's kids (who'd given up on Ralph). Jenny, Ralph's ex, had left with the kids years ago. Johnny said, "It's time to change." Ralph agreed and went to treatment — for three months. Thankfully, Ralph's old union helped; they pitched in to support his treatment at a local residential center.

Ralph hasn't engaged in gambling for five years. He pays his taxes and is getting his life back in order. He's intent on repaying all his debts — financial and emotional.

Relapses, Restarts, and How They Affect Your Family

No plan for change is perfect. All involve slips or relapses. Whether a slip involves you or your family members, the difficult issue of forgiveness inevitably arises.

Technically speaking, relapses are excellent opportunities for understanding your abuse problem better. In contrast to continual use, where it's difficult to determine what the trigger is, the relapse is a specific event where the anatomy of the abuse problem is laid bare for observation. Your counselor will be extremely helpful in analyzing your relapse with you and, if necessary, with members of your family. We also cover relapses in Chapter 16.

Coming to terms with a relapse

The more willing you are to understand how the relapse occurred, the more able you are to prevent future occurrences. The more you can communicate about your relapse to family members, the more able you'll be to regain their confidence and trust.

Often, very little is accomplished immediately after a relapse. Family members are usually in a state of shock. The question of whether the addiction can be beaten resurfaces as a real question. Heavy doubts and powerful fears are evoked. Family members may find little to talk about sensibly. After a relapse, the specter of the addiction, and all the associated hurt and pain, is at its most powerful.

If you're the one who has relapsed, simply work with your counselor at first, learning as much as you can about what triggered the event. Often, your own situation is emotionally charged — perhaps an argument or a deep-seated conflict has surfaced or you experienced failure at work or with a project you set out to accomplish. Or perhaps it was a party or celebration that got out of hand or a situation where you faced a temptation you couldn't resist. Whatever the situation, the better you understand your relapse, the better you're prepared to prevent another one.

You must wait until you feel confident that you've learned from the relapse before trying to persuade anyone else that you're back on the path to recovery. If you try to be too persuasive, too soon, before you have it together within yourself, you'll come across as unconvincing. As a result, you may bring on more distrust, rather than less.

Instead, take your time. The strong emotions that dominate immediately after relapse eventually reduce in intensity. And your family is better able to listen and understand — and forgive — when they're less affected by shock, disappointment, and anger.

Many people who have proceeded with the treatment of addiction have relapsed at least once. Few have a perfect record. If you relapse, listening to and really understanding your family is crucial. Let them ventilate their reactions — it hurts to feel their pain, but it doesn't result in any permanent injury. You will realize, ultimately, that their hurt is linked to their love. And your realizing this can be a strong factor in preventing another relapse.

Restarting with the help of your family

Of course, there is no point dealing with the emotions of your family if you don't get back on the path to recovery. Once again, the single most important thing to do for them is to stay in treatment. That means getting back with your program.

After analyzing your relapse, you're usually better able to see your abuse as a reaction to problems; not a desirable situation in itself. The good news of this view is that the more problems you solve, the less susceptible to relapse you are.

When your family sees you re-engage with your program, they're relieved, and their confidence in you increases. And as they come to understand more about how and why you were triggered into a relapse, the more they'll be able to help you in averting future relapses.

The successful response to a relapse and a strong restart of your program helps you feel less brittle and more resilient. In place of anticipatory anxiety about the future, you have more knowledge about how to effectively reduce problems that may occur. This experience can be communicated to, and adopted by, your family as well.

Chapter 18

For Families and Friends: Ways to Make a Difference

*T*his chapter is oriented toward families and friends who want to make a difference. There is a lot of emphasis in "pop psychology" literature on taking care of yourself — first and foremost. Many people make excuses for emotional cut-offs of family members as necessary to their mental health — and cut-offs are common in families dealing with addictions.

But in our view, the very opposite effect, to mental health, is likely to happen. The cut-off is a dissociation of self — a distancing and deadening. What we advocate here is realizing that recovery is a long climb. But that doesn't mean giving up on your addicted friend or family member, it means getting used to the shared family struggle to help him or her recover. Sometimes, you may need to let go of the struggle, but you also may need to come back to it.

Family power can make a big difference when harnessed. In this chapter, we focus on how families and friends can channel their concern and love into effective action. We also focus on how effective helping can be healthy for you, as a family member or friend. We first focus on attitudes and how you can exert a positive influence on an addicted person.

Focus your compassionate efforts on helping your loved one get treatment for his or her addiction. Because you care, you may sometimes be tempted to support your loved one in ways that actually enable addiction. This can take the form of financial support (paying bills, paying rent) or practical support (offering a place for your loved one to stay, ensuring your loved one eats well).

These well-meaning rescue efforts can be enabling because in some cases, your support permits the loved one to continue using and prolongs addiction. If in doubt, ask for professional advice about how to provide support.

Breaking Through Denial and Codependency

The first modest step you can take toward changing your loved one's attitude is to get him or her to think and talk differently. Although it's easier said than done, *it can be done.* There are issues that you can talk about with your loved one that don't directly relate to addiction but that are important to overcoming an addiction, nonetheless. Without engaging in any talk of use, abuse, or abstinence, you can discuss moods, work performance, relationships, and other issues. You don't need to insist on raising questions about using alcohol or drugs or engaging in another addiction if your loved one isn't ready for this kind of discussion.

Express concern with closer inquiries about what's happening with your loved one. Remember that what we're talking about is inquiry and not an interrogation. These inquiries help the loved one actually examine what's happening in his or her life more closely. When an addicted person begins to examine issues more closely, it gets harder to continue to remain in denial.

This approach entails trusting the human instinct for getting down to the truth. Certainly, people reroute their thinking and talking to avoid the truth, but it takes more effort to do so when someone you care about is asking intelligent questions in a caring way. Remember also that it is important to set the stage for your talk. Jumping out with a series of questions may cause a shut-down in your loved one.

Prepare yourself for the talk. For example, you may decide to have the talk in the evening over a cup of coffee in the kitchen. In this situation, you may face fewer interruptions and you can sit down and not be rushed. Have a number of questions framed in your mind and express them in a kind, unintrusive way. If you ask about the day, ask for details. Inquire about how work is going and how your loved one is getting along with managers and peers. Seek more details about the stresses or difficulties that have been passed off as no big deal. Whatever is difficult in your loved one's life, use or abuse is making it even more difficult. The more you talk about change, generally, the more you're addressing within your loved one, indirectly, the addictive process that's hampering needed change.

Above all, you want to get your addicted family member or friend to talk. You have to give him or her a lot of airtime because the first step in persuading someone to think differently is listening. If you listen well, you'll spot conflicts in the person's experience. By continuing to listen, you'll learn how to use your understandings of these personal conflicts and discrepancies to be positively influential.

Facing denial

Recent research suggests that people go through stages in approaching change. This is true for nearly every change and every person. Of course, no one can change all the time. There has to be a yes to some changes and a no to others. Denial is one way of saying no.

Denial, however, is a *big* no, a no that hasn't truly contemplated the alternative of yes. As a result, people in denial are defensive. They often react to efforts to influence them with extreme actions that shut down contact. When you realize how destructive the addiction is getting, your loved one's denial can be devastating. You can feel hopeless. But if you want to exert influence, you have to overcome your hopelessness. Perhaps, after all, your hopelessness is ill-founded.

Why should you continue to hope and work for change? Well, remember that people's attitudes don't change gradually. Instead, there's often a darkest-before-the-dawn pattern, with the strongest negative reactions occurring right before a reversal of attitude. People try harder to resist until they see resistance is futile — then they change.

In order to be influential, you must keep believing your loved one's attitudes can and will change. Furthermore, you must continue your efforts without relying on particular signs of progress. You may shift strategies, and you may take time off from the struggle, but if you believe your loved one needs to change, you can't let your efforts or hopes lapse. Being helpful, at any given moment, means keeping in view the long haul – because real change usually takes place over time. It's like good wine: Some aging is necessary. Overnight declarations of change may be important, but real changes, sustained for extended periods, are how we evolve into healthier people.

Don't nag your loved one, because nagging fuels resistance. Just being negative doesn't help. And you don't wish to be an enabler, either. One who keeps helping pay the car loan payments and rent, for example, and thus assisting your loved one to continue on the addictive path. You must act with an unyielding belief in a vision of positive change in your loved one if you want to be effective.

Dealing with resistance

Members of families affected by addiction tend to overlook troubles (like abuse) while upholding an artificially positive view of family life. (For more on this, see Chapter 17.) So when you start talking about what's really going on in your family, get ready to take a stand.

In overcoming resistance, you must, again, be prepared for the long haul. You may not be successful the first month or the first year. But counteracting your loved one's addiction is important enough to never let your influence lapse. Ancient Confucian texts refer to the gentle, consistent influence of the wind. Over time, because its influence is unrelenting, the wind exerts a powerful influence, and over time, even stone is eroded by the wind. Use this approach in influencing your loved one. Be unrelenting and consistent, and you will be gentle and powerful.

Fundamentally, you're doing two things to disrupt the status quo. First, you're confronting, rather than avoiding, troubles. And second, you're projecting a realistic, rather than rosy, view of the family. There will likely be resistance to both. Your efforts may not bring rewards. The resistance you meet will predictably take several forms. To overcome each one, you'll have to muster resources.

"It's none of your business"

The first form of resistance follows the view that taking your stand violates privacy. "Who asked your opinion?" is a question you may be asked. "It's my business, not yours!" is another defensive phrase you may hear.

In this resistance, the addicted person is maintaining that his or her behavior doesn't affect anyone. The addiction is a private matter. Although the logic is flimsy, it can slow things to a standstill by making you feel you have an illegitimate interest. This is exactly when you need to stick to your guns. Addiction isn't a private matter at all — it involves the whole family and all the friends. You have a right to persuade your family member or friend to change her behavior and obtain treatment. You also have a responsibility to be persuasive.

"You're breaking up the family"

The second form of resistance may come from the addicted member or from other family members. You may hear family members say that the stand you're taking is threatening to break up the family. Consequently, they try to get you to stop your efforts in order to preserve family harmony.

Joanne gets help to deal with her mother's alcoholism

Joanne was the eldest of three children whose parents had allowed their drinking problems to spin out of control. When her father was hospitalized for an unrelated illness, her mother drowned her anxiety and despair in alcohol. Joanne felt abandoned and alone. But she began to function as the primary caretaker of her younger siblings. She was also no longer able to deny that her mother had a serious problem. Fortunately, she contacted a trusted family friend who referred her to a drug and alcohol counselor. When she confronted her mother with the need to get help, her mother rejected the idea. But she acknowledged that she was not providing enough support for the children during this anxiety-filled period. She agreed to take all the children to see the counselor.

Fortunately, the counselor had extensive experience with the denial problems associated with alcohol abuse. He also had experience counseling families with addicted members. Accordingly, he began counseling the children and relating to their anxieties about what was happening. The younger children and Joanne responded and began to organize themselves better — caretaking each other. Still, their mother was adamant that she neither needed help nor had to stop drinking.

Joanne persevered with the counseling, scheduling several personal sessions, and the counselor was willing to advise the family without obtaining mother's promise to seek treatment. Gradually Joanne's mother began to respond. A turning point came when Joanne refused to buy her any more liquor. Without an enabler, her mother had to confront the fact that she was drinking heavily, and that her drinking was gravely impairing her capacities as a mother. After several weeks of consistent response, the mother agreed to start treatment.

Here again, you need to be persistent. You're not breaking up the family: If there's an addiction, that addictive process is breaking up the family. What you're doing, in initiating change, is the right thing for the whole, entire family.

Preparing for Change

If you're unrelenting and patient in how you approach your loved one, there may come a point when your loved one is ready for change. Sometimes, the signals are indirect and vague. Sometimes, you see a dramatic shift. Sometimes, you feel something is different without being able to put your finger on what it is. Trust your feelings. Prepare for change.

What do we mean by "prepare"? The change process, as we know it, is never one-directional. People can move forward, and they can also fall back or relapse to earlier stages. They can always slip back into denial. So keep the process moving forward. You can move slowly and cautiously, but you must keep moving ahead.

An important step in preparing your loved one for treatment is to assist in the search for the right treatment setting. Each step along the path of change can be a misstep, no matter how positive it starts out. Some people thrive in certain kinds of treatment settings, and other people shrivel up in the same ones. As much as possible, work with your loved one to clarify the kind of treatment that is likely to be the best.

 Carefully review the previous chapters that help you understand the differences in treatment and recovery processes. These include Chapters 7 through 13. If your addicted family member or friend is a teen, read Chapter 14.

The more you learn, the more able you are to understand the kind of treatment your loved one will respond to — and to talk with your loved one when he or she falters. You need to be there when the whole process feels painful. You will have to supply that extra love and encouragement that often makes the difference between your loved one sticking with it or falling back into relapse.

 At every step of your assistance to your loved one, you need to keep checking your own well-being. Make sure that you're not becoming ill yourself. That in your efforts to help, you're not denying yourself sleep, rest, and a personal life.

Helping Your Loved One Follow Through

Finally, when your loved one makes a commitment to go into treatment, and when a choice has been made for the treatment setting, the action begins. You can prepare (as we discuss in the last section), but sooner or later, you must leap into action. There is a critical period for getting into treatment and sustaining treatment. Now the whole family can make a big difference.

Treatment for addiction is like a long mountain climb. You encounter narrow precipices and slippery surfaces (and beautiful landscapes) and you face important questions about why the climb is being made — and why it should continue. We call it a climb because recovery produces, at times, an enormous strain. Healing can be difficult and sometimes seems like an uphill battle. The hardest part is facing up to the negative emotions that frequently arise.

Recognizing negative emotions

Addicts often attempt to escape from emotional difficulties for years. Any confrontation with emotional upset is delayed or derailed. A process of avoidance builds over time and when treatment is obtained, there are two important changes from this previous pattern:

- ✔ You use negative emotions as signals for problem solving rather than avoidance. In treatment, negative emotions are focused on as signals of underlying problems that must be addressed.

- ✔ You confront an accumulated backlog of negative emotion. The addicted individual in treatment confronts the bad dealings and angry reactions that have accumulated over the entire addiction. As long as the addictive process continued undisturbed, a precarious balance was maintained — the addict had a way of communicating that kept negative emotions at bay. Acknowledging an addiction changes that balance. The individual now must relate to negative emotions that are historical, as well as those arising in the immediate situation.

These changes may have so much impact that treatment can be experienced as too painful. Your family member may complain that a particular counselor is too hard and tough or that the whole program is too grim and offers too little hope.

Empathizing: "I feel your pain"

In treatment, your friend or family member must counteract and manage the pain involved in dealing with all the negative emotions. This may be difficult, but it's crucial to treatment success. The critical tool in your support is *empathy,* an awareness and understanding of the thoughts and feelings of another person.

Perhaps the worst part of emotional pain is that it makes you feel isolated and unworthy. The pain makes you feel you *should* be left alone. Why would anyone want to be in contact with someone so burdened? The individual in pain can feel radioactive and toxic.

The addicted person in treatment often feels that level of pain. You may see the world as promising now that your family member is in treatment. But you're not confronting the pain and emotions of treatment.

Because he or she is in treatment, life can seem, for the time being, much more painful. Your family member can be in so much pain that he feels that any chance for a good life is over — that all that's left is confronting the agony of past mistakes. Under such conditions, the individual can feel unloved and unlovable.

Although you may feel ready to share the pain, it's frequently not that simple. Some past bad dealings, under the influence of the addiction, possibly involved you. You, yourself, possibly carry pain from your family member's past problems. You can't just forget. You have to deal with it yourself, with or without a counselor. You must deal with it to get past it, if you want to be helpful. Dealing with such pain isn't easy, but it is incredibly liberating.

In other words, empathy begins with you. It begins with the experience of facing and overcoming hurt, and finding good feelings, the feelings of resolution, that exist on the other side. After you know how the process unfolds, you're ready to be empathic with someone else. You're ready to listen as your family member really tells you what it's like without trying to be polite or having it sound good. You're less likely to turn away or cave in when it gets painful — or when you're having difficulties yourself.

As we've said, you must be ready for the long-term, for the long haul, the long climb. It doesn't help to be available when it's convenient. The important feeling for your loved one is that you are fundamentally there to share experiences, in good times and bad. That feeling directly counteracts isolation and unworthiness — and feelings of being unloved and unlovable. *There is magic to empathy and that magic transforms pain.* You also learn from pain when you're empathic and what you learn makes you a more sensitive, responsive, and sane person.

If you need to take time to recoup your energy or resolve an issue for yourself — do it. The point is that empathy, as a resource, starts within and radiates outward to the others you care about. If you feel empty (which can occur sometimes), focus back on yourself with caring. Seek the support of others like yourself — family members or friends of people who are struggling with addictive problems. One Web site that arranges online support meetings for family members is www.familiesanonymous.org.

Supporting Change over the Long-Term

So, it's important to be supportive over the long-term. What does that mean? How long is long-term and how much stress and strain are involved?

The first six weeks

We have found in our research that when a family member enters treatment for a serious illness — like cancer, heart disease, or addiction — most families provide meaningful support for six weeks. After six weeks, many family members can no longer keep up with the time demands, the emotional demands, and the stressful inconveniences.

After six weeks the process of addiction treatment is definitely started. People involved have an understanding of what full recovery requires. After six weeks of being clean, your family member has had an important taste of what life is like without the plague of an immediate addiction.

But this period of six weeks is usually much too short a span in relation to how much support is truly needed by a family member suffering from addiction. You often need to support your family member's engagement in treatment for several years — and sometimes for the rest of his or her life. We have to be realistic about the amount of change involved in recovering thoroughly.

You don't have to supply all the emotional support yourself. You can find different companies that provide psychological and social support to individuals in recovery, largely by telephone. These services offer several advantages, the most important one being that services are provided by an excellent counselor who can sustain the relationship over long periods of time, no matter where the addicted person travels.

Expecting and getting through relapse

The long climb toward life without addiction is often likened to starting a new life. So a series of "firsts" mark progress. The first month, the first return to living in the real world, the first set of temptations to use again that the individual is able to resist, the first six months, and the first year without use. And of course, the first slip and possibly, the first relapse followed by a renewed commitment to recovery.

No recovery record is perfect, and most involve, at some time or another, a slip or relapse. Whether there is a temporary slip or a turning back to use for significant periods, the difficult processes of acceptance and ultimately, forgiveness, inevitably arises.

We know people who have stopped their addictive behavior and have never relapsed (even 20 years later). But we think that if you prepare for a relapse, you do yourself no harm.

From the point of ultimate recovery, relapses are excellent opportunities for personal change. In contrast to consistent addictive behavior (where determining triggers to use is difficult), the relapse lays bare the anatomy of addiction. Your family member's counselor will be helpful in analyzing the relapse with her or him and, if necessary, can help you understand it as well.

Even though relapse is part of recovery, relapse is often a bitter and upsetting experience for families. The recovery process is an enormous strain for everyone. After all, the strain of watching your family member slip back into the pit of addiction is almost unbearable. You can easily feel like washing your hands of the relationship. Relapse can hurt that much.

But this is the difference between immediate support and long-term support. From the perspective of long-term support, your family member's relapse is exactly when he or she needs support the most. Again, the important resource is empathy, which starts with imagining how painful the treatment process must be for the relapse to occur. Although the addicted person often re-engages in denial, you can imagine how difficult things will be when his recovery resumes and he comes out of denial.

Empathy for your relapsed family member is important, but insistence on the resumption of treatment is essential at this point. Conversations, by necessity, become oriented around several questions:

- ✔ When will you re-enter treatment?

- ✔ What will it take to convince you to re-enter?

- ✔ What is happening now to make you resist getting back into recovery?

Until these questions are properly and thoroughly answered, no additional discussion is worth having. Empathy, at this stage, must take the form of toughness, with a consistent insistence on solutions being applied as soon as possible. The primary solution is getting back into treatment. There is no other solution.

The Ups and Downs of Change

Up to this point in the chapter, we have discussed how to deal with your addicted family member or friend. Now we focus more broadly on how your family is affected by addiction, and how these effects contribute to ups and downs. Not everything in this section will be relevant. However, some information will likely fit. When it does fit, use it to full advantage in helping your loved ones and yourself.

Dropping expectations and falsely positive images

There is one basic idea underlying behavior change in all families: Family members are reacting to each other all the time. As a result, we feel we can take certain reactions for granted. We develop expectations that a family member always reacts a certain way. What we don't realize is that our expectations influence people to *keep* reacting the same way.

On the other hand, positive change happens in families when we drop expectations and observe realities carefully. Change happens when people do things differently — at first, small things. If you observe the details of how your family operates, you can consistently reinforce small changes until they add up to significant ones.

The process of change is more difficult in families with an addicted member because of the tendencies to deny problems and camouflage them with falsely positive family images. In meaningful change, the pattern is reversed. The positive camouflage is lifted, and the underlying personal and family problems are identified and resolved.

Originally, the patterns of denial may have largely related to addictive behaviors. Efforts were directed at denying that the addiction was affecting anyone. Gradually, these patterns progressed to include other situations. Avoiding problems became habit. The pretence that "everything's fine" became the convenient camouflage.

Turning downs into ups

When interested in change, one deliberately and carefully looks at the downs (one's emotional problems) to transform them into ups. It is just the opposite when avoiding change. In these cases, one avoids downs, pretending to see ups and not even acknowledging one's avoidance.

If you're going to support positive change in your family, you must be willing to see the downs as opportunities for change. That process begins with yourself and entails mustering the courage to see where your pain is and to look into your pain until you understand its origins.

More about Joanne

Joanne was pleased that both parents entered treatment for alcohol addiction and that her father made a full recovery of his health. She was especially pleased with the results of her own counseling. By trusting her parents to remain in treatment, she was able to direct more attention to her own life. She came to a decision to attend a university in a nearby city and to gradually relax her vigilant observation of her parents, limiting herself to biweekly telephone calls. During these consistent contacts, she was alert for any signs that her parents had resumed drinking and therefore quickly picked up on her father's brief relapse. She joined with her mother in persuading him to resume and intensify his commitment to treatment.

But things were not all positive with Joanne, because she experienced a bout of chronic fatigue halfway through her second semester. It wasn't surprising — she had been through several stressful events. The caretaking of her family had also required a great deal of energy, although there was much less energy expenditure currently. Added to it all were the usual academic demands of student life, and her interest in spending time with the boyfriend she had met during her first semester. For a while, her individual life ran rough, and she had no reserve energy. She also was lacking support from her friends, because most had never had family experiences like those she encountered.

Over time, avoiding the potential codependency trap by making sure that she had a life of her own and with ongoing counseling, she began to return to her natural equilibrium. Her parents continued to progress with treatment, and she was able to trust them to the point where, once again, she asked them for support and guidance.

It had taken 18 months to influence her parents to enter and stay in treatment. She would not have traded the 18 months for anything, but it had been, as she described it, "A long, hard climb with lots of uncertainty."

One reason you must start with yourself is that when you point out family problems, family members will inevitably point to *your* personal difficulties. You acknowledge them and then undertake a personal change that models what you want your addicted family member or friend to do.

After the reversal is made and the downs are confronted as transformative opportunities, the pace of change becomes an issue. How much change can occur within a given period of time? How do the paces of different family members vary? How much time should be devoted to confronting downs versus celebrating the ups?

Sustaining Optimism and Support in Your Family

How do you stay optimistic through it all? How do you keep believing that things will work out? How do you keep believing that treatment will work for your family member, for your family, and yourself?

Staying out of fantasy land and finding realistic optimism

Recognize the important difference between optimism that is propped up by fantasy and optimism that is realistic. Fantasy optimism, in the end, gets you nowhere. It supplies momentum, temporarily, but the momentum fizzles when the nitty-gritty is denied. It fizzles whenever you put on rose-colored glasses and avoid realities.

Realistic optimism, on the other hand, involves envisioning a best-case scenario while continually testing reality. You face all the possible disappointments while envisioning positive outcomes.

How does one generate this realistic optimism while dealing with the uncertainties and stresses of addiction?

We believe optimism is a natural human resource. Realistic optimism doesn't need to be propped up by pretence or avoidance. We believe that the more you nourish your self-esteem and understand your strengths and successes, the more resilient your optimism is.

Being deserving of victory and success

When we work with elite athletes, they generate realistic optimism by training to be deserving of victory. In other words, with some guidance, they ingrain in themselves their various strengths and various components of previously exhibited successes and thus train and prepare for victory. They may not win, but if they feel deserving in every game or match, they do get their fair share of victories. When they train to deserve victory, their optimism becomes realistic; after all, their optimism is based on their realistic experiences. This optimism proves very durable through their hard times.

In working with your addicted family member or friend, you must aim to be deserving of success, however you define it. You must prepare thoroughly, and you must be precise and consistent in what you do. You must think every action *through* and get the best advice and find the best strategy.

Above all, although you need to be ready to accept temporary setbacks, you must not personalize them as your own defeats. After all, it is the addicted loved one who chooses to continue with the addictive behavior and not you. However, do continue to believe in the possibility for recovery.

You can develop realistic optimism and you can positively influence your family member and your family. Your well-directed hard work is what is needed — and it's all worth it when you experience the well-earned victory.

Part V
The Part of Tens

The 5th Wave
By Rich Tennant

"I don't think the crackling sound coming from
your lower back is as serious as you thought.
Just relax and I'll have this Rice Krispie Square
out of your back pocket in no time."

In this part . . .

*A*ll *For Dummies* books end with top-ten lists, and this one is no exception. If you are a friend or family member of a loved one who has an addiction, we tell you ten ways to help him or her overcome an addiction problem. We also provide a list of books and Web sites that offer additional information on overcoming addictions and maintaining recovery.

Chapter 19

Ten Ways to Help a Friend or Loved One

ddiction is so powerful that it often takes a whole family group plus the help of an interventionist to get an addicted person to the crucial point of accepting that a problem exists. Also, you aren't going to get the addicted person to change unless he or she wants help, and that usually only happens when the addicted person reaches a point of significant despair.

This chapter focuses on ten key ways to help a friend or loved one recover from an addiction problem. We also focus on what you can do for *your* mental health.

Talk Things Over Truthfully

Knowing your friend or family member has a problem and knowing what the problem is are two different things. You need to break through the communication barrier to find out whether the problem is an addiction and, if so, what kind of addictive process is involved.

If you feel something isn't right with your family member or friend, get him or her to start talking and opening up emotionally. As long as you're listening attentively, you can be certain you'll learn more. The more you listen, the closer he or she will be to telling you the truths that need to be told. When these truths are shared, you can, as a team, get appropriate help.

Recognize the Telltale Signs of an Addiction

Does your friend or loved one have an addiction problem? Here are some signs that he or she does:

- ✔ Forgetting commitments or being frequently, uncharacteristically late
- ✔ New or more frequent illnesses
- ✔ Unexplained work and relationship difficulties
- ✔ Increased absences or erratic breaks from routines
- ✔ Spending hours with new friends who, themselves, keep unusual hours and don't have regular jobs
- ✔ Financial troubles
- ✔ Memory or concentration problems
- ✔ Sleep disturbances or major changes of sleep habits
- ✔ Surprising secrecy

If you've noticed one or more of these issues, be concerned. Continue observing even more closely. See Chapter 5 for more guidance about other signs that may be of concern.

Confront Denial

Your loved one is probably denying that any problems exist. The most common response from a loved one when confronted about possible use and abuse is a mixture of denial and rationalization. Problems that keep recurring are called "just temporary." And you may be in denial too.

However, as frightening as it is to see that a friend or loved one is addicted, acknowledging it is the first step to helping that person onto the road to recovery.

This is where an interventionist may be helpful. An *interventionist* is a professional who assists family members in confronting a loved one about addiction problems. The interventionist comes to your home and prepares you and your family to communicate about suspected addiction with your loved one. He or she also leads family meetings where the loved one is confronted in a supportive and direct way. The interventionist helps you talk about the addiction and the devastating effects it has been having and will have on everyone concerned. Chapter 9 provides more information on the role of an interventionist.

Help Get Treatment

After your loved one acknowledges the need for treatment, the next step is figuring out what kind(s) of treatment will work best. Part III of this book describes a whole range of different addiction treatments.

Sometimes, the best thing you can do is assist in the search for the right treatment. See Part III for information on the variety of treatment methods available. And don't forget to look into alternative treatments that are different from what's been tested and tried in the mainstream. See Chapter 14 for more information on alternative treatments.

Initially, hospitalization may be necessary to enable your loved one to safely withdraw and detox. (See Chapter 10 for information on detox.) A residential treatment program may further ensure that your loved one starts on the recovery road with a solid foundation of abstinence. Residential programs can last for 28 days or longer. In some cases, programs may be more brief but still very effective. (See Chapter 9).

Addictions affect every area of a life, and so it may be important to think of a combination of treatments rather than thinking that "this one will do it." Recovery may be a lengthy process. You have to be ready for the long haul. Self-help approaches may also provide excellent assistance for sustaining progress. Some have minor fees, but most operate without any fees. (See Chapter 12 for information on self-help approaches.)

The addicted person may not be the only one who needs help! You too may need professional assistance. Family members can easily get caught up in their loved one's problems, sometimes becoming codependent. Codependence can occur unconsciously when you start behaving in a way that supports your loved one's addiction (but smoothes things over in the immediate situation). Or you can become so enmeshed in your loved one's problems that you forget your own needs. You can pay a high price for too much self-sacrifice.

Let Go of Your Need to Control the Situation

Chapter 18 provides more information on what you can do to take care of yourself. Perhaps the hardest lesson for family members is figuring out how to motivate a loved one without trying to become motivated *for* that person. Also, some of your efforts to support your loved ones in getting clean may not actually work until the situation worsens. Why? The addicted person needs to hit rock bottom, a point of ultimate despair where more use and abuse ceases to be an option, and the only alternative left is seeking help and getting into treatment.

Terrifying? Yes, of course. Seeing your loved one risk harm, prison, and even death is frightening. Dealing with the fall-out of addiction is very difficult, no matter how strong you are. Here are some pointers on what you can do to take care of your own needs:

✔ Maintain *your* normal routines.

✔ Keep up *your* social and recreational activities.

✔ Find a trusted confidant and talk as much as he or she is willing to listen.

✔ Don't blame yourself for your loved one's problems.

✔ Acknowledge your own problems. It may be easier to focus on your loved one's problems. But you'll feel better and function better when you deal with your own issues.

✔ Consider some professional help for yourself. (See Chapter 21 for Web site links and books for help for family members.)

Hold Criticism at Bay

Criticism often increases the strength of the addiction. Specifically, criticism often provokes greater resistance to change. Your loved one knows addictive behavior is unhealthy and dangerous. But the addiction has taken hold and become hard to resist. Your loved one may still be denying that he or she has lost control. Communicate your concern directly without stinging criticism. It may well take more than your voice alone to motivate this person to get help. But he or she will listen better if talked to sincerely with a minimal amount of criticism. (See Chapter 18 for more about how to communicate directly and supportively.)

Offer Balanced Support

You may be hitting a wall. Your loved one may have put you through a very hard time. Under these circumstances, it may be hard to remain caring and supportive, especially after you've been hurt badly. Sure, deep down, the care is still there, but you're only human, and you feel anger and frustration. Don't despair, here are a few tips that may help you continue to give constructive support and care:

- ✔ Don't get burnt out from focusing all your efforts on your loved one's problems and neglecting your own needs. Balance your support for him with self-care. Self-care activities naturally include having fun and nurturing yourself. Self-care also means getting help for your psychological, financial, and physical needs.

- ✔ Provide love and support, but be careful not to do things that enable your loved one to continue with the addiction. This is what is meant by *tough love*. For example, you may feel that you ought to provide bail money to get your loved one released from jail. But consider whether you're actually softening the penalties and prolonging the addiction. See Chapter 18 for information on the fine line between supporting a loved one and enabling the addiction.

Understand What You're Fighting

This book provides a great deal of information on the nature of addiction and addiction treatment. Take your time and read it thoroughly. The more you understand about the nature of addictions, the less you will be overwhelmed by the associated uncertainties. Knowing about treatment options helps you feel less isolated in the fight against addiction. The various treatment options are described in Part III of this book.

Because of the high prevalence of addictions in our modern age, many communities offer some sort of group therapy for the relatives or loved ones of addicts. Participating in a group session permits you to share experiences with others in your situation and to learn techniques that help you self-nurture and self-sustain in the face of addiction.

In Chapter 21, we provide a number of Internet links and reading resources for information on addictions and treatment. You can also find information by going to your favorite Internet search engine and looking for information about treatment.

Remain Optimistic

Optimism is a natural human resource, and realistic optimism doesn't need to be propped up by pretense or avoidance. The more you grasp and understand your reality and that of your loved one, the more resilient your optimism becomes. (See Chapter 18 for more specific guidance on remaining optimistic.)

Because relapse is pretty well a given, family members may give up hope and lose optimism about their loved one's recovery. Hope and optimism can be sustained when you remember that many addicts eventually overcome addiction. Each positive story you hear teaches you and supports your courage and optimism. Each relapse is an opportunity for your loved one, and possibly you, to learn what to do differently in the next recovery attempt. Your loved one may have to hit bottom (sometimes more then once!) to find the motivation to seriously confront addiction. Treatments that greatly increase the chances of successful recovery are available. The key is matching the treatment to the individual.

Part of being realistic is realizing that on the road to recovery, relapse is the norm, not the exception. Most addicts make several quit attempts before quitting for good. Many continue to slip from time to time even though the slips get fewer and fewer with more and more time in-between.

Know What to Do When Treatment Efforts Fail

Sometimes, the best that you can do for your loved one is to reduce the immediate risk to her life. Chapter 9 discusses various harm reduction measures. These include strategies such as needle and syringe exchange programs, encouraging safe sex to reduce associated health risks (such as acquiring an infectious disease), providing drugs such as methadone under controlled conditions, and decriminalizing certain substances so that the addict isn't faced with a lifelong criminal record. The goal of the harm reduction approach is to reduce the risk of serious health or social consequences of addictive behaviors.

Chapter 20

More Than Ten Self-Help Resources

*I*n this chapter, we provide some additional resources and Web links to help you learn more about addictions and how to overcome them. We also make suggestions for resources to help with problems related to addictions such as anxiety, depression, relationships, and work stress. These are the resources that we're most familiar with, but we certainly may have overlooked other helpful sources of information. Therefore, we encourage you to explore other books and Web sites on your own.

Self-Help Books

Bien, Thomas, and Beverly Bien, *Mindful Recovery: A Spiritual Path to Healing from Addiction* (Wiley)

Fleeman, William, *The Pathways to Sobriety Workbook* (Hunter House Publishers)

Kirkpatrick, Jean, *Turnabout: New Help for the Woman Alcoholic* (Bantam) (describes the Women For Sobriety program)

Trimpey, Jack, *Rational Recovery: The New Cure for Substance Addiction* (Pocket)

Volpicelli, Joseph, and Maia Szalavitz, *Recovery Options: The Complete Guide* (Wiley)

Self-Help Books for Problems Related to Addictions

Beck, Aaron T., *Love Is Never Enough: How Couples Can Overcome Misunderstandings, Resolve Conflicts, and Solve Relationship Problems Through Cognitive Therapy* (Harpercollins)

Beck, Aaron T., A. John Rush, Brian F. Shaw, and Gary Emery, *Cognitive Therapy of Depression* (Guilford Publications)

Burns, David D., *The Feeling Good Handbook* (Plume)

Elliot, Charles H., and Laura L. Smith, *Overcoming Anxiety For Dummies* (Wiley)

Gottman, John M., and Nan Silver, *The Seven Principles for Making Marriage Work* (Three Rivers Press)

Gottman, John, with Nan Silver, *Why Marriages Succeed or Fail* (Simon & Schuster)

Greenberger, Dennis, and Christine A. Padesky, *Mind Over Mood: Change How You Feel by Changing The Way You Think* (Guilford Press)

Prochaska, James O., John C. Norcross, and Carlo C. DiClemente, *Changing for Good: The Revolutionary Program that Explains the Six Stages of Change and Teaches You How to Free Yourself from Bad Habits* (Harpercollins)

Ritvo, Paul G., M. David Lewis, M. Jane Irvine, Laura J. Brown, A. Matthew, and B.F. Shaw "The Application of Cognitive-Behavioral Therapy in the Treatment of Substance Abuse" in *Primary Psychiatry,* Vol. 10, May 2003

Segal, Zindel V., J. Mark G. Williams, and John D. Teasdale *Mindfulness-Based Cognitive Therapy for Depression: A New Approach to Preventing Relapse* (Guilford Press)

Smith, Laura L., and Charles H. Elliot, *Depression For Dummies* (Wiley)

Self-Help Web Sites for Managing Addictions

The Secular Organizations for Sobriety (SOS) has a Web site (www. secularsobriety.org) that provides links to SOS programs worldwide.

You can learn AVRT (Active Voice Recovery Technique) by either reading *Rational Recovery* or by taking a course on its Web site (www.rational.org).

You can find information on Self-Management and Recovery Training (SMART) at www.smartrecovery.org.

You can obtain information on Women For Sobriety (WFS) groups in your community and on other services of WFS at www.women forsobriety.org.

The Narconon Network (www.narconon.org) is an association of over 100 drug rehab and prevention and education centers worldwide.

The Substance Use Counseling and Education (SUCE) Program (www.gmhc.org) provides information for gay men who want harm-reduction counseling particularly focused on help with the impact of drug use on sexual behavior.

Christian Recovery International has a Web site at www.christian recovery.com.

The National Association for Christian Recovery provides advice at www.nacronline.com.

You can find information on Jewish Alcoholics, Chemically Dependent People, and Significant Others at www.jacsweb.org.

Research funded by the National Institutes of Health in the United States on treatments for addictions and related topics is provided on the National Institute on Alcohol Abuse and Alcoholism Web site at www.niaaa.nih.gov.

The American Society of Addiction Medicine (www.asam.org) provides information on a wide rage of addiction topics as well as links to treatment programs.

Web Sites for Treatment Models

The U.S. National Institute on Drug Abuse (www.drugabuse.gov) is one of the best Web sites for current research information on drugs and drug treatments. It also offers links for family members and for teens.

Another excellent Web site for drug and alcohol information for all age groups and for family members is the U.S. Department of Health and Human Services and SAMHSA clearinghouse (http://ncadi.samhsa.gov/govpubs/rpo926).

National Alliance of Methadone Advocates (www.methadone.org) provides information on methadone treatments and links to methadone providers across the United States.

Alcoholism and Addiction Resource Guide (www.hubplace.com/addictions) provides links to twelve-step-oriented treatment facilities.

The Drug and Alcohol Prevention Network (www.drugnet.net) provides links to an extensive array of self-help treatments, treatment centers, research, and other related topics.

Drug and Alcohol Recovery Network (www.darnweb.com) allows you to search for links to different types of addiction treatment facilities and groups.

Practical Recovery (www.practicalrecovery.com) provides links to non-AA treatment groups and referrals.

The Harm Reduction Coalition Web site (www.harmreduction.org) provides links to many of the needle exchange programs across the United States.

The Lindesmith Center (www.lindesmith.org) is another good site for information on harm reduction approaches.

Alcoholics Anonymous Worldwide (www.aa.org) provides links to AA programs across the world including the United States and Canada.

Oxford House (www.oxfordhouse.org) provides a worldwide directory of Oxford Houses, which are self-managed houses for the twelve-step program.

Dual Recovery Anonymous Central Service (http://dual recovery.org) provides links to twelve-step programs for help with multisubstance addictions and/or mental health problems.

Cocaine Anonymous (www.ca.org) is a twelve-step program for cocaine addiction.

Marijuana Anonymous (www.marijuana-anonymous.org) is a link to twelve-step programs for overcoming marijuana abuse.

Narcotics Anonymous (www.narcoticsanonymous.org) is a peer support organization for people recovering from drug addictions. It too is based on the twelve-step program model. Its Web site provides links to support group meetings held in over 100 countries worldwide.

Behavior Therapy Associates (www.behaviortherapy.com) offers a list of therapists who can provide motivational enhancement therapy (MET) and cognitive behavior therapy (CBT).

Interactive-Health.Com, Inc. (www.interactive-health.com) offers cognitive behavior therapy for relapse prevention.

The National Council on Problem Gambling (www.ncpgambling.org) offers information on pathological gambling and provides links to gambling treatment programs.

Several state government Web sites provide information on problem gambling and links to treatment (www.addictionrecov.org/addicgam.htm).

Gamblers Anonymous (www.gamblersanonymous.org) is an organization of individuals providing support to one another to help each other recover from gambling problems.

Peer group support for help with online gaming is offered by On-line Gamers Anonymous (www.olganon.org).

A group that provides information on recovering from problems with debt is Debtors Anonymous (www.debtorsanonymous.org).

The Overeating Support Group Networking Web site provides information about peer support group networks throughout the United States (www.overcomingovereating.com/groups.html).

Overeaters Anonymous (www.overeatersanonymous.org) offers support based on the twelve-step model.

Greysheeters Anonymous (www.greysheet.org) also offers peer group support for recovering from an overeating problem.

A Web site that provides useful health-related links for those with eating disorders is http://open-mind.org/ED.htm.

Dealing with emotional problems like depression, anxiety, and compulsive behaviors can feel like a life-long, and possibly lonely, struggle. An organization focused specifically on supporting individuals recovering from emotional problems is Emotions Anonymous (www.emotionsanonymous.org).

There are several peer support organizations aimed at helping men and women recover from sex and love addictions. These include Sexual Addicts Anonymous (www.sexaa.org); Sex and Love Addicts Anonymous (www.slaafws.org); Sexaholics Anonymous (www.sa.org); Sexual Compulsives Anonymous (www.sca-recovery.org); and Sexual Recovery Anonymous (www.sexualrecovery.org).

A twelve-step program-based organization for workaholics is Workaholics Anonymous (www.workaholics-anonymous.org).

Web Sites for Families

Families should check out the Web site links listed under addictions, because most also offer information and services for family members.

One such link is the drug-rehabilitation Web site (www.drug-rehabilitation.com/family_program.htm).

Al-Anon Family Groups (www.al-anon.org) offers twelve-step support for families of alcoholics.

Alateen is a Web site linked with Al-Anon (www.alateen.com) that provides support to family and children of alcoholics.

Codependents Anonymous (www.coda.org) also offers support and guidance to families and partners of people with addictions. Its specific focus is helping individuals to develop healthy relationships. On its Web site you can find information on possible meeting groups in your community.

Another peer support group organization for families and partners of people with an addiction that is based on the twelve-step program is Nar-Anon (www.nar-anon.org).

Sexual Recovery Anonymous (www.sexualrecovery.org) provides a link to peer support groups for family members of a sex addict.

Mothers Against Drunk Driving (MADD) is an advocacy group fighting for greater protection against drunk drivers (www.madd.org/home).

Mothers Against Misuse and Abuse (www.mamas.org) is an advocacy and educational group that aims to provide current, scientific education about drug abuse to all ages and that promotes healthier alternatives to drug use.

Web Sites for Teens

Al-Anon/Alateen is a family support site for families of teens (www.al-anon-alateen.org).

National Association for children of alcoholics (www.nacoa.org) provides information and links to assistance for children of parents who have alcohol or drug addictions.

Web Sites for Problems Related to Addictions

The American Psychiatric Association (www.psych.org) provides information about mental health problems.

The American Psychological Association (www.apa.org) provides information about psychological problems as well as links to related resources.

The Anxiety Disorders Association of America (www.adaa.org) provides links to self-help groups for anxiety problems.

The National Foundation for Depressive Illness (www.depression.org) provides information on help for depression.

The National Institutes of Mental Health (www.nimh.nih.gov) reports research results of studies on mental health issues.

WebMD (www.webmd.com) provides information on very a wide array of mental and physical health problems.

Information on many of the prescription drugs that interact with drinking alcohol is provided at http://alcoholism.about.com/library/bldrug_la.htm.

The American Association for Family and Marital Therapy (www.aamft.org/index_nm.asp) provides information and links to marital and family therapists.

Web Sites for Related Health Resources

There are many Web sites that offer health information. The government provides guidelines regarding healthy dietary goals at www.health.gov/dietaryguidelines/dga2000/document/build.htm#pyramid.

The United States Food and Drug Administration Web site (www.fda.gov) is also an excellent source of information about both food and drugs.

Web Sites for Legal Issues

The U.S. Department of State provides information on a range of legal topics, including getting legal help if you're dealing with a foreign legal system at www.state.gov/other.

Most state government Web sites have links to legal assistance programs. Rather than list the individual Web sites here, we encourage you to google the Web site of your state, province, or country.

Treatment Centers

The following are notable treatment centers:

- ✔ The Betty Ford Center: www.bettyfordcenter.org
- ✔ Hazelden: www.hazelden.org
- ✔ ASAP Family: www.asapfamily.com

- ✔ Visions Adolescent Treatment Program: Malibu, CA, 866-889-3665, www.visionsteen.com

- ✔ Harmony Place: Malibu, CA, 888-866-9778, www.harmony place.net

- ✔ Lake Chelan Community Hospital: Chelan, WA, 509-682-3300, www.lakechelancommunityhospital.com

- ✔ Caron Foundation: Wernersville, PA, 610-678-2332, www.caron.org

- ✔ Renaissance Institute: Boca Raton, FL 561-241-7977

- ✔ Malibu Coast Treatment: Malibu, CA, 310-457-7229

- ✔ Las Vegas Recovery Center: Las Vegas, NV, 800-790-0091

- ✔ The Canyon: Malibu, CA, 888-922-6966, www.thecyn.com

- ✔ Milestone Treatment Program: Calabassas, CA, 818-879-9873

- ✔ Sober Living by the Sea: Newport Beach, CA, 800-647-0042

- ✔ Silverhill Hospital: New Canaan, CT, 800-899-4455

Index